ECONOMICS WITHOUT ILLUSIONS

ALSO BY JOSEPH HEATH

Nation of Rebels
(WITH ANDREW POTTER)

The Efficient Society

ECONOMICS
WITHOUT ILLUSIONS

DEBUNKING THE MYTHS
OF MODERN CAPITALISM

JOSEPH HEATH

BROADWAY BOOKS   NEW YORK

FOR OSCAR

BROADWAY BOOKS and the Broadway Books colophon
are trademarks of Random House, Inc.

Originally published in slightly different form in Canada by
HarperCollins Canada, Toronto, in 2009.

Cataloging-in-Publication Data is on file with the Library of Congress.

ISBN 978-0-307-59057-2

Printed in the United States of America

10   9   8   7   6   5   4   3   2   1

First U.S. Edition

CONTENTS

PART II. LEFT-WING FALLACIES

As a nail sticketh fast between the joinings of stones,
so doth sin stick close to buying and selling.

ECCLESIASTICUS 27:2

INTRODUCTION

I was in high school when the movie *Blade Runner* first came out. It's difficult to explain to people now why the film was such a shock for audiences at the time, or how deeply it revolutionized science fiction as a genre. I can still remember the surprise I felt seeing the first panoramic view of the future city of "San Angeles," where the entire side of a skyscraper hosted a giant video screen showing an advertisement with a smiling Japanese woman popping pills. Enormous dirigibles cruised through the night sky, with intrusive searchlights and a booming sound track advertising off-world emigration (the apparent objective being not so much to entice people off the planet as to drive them away).

Why was this so shocking? Because it was the first time anyone had ever suggested that there might be *advertising* in the future—or worse, that there might be *even more of it* in the future than in the present. Nuclear holocaust? Sure. Everyone assumed there was going to be an apocalyptic nuclear war. But advertising? Now *that's* bleak.

Science fiction at the time was dominated by dystopian visions of the future—*Battlestar Galactica* was set just shortly after the near-annihilation of the human race by renegade robots; *Space: 1999* occurred after catastrophic explosions knocked the earth's moon out of its orbit;

Planet of the Apes was, of course, none other than Planet Earth, several generations after the seemingly inevitable nuclear war. Yet no matter how depressing the vision of the future, the dominant assumption was that we would not still be buying and selling things from one another. Capitalism, along with all of its gaudy accoutrements, was regarded as merely a step on the road to a higher level of civilization.

In the old *Star Trek* series, capitalism was forthrightly dismissed as a primitive stage of human social evolution. This was often played for comic effect, as when members of the *Enterprise* beamed down to the surface of some backward planet and acted confused when confronted by a demand from an alien merchant for something called "money." The closest thing we ever saw to capitalism was in the first *Star Wars* movie, when Obi-Wan Kenobi and Han Solo settled on a price of 17,000 "credits" for the hire of the *Millennium Falcon*. But even then, in the famous Mos Eisley Cantina, where the scum of the galaxy assembled for drinks and intrigue, there were several notable omissions. Not only was there no advertising at all in the bar, but there didn't seem to be any brands either. In the future, we were led to believe, people would drink just plain old beer, not Jedi Lite.

These omissions were highly characteristic of the science fiction of the time. There were two things that science fiction writers almost uniformly failed to anticipate, right through to the end of the 1970s.[1] The first was the impact that information technology would have on everyday life. It was generally assumed that the development of *mechanical* technology would be the most powerful force for change in human society: robots were to have been the big story, not computers. The second major assumption was that the market would fade away. No one could quite believe that, in the twenty-first century, we would still be living in an old-fashioned capitalist economy. It was almost universally assumed that the future would be some kind of post-scarcity socialism, not information hypercapitalism.

If people had a hard time believing that we would still be living in a capitalist economy in the twenty-first century, imagine how much more difficult it would have been for them to believe that we would still be having exactly the same debates about the pros and cons of the market. Indeed, if you look at the state of this debate at the time of Karl Marx's death, and compare it to today, it would be easy to come to the conclusion that we have gotten precisely nowhere. People may be a lot more resigned to the market now than they were a hundred years ago, but they are not necessarily any more comfortable with it.

So what are we to make of this unexpected persistence of capitalism? John Kenneth Galbraith once observed, with respect to American capitalism, that "in principle the economy pleased no one; in practice it satisfied most."[2] Behind this observation is the familiar story of economic growth and diminished material scarcity. People didn't like the concept of a market economy, but they had to admit that it did a good job of putting bread on the table. Yet the unease and suspicion have never gone away. A recent study by moral psychologists showed that a solid majority of Americans think it is immoral for businesses to raise prices in response to scarcity (say, charging more for shovels after a big snowstorm).[3] But since having prices that will go up in response to scarcity is the single most important advantage of having a capitalist economic system, this moral intuition reveals something of a public relations problem for fans of the free market.

Indeed, everyone has at least some moral intuitions that are implicitly, if not explicitly, anticapitalist. This is why there has always been good money to be made from pandering to popular anticapitalist sentiment (Hollywood does it quite relentlessly, mainly by romanticizing "the good old days," when life was about more than just money). Against this tide of popular opinion, who is willing to speak up for the free market? Probably the most sustained campaign against popular anticapitalism has been waged by members of the economics profession. According to the standard refrain, people are uncomfortable with markets only because they don't understand them. The solution is more education, or, more specially, more economics classes. (Bryan Caplan, an economist at George Mason University, has recently suggested that the votes of people who lack basic economic literacy should be given less weight in elections.)[4] Hence the hallowed status of Economics 101—the course that introduces students to "the model," or the way of looking at things that makes capitalism seem like not just an acceptable compromise, but the best of all possible worlds.

Of course, not everyone goes to university, and not everyone takes Economics 101. For those who miss out, there are shelves full of "popular economics" books, like *The Armchair Economist* or *The Undercover Economist* or *Naked Economics*. Think of these as the poor man's Economics 101. In each case, the goal is to present "the model," either in part or in whole, for those who have missed out on the textbook version.

This book is different. I'm not interested in selling anyone on the virtues of private enterprise. There will be no pat lectures about the wonders of free trade or the evils of government intervention. This is primarily because I share the unease that most people feel with the capitalist system. And I would like to see us come up with something better than what we have right now.

However, I also think that economics is important—as important for critics of capitalism as it is for its cheerleaders. Furthermore, I think critics of capitalism have not done nearly a good enough job at learning their economics. Marx clearly understood the "mainstream" economics of his day, yet, in part due to his influence, very few left-wing or "radical" theorists can say the same. Perhaps people have been hoping that this whole capitalism thing will blow over soon, so it won't be necessary to learn about Leontief production matrices or separating hyperplane theorems or any of the other gizmos that economists insist are essential to understanding the price of milk.

There are two unfortunate consequences of all this. First, most people on the left are incapable of spotting the garbage arguments that are routinely trotted out by conservatives in support of their views. For example, a common argument made against reducing greenhouse gas emissions is to point out that doing so would decrease the rate of growth, and that since growth creates employment, fighting climate change will cause unemployment. This is what's called a *non sequitur*—an argument in which the premise fails to provide any reason whatsoever for believing the conclusion. Yet environmentalists respond to this argument not by laughing and pointing their finger at the person who made it, but by adducing some other set of considerations ("But what about the *benefits* of avoiding climatic instability?" or "What about the jobs that will be created developing new, green technology?"). As a result, "economics" winds up serving as a magic hat, allowing people on the right to pull out support for any policy that they happen to like, even when it doesn't follow from any coherent set of economic principles. (The best, and by far the most common, is the suggestion that tax cuts "stimulate" the economy. I sometimes wonder if economists who encourage this misconception—as a convenient fiction, simply because they don't like taxes—ever lie awake at night feeling guilty about the setback they are helping to inflict on the cause of economic literacy.)

The second problem with the prevailing state of economic illiteracy on the left is that it leads people of good will to waste countless hours promulgating or agitating for schemes and policies that have no reasonable chance of success or that are unlikely to actually help their intended beneficiaries. Consider, for example, *The Take*, a documentary on worker cooperatives in Argentina put together by Naomi Klein and Avi Lewis. While the material is quite affecting and some of the footage is remarkable, the events of the film are presented in what can only be described as an intellectual vacuum. Klein and Lewis don't even bother to explain basic features of how these cooperatives are structured and financed, much less how an economy organized this way is supposed to function. Yet they present the movement as a "new kind of economy" and as an "alternative to global capitalism." You would never know, watching the film, that there is an extensive economic literature on the subject of cooperatives—written by socialists and nonsocialists alike—dating back over a century, that raises serious doubts about the possibility of structuring an economy along these lines. Rather than heading to Argentina, Klein and Lewis might have profited more from a visit to their local library. Unfortunately, they are so enamored of the activist ethos—the seizure of the factories, the confrontations with police, and so on—that they simply don't apply any intellectual energy to the question of whether the people involved are tilting at windmills.

The standard reflex on the left when confronted with an economic question is to change the topic. Consider, for example, the economic argument against paper recycling.[5] People say that recycling is a way of "saving trees," yet, in practice, it has exactly the opposite effect. Why are there so many cows in the world? Because people eat cows. Not only that, but the number of cows in the world is a precise function of the number that are eaten. If people decided to eat less beef, there would be fewer cows. Yet the same is true of trees. "Old growth" timber is not used for pulp and paper—the trees that go into making our paper are a cash crop, just like wheat and corn. So one way to increase the number of trees being planted is for us to consume more paper. Furthermore, if we dumped used paper down an old mineshaft, rather than recycling it, we would in effect be engaged in carbon sequestration: taking carbon out of the atmosphere and burying it in the ground. This is exactly what we need to be doing in order to combat global warming. So recycling paper would appear to be bad for the planet, on numerous levels. *Aluminum* recycling makes sense (as suggested by the fact that it is profitable). But why *paper* recycling?

It's possible that there is a coherent response to this argument, but I've never seen one. Most environmentalists focus on how recycling reduces deforestation in the short term but ignore the long-term consequences of diminishing the incentive to reforest. More often people just change the topic, decrying how tree farming promotes monoculture, criticizing logging practices, or complaining about the wastefulness of consumer society. What is conspicuously lacking is a simple, cogent line of reasoning that defends the practice against the "economic" objection. Again, this isn't to say there is no argument, just that I've never heard it. What I have heard is a whole host of increasingly ingenious ways of changing the subject.

s s s

"Economics is haunted by more fallacies than any other study known to man." This is the opening sentence of Henry Hazlitt's classic *Economics in One Lesson,* a book that is as valuable today as it was when first published in 1946.[6] The fact that this remains true is, in a sense, a sad reflection on the state of intellectual development in our civilization. Hazlitt's book consists of a discussion of twenty-odd popular arguments used in political debate, all based upon economic fallacies. What makes it discouraging to read is the fact that the modern twenty-first-century reader will still be familiar with most of these arguments, since the central ideas enjoy almost undiminished popular currency. (A few fallacious claims, primarily ones dealing with the prices of agricultural products, have faded in importance.)

Hazlitt's book should still be essential reading for anyone interested in knowing which way is up and which way is down in the world of economics. Yet it also has its flaws. Its central problem is that Hazlitt is an unqualified cheerleader for the free market. He tends to regard anyone with any misgivings whatsoever about the virtues of unbridled capitalism as either beholden to special interests or simply a bonehead. Not once in the entire book does he entertain the possibility that anyone might have any legitimate *moral* concerns about the way the market works.

The result is a failure to appreciate the extent to which individuals can have reasonable doubts about the capitalist system. Anyone who does have such doubts is therefore unlikely to pay much attention to Hazlitt's arguments. Having one's deeply felt moral convictions about social justice dismissed as either rationalized self-interest or unadorned stupidity is unlikely to put many people in a mood that is receptive to argument, much less create a willingness to follow some rather abstruse lines of economic reasoning. Yet time and again, this is the rhetorical strategy that Hazlitt employs.

Most economic popularizers have followed Hazlitt in this strategy. Economists constantly lament the fact that there is so much economic illiteracy. Yet the major attempts to communicate with people outside the profession have been marked by such profound disregard for the reader—and, in particular, for the reader's moral sensibilities—that they have largely failed in their purposes. Reading most works of "popular" economics, it is easy to get the impression that one is being sold a bill of goods, and a rather unsavory one at that.

This is unfortunate, since the failure to address these underlying moral concerns is one of the primary reasons for the persistence of so many of the fallacies that Hazlitt diagnoses. The economic proposals that he excoriates are for the most part motivated by a concern over fairness, or social justice. Rather than acknowledging the legitimacy of the underlying moral concern while showing how the proposed remedy will nevertheless fail to achieve the desired results, Hazlitt heaps scorn upon both the concerns and the proposals. The result is a complete failure of communication. People don't accept the arguments because they find the premises—not to mention the overall line of reasoning—morally repulsive. And so the fallacies persist.

I'd venture to say that pretty much everything that the average person thinks he or she knows about how the economy works is wrong (or is one degree of separation from something that is wrong). I'm sure this is what makes economists such cranky people. After all, it's impossible to read the morning newspaper without running into at least three or four glaring economic fallacies, even in the business pages. It must drive economists crazy. Whenever you see a journalist, politician, or lobbyist doing a "cost-benefit analysis," for instance, it's almost always wrong. Typically, the way people do it is by adding up all the costs of some policy they don't like, disregarding all the benefits, then declaring it a great social evil. I call this the "count the costs, ignore the benefits" fallacy.

My favorite example of this is when people talk about the "costs" that smoking imposes upon society. Usually the intrepid antismoking crusader will add up such things as the value of lost wages due to sickness and absenteeism, along with the cost to the public health care system of treating smoking-related illnesses like emphysema, lung cancer, heart disease, and various vascular disorders. Yet they ignore one absolutely fundamental principle: everyone has to die of something. This has some immediate and obvious consequences. Anyone who doesn't die of one *particular* thing dies of something else. Thus all those smokers who don't die of lung cancer, or who don't die of heart attacks, are bound to die of another cause. Whatever this other cause is, it's likely to be a whole lot more expensive, since lung cancer is basically untreatable and heart attacks are one of the cheapest, fastest ways to die. A moment's reflection is enough to suggest that smokers probably save "society" a lot of money. Proper cost-benefit analysis has shown the same thing: In 1995 an American analyst concluded that the average smoker generated a net *benefit* to society of 30¢ per pack, before even factoring in the taxes paid.[7]

It used to be the case that coroners would classify deaths in terms of "natural causes." For example, a famous "bill of mortality" compiled in England in 1655, while it used exotic categories like "dropsie," "rising of the lights," and "King's evill" to describe various causes of death, also included such categories as "found dead in street" and simply "aged."[8] Nowadays, however, people don't just die in the street or expire of old age; they die of some kind of medical condition. As a result, whenever we remove one cause of death (plague, polio, tuberculosis, cholera) the rates of everything else go up. Yet people constantly ignore this fact.

Environmentalists, for instance, are fond of pointing to skyrocketing rates of cancer throughout the industrialized world in the twentieth century as evidence of impending catastrophe. Yet this increase in cancer has coincided with dramatic improvements in average life expectancy. How is this possible? It's because a lot of the increase in cancer is *due to* increased life expectancy. Live long enough and you're guaranteed to get cancer, just because of accumulated copying errors in your cells. "Dying of cancer" is, in many cases, just a medicalized way of describing "dying of old age." The overall trend in cancer rates has been up because more people are now making it to an age where they are likely to develop it—because they are *not* dying of other things that used to kill significant percentages of the population.

I'm tempted sometimes to start a campaign against seat belts, on the grounds that they cause cancer. I'm sure I could find statistics to back up the claim. The rate of motor vehicle fatalities in Canada has fallen by about half in the past 30 years, largely due to improvements in automotive safety. Eventually some of these people who don't die in car accidents have to get cancer, so it's just a matter of time before a slight uptick in cancer rates is registered (or diabetes, heart disease, or something else). Isn't it strange, I can then argue, how the new mandatory seat-belt laws *just happen* to coincide with an increase in cancer rates?

I'm not trying to pick on environmentalists. There are certain types of cancer that are a result of exposure to environmental contaminants. My uncle, like most farmers back in the '60s, used to handle huge volumes of herbicide without even gloves on, much less a mask. That (alongside the three packs of cigarettes he smoked every day) no doubt contributed to his death from lung cancer. But to try to blame the overall trend in cancer rates on "the chemical industry" or some other environmental evildoer is to commit an elementary conceptual error. Of course, there is nothing particularly "economic" about this fallacy. It is just that confusions of this type are among the sort that economists, because of their disciplinary training, are particularly good at avoiding.

Each chapter in this book is based upon one such confusion and the fallacies that can result. The first half can be thought of as "favorite economic fallacies of the right"—arguments routinely peddled by conservatives not because those arguments make any sense, but because the conclusions are so agreeable to them. The second half consists of "favorite economic fallacies of the left."

$ $ $

One of the most unfortunate misunderstandings of economics is the idea that it's all about money. In fact, economists have distinguished themselves in the past century not so much by *what* they study as by *how* they study it. It is the methodology they employ, the way they try to model social interactions, that generates useful insights. This methodology is applicable in areas of social life that have nothing to do with buying and selling. Traffic is a good example, since driving seems to bring out the rational utility-maximizer in all of us. I once had an idea for a book called *All I Really Need to Know I Learned Sitting in Traffic.* This is only a slight exaggeration. What I did learn was that there are four big ideas you need to keep in mind, whenever you think about "society."

I. PEOPLE AREN'T STUPID

It's surprisingly easy to forget that there is other intelligent life on this planet, in the form of other people. When you sit around making little plans and schemes, you need to remember that everyone else is planning and scheming as well. They may not be doing a great job of it, but they are doing it, and in order for your plans and schemes to work out, you're going to have to take theirs into consideration. Economists call this the *strategic* dimension of social action.

Consider, for example, how people behave when sitting in traffic jams. You're in your lane, inching along, getting nowhere. Suddenly cars in the lane right next to you start pulling ahead. The truck that you've been watching in your side mirror zips past. What's the obvious thing to do? Change lanes, of course, to get into the one where the traffic is moving faster.

This is a seductive line of reasoning, but it ignores one crucial fact: you're not the only person on the road trying to get home. In fact, almost all the people in your lane, both in front of you and behind you, would like to get home sooner rather than later. And they're all sitting there, just like you, watching the traffic in the other lane zip by. Everyone has an incentive to switch lanes. But if the people in front of you switch, that makes your own lane go faster. So in fact you have two choices. You can switch lanes, or you can just sit tight and let the people in front of you switch. Either way, you'll probably get the same increase in speed. (In general, one can expect all lanes to move equally fast, for the same reason that one can expect all supermarket queues to be equally long.)

The real question, therefore, is not whether you want to get into the faster lane, but simply how many lane changes you want to make. Since lane changes are comparatively dangerous, the answer to that question depends really upon how averse you are to the thought of having an accident. Not surprisingly, it was an economist[9] who made this observation, and who offered the following bit of advice: If you're driving a beat-up old car, you should make the change; if you're driving a brand-new Mercedes, you're better off sitting tight and letting the people in front of you run the risk of an accident.

2. THE IMPORTANCE OF EQUILIBRIUM

Because economists pay careful attention to the strategic aspect of social interaction, they tend to be less interested in mere patterns of behavior or statistical correlations than other social scientists. The central concept in economic analysis is that of *equilibrium*—understood as an outcome that has no tendency to change. Because people adjust their behavior in response to changes in their environment, you can't predict what they're going to do just by looking at what they are currently doing. You have to figure out how they're going to respond to the change (and whether this response is going to cause further changes, and so on).

Ignoring these responses is one of the most significant sources of public policy failure. I am reminded of this whenever I'm sitting in my car waiting to turn left at a traffic light. I almost never make it through on yellow anymore, but this wasn't always the case. When I was growing up, traffic lights followed a fairly simple pattern. When the light going one way turned red, the light going the other way immediately turned green. Because of this, it was a very bad idea to run a red light, simply because you were likely to get clocked by a car going in the other direction. In this world, yellow meant yellow. Nowadays (or at least in Toronto, where I live), the pattern is different. When one light turns red, the other does not turn green right away. Instead, they both remain red for about two seconds.

I can just imagine how this scheme came about. Some well-intentioned bureaucrat somewhere, looking at the number of collisions in intersections, thought it would be a good idea to have a little cooling-off period, so that everyone could adjust to the big change that was about to happen. Therefore it was decreed that both lights should stay red for a few seconds, so that everyone could come to a stop. But of course the policy had no such effect. Motorists, knowing that they have an additional two seconds after the light turns red, simply treat yellow lights as though they were green and treat the newly switched red light as a yellow. In other words, the equilibrium changed. The result has been an epidemic of red-light running (not to mention the near-impossibility of turning left on yellow).

Because of this failure to anticipate the shift in equilibrium, the policy added absolutely no benefit from the standpoint of traffic safety, and probably made things worse. All this because some bureaucrat somewhere failed to realize that people were going to change their behavior as a result of the policy being proposed. This is an incredibly common mistake made by social engineers of all stripes (the fancy term for it is *parametric thinking*, or treating the social environment as though it were exogenously fixed). Say what you like about economists—love them or hate them—they are the people least likely to make this sort of error.

3. EVERYTHING DEPENDS UPON EVERYTHING ELSE

If you listen to economists talk, one of the things that you'll hear them say a lot, in response to questions, is "It depends . . ." This isn't because they're being shifty. It's because the answers to a lot of questions really do depend upon the answers to a lot of other questions. And this is because, out there in the real world, a lot of things actually depend upon a lot of other things. Economists tend to be more alert to this than many others because the market economy represents such a vast system of interdependency.

As a result, whenever something happens and we want to consider its effects, we have to make sure that we're tracing them back far enough. A classic mistake is to look at only the immediate effects without considering what effects those effects will have. Take, for example, the phenomenon of "induced traffic." If you ask a traffic planner whether a network of urban roads has "enough capacity," the answer will be "It depends . . ." If you keep the volume of traffic constant and take away some of the roads, then the system will have suffered a decrease in capacity. But whether or not removing roads *actually* makes a difference to anyone will depend upon whether volume remains constant.

After the destruction of the Embarcadero Freeway in San Francisco by the 1989 earthquake, residents decided not to rebuild it. Planners kept an eye on the alternate routes to see where all the traffic would go. What they found instead was that most of it disappeared. Contrary to initial expectations, no spike in congestion was registered anywhere in the Bay Area. (In New York, the Department of Transportation made an accurate assessment after the collapse of the West Side Highway in 1973 and discovered that 93% of the traffic disappeared.)[10]

What these observations point to is the fact that the volume of traffic at any given moment is part of an equilibrium, one that rests on a number of factors. Congestion is one of them. Because (non-toll) roads are free, people "pay" to use them with their time (just as people do when they line up for any underpriced commodity, such as a concert ticket). As the amount of time that it will take to get somewhere increases, people with better things to do stop driving—they reschedule, consolidate trips, take transit, or find other alternatives (in the longer term, they may choose to live closer to work or shopping or transit). Adding more capacity to the road network thus "induces" traffic. By decreasing congestion, you encourage more people to drive, lead people to live farther from work, and so on, which simply brings the level of congestion back to where it was before.

But what happens if you pump a whole lot of money into public transit? This is also unlikely to relieve congestion. If more people start riding transit, because it's now subsidized or more convenient, that will free up space on the roads, which in turn reduces the "cost" of driving. If trips start to take less time, more people will drive (or those who do will drive more often). As long as roads are free, there's no way to square this circle.

4. CERTAIN THINGS HAVE TO ADD UP

I once saw a cute advertisement for a clothing company featuring snappily dressed protesters waving placards calling for a variety of improvements in society, including "more green lights." I thought it was a nice portrayal of youthful idealism. I hate red lights as much as the next guy, but since one person's green light is someone else's red light, increasing the sum total of green lights is not just a practical impossibility, it's a conceptual impossibility. Still, the *message* is a hopeful one.

If this seems a bit uncharitable, it is worth observing that all sorts of people campaign for the economic equivalent of more green traffic lights. It comes from a failure to recognize that some things have to add up. The total number of green traffic lights must be the same as the total number of red traffic lights, because one person's green light just *is* someone else's red light. The same is true of economic exchange. Every time someone sells something, someone else must buy something. Why? Because the only way to sell something is to sell it *to* someone else. This may seem obvious, but a staggering percentage of the popular commentary on all sorts of economic issues loses track of this elementary equivalence.

For example, while individuals are able to spend more than they earn (and thereby go into debt), society as a whole is unable to. That's because one person's spending just *is* someone else's earning. This is why the GDP—the gross domestic product—can be calculated in two different ways: the first by adding up the value of goods and services produced in the economy, the second by adding up all the income that is earned. This is something activists for the annual Buy Nothing Day keep forgetting. Reducing consumption for one day does not reduce total consumption unless you also reduce *income*. You would have to have an "Earn Nothing Day" in order to have any impact.[11] Trying to reduce consumption merely by spending less is a conceptual impossibility.

These equivalencies can often be tricky. When people talk about taxes, for instance, there is a tendency to forget that—setting aside bequests—people spend their entire incomes. A "consumption tax" is nothing but an income tax with an exemption for savings. Even this exemption is not really an exemption but just a deferral, since—again, setting aside bequests—people eventually spend their savings. Yet when the Conservative government in Canada recently cut the GST (Canada's "value-added" consumption tax), some commentators, even those writing in rather highbrow newspapers, observed that this would be useful only to consumers who were contemplating a major purchase, such as a car. The rest would have been better off with an income-tax cut.

Now there may have been a good argument to be made for an income-tax cut, but this certainly wasn't it. Whether or not you spend $10,000 on a single big item or $10 on a thousand small items, you still pay the same amount in consumption tax. This is easy to forget. A couple of years ago, I paid over $8,000 in tax on a new car. I looked at the invoice and thought, "Holy crap!" In fact, there was no reason for alarm. One way or another, the $8,000 would have gone to the government. If I hadn't bought the car, I would have bought all sorts of other stuff, and all those other purchases would have been taxed at exactly the same rate. The appropriate response, I realized, was not nervous agitation, but Zen-like tranquillity.

$ $ $

If it makes anyone feel better, I should mention that I'm not an economist. This is why I consider myself free to make all sorts of wild generalizations about what "economists" think. (I work in a department of philosophy, sometimes known as "the department of data-free speculation"—which, come to think of it, is one thing that philosophers and neoclassical economists have in common.) I hope that this will be taken in the right spirit and that the relevant qualifications and caveats will simply be assumed: naturally, not all economists think alike, not all economists are apostles for the free market, the views I criticize were more strongly held twenty years ago, there have always been active debates within the profession, and so on.

It is perhaps also worth mentioning that, apart from not being an economist, I have essentially no formal training in the subject. I did take the usual Economics 101 course as an undergraduate, but I only went to class a couple of times. The professor got on my nerves. Once I discovered that the exams were going to be multiple-choice, generated by some software that accompanied the textbook, I never went back. That was the end of my official training. Since then, I've just been reading on my own. I also have no mathematics beyond high school. I did learn calculus, but I can't remember how to do it.

I mention this not to undermine anyone's confidence in the arguments that follow, but merely to show that the barriers to economic literacy are not as great as they are sometimes made out to be. Make no mistake, economics can be extremely tricky. Nevertheless, the central ideas can all be grasped through the exercise of general intelligence. There is no secret code that needs to be learned. Nor is there a need for an advanced degree in the subject in order to avoid the pitfalls that are detailed in the chapters that follow.

What I am presenting in this book are all very basic arguments, based on simple models, illustrating mistakes that any educated person should be able to avoid. But of course, for every one of these simple claims there are dozens of exceptions, caveats and qualifications, and all sorts of more exotic models that behave somewhat differently. The fact that I don't stop to deal with all these possibilities should be understood in context, and with respect to the type of work that this is. Every time a person makes a fallacious inference, it is possible to invent some more complicated or circuitous chain of reasoning that "might be what he had in mind." Nevertheless, if it looks like a duck, swims like a duck, and quacks like a duck, it probably is a duck. People make a lot of mistakes when it comes to economics, and getting past these mistakes is an essential step for anyone hoping to make the world a better place.

PART I
RIGHT-WING FALLACIES

In which the false beliefs and fallacious inferences of the apostles of the free market (including, but not limited to, members of the notorious "Chicago School") are unveiled, debunked, and overcome.

CHAPTER 1

CAPITALISM IS NATURAL

Why the market actually depends on government

People often complain about the absence of "big ideas" in contemporary political debate. There is some truth to this. Politics in the twentieth century was often characterized by sharp disagreements over fundamental issues, with various factions wanting to completely overhaul society in all sorts of dramatic ways. In the 1920s, for instance, eugenics—the selective breeding of human populations—was all the rage in political circles. Winston Churchill, an enthusiastic proponent, thought it was essential to stem what he called, with a candor typical of his era, "the unnatural and increasingly rapid growth of the feeble-minded and insane classes."[1]

Then, of course, there were fascism and the "world communist revolution"—both of which involved what were, in retrospect, rather unlikely proposals. Consider V. I. Lenin, in 1918, still confidently predicting the "withering away of the state" under communism. Getting rid of the market economy and replacing it with central planning would be no big deal, he thought—a matter of "watching, recording and issuing receipts," tasks that were "within the reach of anybody who can read and write and knows the first four rules of arithmetic."[2]

In the '50s, it seemed there wasn't a problem in the world that couldn't be solved by "science." Women in the United States stopped breastfeeding en masse, figuring that baby formula had to be better—after all, *it was made by scientists!* How much longer could it be before they solved other social problems, like crime or disease? John F. Kennedy spoke for many when he predicted that technocracy, not democracy, was the future. "Most of the problems that we now face," he claimed, "are technical problems, are administrative problems" best dealt with by experts.

This technocratic consensus lasted long enough for Daniel Bell to publish his famously ill-timed book, *The End of Ideology*, in 1960. The ink was barely dry on the page before things went completely haywire, ushering in one of the most intensely ideological periods in Western history. The '60s counterculture arose, promising no less than a complete transformation of both human civilization and consciousness. Sex, drugs, and rock and roll were presented not just as entertaining distractions from the serious business of life, but as forces that would fundamentally transform the family, the economy, the state, and the geopolitical system.

While the boomers didn't exactly deliver on these promises, one must admit that they gave it a college try. To take just one tiny example, by the early 1970s there were thousands of communes across the United States engaged in various forms of collective child rearing, trying to render the nuclear family obsolete through communal parenting.[3] (A friend of mine in grad school had, in his youth, belonged to an ill-starred venture of this sort. He wound up with a dozen or so "kids" from this period, some of whom would occasionally drop by to visit him. Only one was his biological daughter.)

The point is this: There was a time, not so long ago, that when people talked about changing society, they generally had Big Plans. These plans were big in the sense that, had any of them worked, the world we live in would have been changed almost beyond recognition. Things are different now. People may complain just as loudly, but they generally lack big ideas about how things should be redone. Or to speak more precisely: The big ideas that do remain are so *obviously* bad ideas (such as Islamic theocracy) that almost no psychologically well-balanced individual feels tempted by them. There is a stark difference between this ethos and a time when mild-mannered, middle-class people actually thought it might be helpful to tear down various pillars of Western civilization and rebuild everything from the ground up.

Nowadays, the disagreements that do remain tend to be over matters of detail. Political protest still carries the trappings of radicalism, but when you scratch the surface a bit, ask people what they really want, you typically end up with some fairly modest proposals. Antiglobalization protesters may still call for the overthrow of capitalism, but they're usually willing to settle for an environmental protection rider or an amendment to the arbitration mechanism of the next free trade agreement. In France, activists have even insisted upon using the term *altermondialisation* to describe the movement, rather than *antimondialisation*, to emphasize the fact that they are not opposed to globalization—they would just like to see it done a bit differently.

Where have all the radicals gone? The movie *The Corporation*, after more than two hours of bluster about the "psychopathic" pursuit of money and power on the part of the modern business enterprise, ends with a call not for workers to seize control of the means of production or for the state to nationalize big business. Instead, it celebrates the outbreak of "grassroots democracy" in the town of Arcata, California (pop. 16,651), where citizens got together to—brace yourself—limit the number of franchise-operated fast food restaurants in the town to nine.

It's a reminder of the old joke about a Fabian socialist rally, where the protesters chant, "What do we want? Gradual change! When do we want it? In due course!"

In a sense, we are all Fabians now.

This state of affairs has been described in a variety of ways. Francis Fukuyama referred to it as the "end of history." Jürgen Habermas, in a slightly less upbeat mood, described it as "the exhaustion of utopian energies." The central element is the fact that liberal democracy has emerged out of the twentieth century as the only credible form of political organization, alongside some sort of regulated capitalism as the only plausible form of economic organization. As a result, all the serious participants in the political process—and even a fair proportion of the wacky ones—find themselves espousing what are essentially variations on the same basic blueprint for society. Everyone winds up defending—or, better yet, presupposing—some version of welfare-state capitalism. Of course, the welfare state has all the characteristics that a woman typically seeks in a husband, not a lover. It's safe, reliable, and a good provider. As a result, it tends to generate a fairly steady stream of grievances. But as everyone knows, there's a big difference between complaining about your husband and actually leaving your husband. Suffice it to say that, right now, divorce does not look imminent.

The successes and failures of the welfare state have forced both the left and the right to swallow very bitter pills—to renounce a core component of the ideologies that at one time set them apart. What are these pills? Simply put, the left has been forced to give up on communism, while the right has been forced to give up on libertarianism. Communism, to simplify somewhat, is the view that, when it comes to the economy, the state should do everything. Libertarianism is the view that the state should do nothing. Both ideas are now thoroughly discredited. The collapse of communism is, of course, somewhat better known, because it made for better television. But the collapse of libertarianism in the twentieth century was just as complete.

The idea that people could get along fine with just markets, and no government, turned out to rest upon a version of what economists call the "compositional fallacy." The basic assumption of libertarianism is that if people share some particular economic interest (such as having a stable system of property rights), they will naturally get together as a group to advance that interest. A capitalist economic system could arise as what Friedrich Hayek called a "spontaneous order."[4] This turns out to be false. A whole bunch of individual interests just don't add up to one group interest. Despite having the same objectives, people often need the "visible hand" of government to step in, in order to get everyone to act in a way that actually promotes their common objectives. This is a somewhat surprising result, and it is one of the greatest triumphs of twentieth-century social science to have finally given it clear expression.

$ $ $

The libertarian sensibility received its clearest legal expression in the 1905 United States Supreme Court decision *Lochner v. New York,* in which the court struck down a state law that prohibited employees in bakeries from working more than 10 hours per day or 60 hours per week. Bakery workers were grown-ups, the majority reasoned, "not wards of the state": they should be free to do as they pleased. A law restricting an employee's work hours represented "an unreasonable, unnecessary, and arbitrary interference with the right of the individual to his personal liberty, or to enter into those contracts in relation to labor which may seem to him appropriate or necessary for the support of himself and his family."[5] After all, if people are free to work *two* jobs, why shouldn't they be free to work 16 hours a day in *one* job?

Some people are tempted to regard this sort of reasoning as simply a smokescreen for the expression of crass commercial interests. Yet this grossly underestimates the intellectual appeal of libertarianism. Setting aside political ideology and social conscience for a moment, isn't it obvious that the Lochner court had a point? Why shouldn't consenting adults be able to enter into whatever contracts they judge to be in their interests? Far from being merely an apologetic, libertarianism is in fact a sophisticated political doctrine, rigorously developed, based upon a set of very simple and intuitively compelling ideas. It's also a house of cards, founded entirely upon a fallacy. But the flaw in the foundations is sufficiently unobvious that generations of very clever people were able to overlook it.

In order to see the attractions of libertarianism, it is important to consider two very powerful images that emerged from the nineteenth century. The first regards nature as an optimizing system, with Darwinian natural selection ruthlessly weeding out the sick and unfit. The second regards capitalism as an optimizing system, with the discipline of the market driving out the lazy, irresponsible, and inefficient. The confluence of these two ideas is summed up perfectly in Herbert Spencer's expression "survival of the fittest," initially used to describe social relations in the market economy but subsequently extended to describe evolutionary dynamics in the natural world.[6]

Indeed, Spencer was not the only one to be struck by the similarities between Adam Smith's "invisible hand" and Charles Darwin's mechanism of natural selection. Both represented systems of "spontaneous order"—situations in which an outcome that *looked* like the product of meticulous planning and design turned out in fact to be the result of a "blind" mechanism. If one looks at bird beaks among different species, for instance, it seems that each was designed for a particular task: cracking seeds, catching fish, tearing meat, and so on. Darwin was the first to propose a mechanism that could achieve this result without positing any sort of conscious design.

The market exhibits a very similar structure. When left to its own devices, the movement of prices ensures that labor and resources migrate to their best employment. If there is a shortage of coal, tin, wheat, or whatever, prices will be bid up until only people who are able to make best use of these inputs are able to afford them. An alien observing from on high might think that some conscious intellect was rationing these goods, but in fact the outcome is nothing more than a consequence of each individual's pursuing his or her own interest under the appropriate circumstances. Tin cans are no longer made out of tin,. and nickels are no longer made out of nickel, not because anyone sat down and decided that these metals would be of greater use in other applications, but simply because the price of these metals was bid up to the point where it became economical to change the way tin cans and nickels were made.

The medieval Christian worldview assumed that all the order in the universe was a product of some underlying divine purpose. Everything from rocks, plants, and animals to humans needed to be understood in terms of the good that was sought, since this good represented the place of each of these creatures in the providential order. Striving for the good was seen to be the "final cause" of all natural and vital motion. In the case of humans, this good was sought self-consciously, taking the form of "natural law." The highest manifestation of this pursuit of the good was the state, which was taken to be the agency through which humans sought to give concrete expression to the dictates of this natural law.

The central success of the Scientific Revolution was its demonstration of how "orderliness" could be explained without divine intention. Newtonian mechanics allowed one to show how heavenly order (the regularity of planetary orbits, their alignment in a single plane) could be explained without God. In the case of living things, Darwin showed how a perfectly "blind" mechanism, such as natural selection, could achieve adaptation and "design." There was no need to assume that living creatures sought some good or pursued some higher divine purpose; a narrow drive for self-preservation was all that was required for natural selection to occur.

In the case of society, Adam Smith showed that a perfectly "blind" mechanism was able to achieve order. There was no need for conscious guidance by the state, since the market mechanism was able to produce optimal allocations on its own. Furthermore, there was no need to assume any pursuit of the good, or any higher divine purpose, on the part of individuals. When seen in this light, "natural law" becomes irrelevant; the narrow pursuit of self-interest is all that is required to achieve what Spencer described as "a constant progress toward a higher degree of skill, intelligence, and self-regulation—a better co-ordination of actions—a more complete life."[7]

Thus twentieth-century libertarianism developed, essentially as an application to society of the principles of the Darwinian revolution. Aristotle thought that "the good" was required in order to have order in either nature or society; as it turned out, it wasn't required for either. What libertarians posited, in the place of the state and of natural law, was simply a system of natural rights, most famously the rights to life, liberty, and property.

From this basic point of departure, two flavors of libertarianism developed. The first claims that self-interest alone is enough to motivate individuals not only to assert their own rights, but to respect the rights of others.[8] No government whatsoever is required; a market economy is perfectly capable of arising in the so-called state of nature. The second claims that a state is required in order to prevent individuals from interfering with one another's rights but that this constitutes the only legitimate role for government. Libertarians of this tendency endorse a minimal, or what Robert Nozick called a "nightwatchman," state—one that has no mandate to take any positive action: it is merely there to ensure that the rights of individuals are respected.

Over the years, libertarians tried various strategies to show that all this could be accomplished entirely through decentralized, self-interested action. Unfortunately, they never quite succeeded in doing so.

§ § §

In order to see the fatal weakness in the libertarian scheme, one can start by looking at the problems with the Darwinian version of "survival of the fittest." Sometimes the competition for survival results in outcomes that are highly adaptive—eyes for seeing, limbs for running, teeth for chewing—but sometimes the results are highly maladaptive. It depends upon how exactly the competition is structured, and how the "competitive edge" of the winners is acquired.

In this respect, the concept of "fitness" harbors an important ambiguity. At a certain level of abstraction, the concept is simple. To say that x is more "fit" than y is simply to say that x is able to reproduce itself better than *y*—it says nothing at all about how this is achieved. One aspect of biological fitness is the organism's ability to survive in its environment and to compete with other species for control of various ecological niches. We tend to think of this as "good" fitness. In this category, we would put things like ruminants' digestive systems, giraffes' long necks, birds' hollow bones, and so on.

Another important aspect of fitness, however, involves the organism's ability to compete against members of its own species for resources and reproductive opportunities. This category contains a lot of "bad" fitness. Consider the habit known as "new mate infanticide," wherein a male kills all of a new partner's existing children before mating with her. It is surprisingly common among animal species. One can see how such a behavioral disposition would be particularly "fit," since it allows the male to avoid wasting time and energy raising genetically unrelated children, which is to say, those who are unlikely to share the same disposition. This, however, we tend to think of as "bad" fitness.

The biggest problem with intraspecies competition of this sort is that it can easily lead to an overall reduction in fitness with respect to the environment. The classic example, noted by Darwin himself, is the peacock's tail. For whatever reason, peahens have a marked preference for males with longer and more elaborate tail feathers.[9] At the same time, these tail feathers both impede flight and demand resources to produce (which is presumably why peahens don't have them). A male with longer, more majestic tail feathers is therefore less likely to survive to adulthood. But since he is more likely to reproduce if and when he gets there, the trait may nevertheless prove to be evolutionarily successful.

The problem is that once this trait becomes successful, it also becomes universal in the population. As a result, any given male with the trait will lose his differential reproductive advantage (since everyone now has equally long tail feathers), even though he continues to bear the cost of that advantage (producing those tail feathers). In other words, the gains to individual organisms cancel out, while the disadvantage to the species persists. The net result is maladaptive. Individuals with such traits are able to survive only because the structure of the trait is such that as they go down, they are able to take every other member of the species down with them.

The peacock's tail is a biological example of what economists call a "race to the bottom." Figure 1.1 shows the results of two peacocks competing against each other, with outcomes a function of the relative length of their tails. Each square of the matrix shows the number of offspring that survive to adulthood (Peacock 1 first, Peacock 2 second). Short tails have a number of survival benefits, which means that five chicks from any given brood will make it to adulthood. Long tails diminish the chances of survival, so only three can be expected to make it. However, long-tailed peacocks have one advantage: If both peacocks have tails of the same length, females will be indifferent between them (and so both can be expected to father one brood); but if one peacock has a tail that is longer than the other's, he can monopolize female attention, and thus expect to father two broods (while the other is denied the opportunity to reproduce).

	Peacock 2	
	Short tail	Long tail
Short tail	(5,5)	(0,6)
Long tail	(6,0)	(3,3)

Peacock 1

Figure 1.1 The peacock's tail

The situation in which both peacocks have short tails is unstable. As soon as a mutation comes along that results in a somewhat longer tail, that individual gains a huge reproductive advantage, and so the trait spreads throughout the population. The trait, however, is collectively self-defeating. In a few generations, when everyone has it, the outcome is worse for everyone (instead of an average survival of five chicks per brood, it is now down to three). And if a different mutation comes along, making the tail even longer, the same selective pressures may continue to favor that new mutation. This cycle can continue until the species is quite literally on the brink of extinction. (One need only contemplate the fate of "megafauna" such as the Irish elk, the largest of which had grotesquely impractical antlers spanning 13 feet.)

Evolution does not optimize. In fact, the world of living creatures is the product of one giant race to the bottom after another. Consider the case of trees. What exactly is the point of growing to be 50 feet tall? It requires enormous resources, as water and nutrients must be pumped from the ground all the way up to the tips of highest leaves. The answer, of course, is that trees are striving for sunlight. But sunlight is freely available much closer to the ground, *so long as nothing else gets in the way.* And therein lies the rub. If all the other trees are growing to be three feet tall, then the tree that grows to be four feet tall will gain a competitive advantage—more sunlight for itself, less for its neighbors. Thus the four-foot variant will slowly take over. But if all the trees are four feet tall, then the tree that grows to be *five* feet tall will gain a competitive advantage. And so it continues.

The important point is that this competition is nonproductive from the standpoint of the overall fitness of the trees. Eventually they reach the physical limits, where it is impossible to get any taller without becoming overly fragile or overly difficult to supply with nutrients. And still, from the standpoint of access to sunlight, they are all no better off than they were back when they were shrubs. One can tell a similar story about the development of movement, consciousness, or even social intelligence. If natural selection was optimizing, life on earth would be one smooth, uniform layer of bacteria. The wild diversity that we see around us is entirely a product of the *failure* of natural selection to favor that which is "best" from the standpoint of species fitness.

Yet despite all these examples, it is still easy to commit the compositional fallacy when thinking about evolution—to assume that because a particular trait enhances the fitness of each individual who possesses it, that it must also enhance the fitness of those individuals taken as a group (that is, as a species). In fact, adaptations that are "good for the individual" need not be "good for the species" at all. Individuals cannot be counted upon to do what is necessary to promote their own interests as a group.

§ § §

Although Darwin himself drew special attention to these examples of suboptimality, generations of evolutionary biologists, not to mention popular commentators, stubbornly clung to the idea that natural selection was optimizing (that it always increased fitness, or that it always favored improvements in the organism relative to its environment). This required rather concerted inattention to the fact that much of the competition in the natural world has a collectively self-defeating character. Particularly when intraspecies competition is involved, forms of behavior that initially maximize individual reproductive success may, when universally adopted, reduce the reproductive success of each individual. We tend to look for external factors, like falling asteroids, to explain species extinction. We should consider internal factors as well.

What is true of evolutionary systems is also true of social relations. The same dynamic that leads evolutionary systems in the direction of collectively self-defeating outcomes undermines the success of many human projects. We tend to blame external factors in this case as well, ignoring the fact that (most of the time) people themselves are, if not individually then collectively, the authors of their own misfortunes.

Take the case of the market. Let us agree, for the sake of argument, with Smith's contention that a properly structured capitalist economy transforms the individual pursuit of self-interest into outcomes that are better for everyone involved. All transactions are voluntary, so exchanges will occur only if each party values the goods purchased more than those sold. This leaves everyone free to attend to their own interests. As long as everyone plays by the rules, no one has to worry about whether others are getting a good deal. The fact that everyone is willing to accept the transaction suggests that they are.

But where exactly do these rules come from? In order for the market to function correctly, people must be willing to refrain from all sorts of nuisance behavior: stealing, defaulting on payment, misrepresenting their goods, coercing others, and so on. Naturally, it is in everyone's *interest* for everyone to abide by these rules. But that doesn't mean they'll do it. Consider Figure 1.2, which shows the options facing two trappers as they decide whether it would be better to spend the afternoon setting traps or poaching from their neighbor. If they both choose to set as many traps as possible, then they will both double their catch. If, however, one decides to spend his afternoon poaching while the other spends all his time setting traps, then the poacher will triple his catch, leaving the other with nothing. The other now has no choice but to start poaching in the afternoon as well, leaving them both much worse off.

| | **Trapper 2** | |
	Set traps	Poach
Trapper 1 Set traps	(2,2)	(0,3)
Poach	(3,0)	(1,1)

Figure 1.2 The state of nature

This sort of interaction is often called a *prisoner's dilemma*, after a tactic supposedly used by police to get suspects to testify against one another. By offering an acquittal on a lesser charge, each collaborator can be persuaded to testify against the other on a major charge. Yet when both rat out the other, the result is more jail time for both. Thus the two suspects face what is known as a *collective action problem:* even though they would both be better off if neither testified, neither has any incentive to remain silent. They therefore wind up with an outcome that is collectively self-defeating.

Some people also refer to these as *free rider problems.* Each of the trappers hopes to benefit from the actions of the other, without making a contribution himself. When they both do this, *neither* makes a contribution. (Note that the "problem" with free riding is not the unfairness that results when one person is able to successfully take advantage of the benefits produced by another; the problem is that no benefits are produced at all, because everyone is too busy trying to take advantage of everyone else.) Thus the competition for individual advantage, far from generating what Spencer described as "better co-ordination of actions," in fact generates an outcome that is worse for all.

In order to get a market economy going, three basic systems of cooperation must be in place. As David Hume described it, there must be "stability of possession," "transfer through consent," and "the performance of promises"—also known as property, exchange, and contract.[10] Yet the free rider problem clearly undermines all three. Why plant your own crops when you can steal from your neighbor? Why pay for your purchase when you can renege after you have taken delivery? Why perform services at the price you have agreed upon when an opportunity arises to demand more?

Naturally, both the buyer and seller can promise each other that they will refrain from doing these sorts of things. But as long as self-interest is the only motive, these promises lack credibility. As soon as either person has the chance to break his promise, self-interest will lead him to do so.

Libertarians have been quick to suggest that, even if promises are not credible, individuals may still respect the property of others, or abide by their contracts, because they fear retaliation. This argument essentially appeals to threats as a way of explaining respect for individual rights, ignoring the fact that if self-interest is the only motive, it is also impossible to make credible threats, for *exactly the same reason* that it is impossible to make credible promises.[11] Exacting retribution is a costly (or at least risky) business. When I say to someone, "Do it or I'll shoot you," the implication is that shooting the person is not something I actually *want* to do (if I wanted to do it, then, being self-interested, I would do it anyway, regardless of whether the person complied with my demand). So if the person that I'm threatening says, "Go ahead and shoot me," then my bluff has been called. Now that the threat has failed, there's no point in shooting him. I might want to carry out the threat in order to gain a reputation as a person not to be trifled with (I might also carry through on my promises, in order to gain a reputation as a person that can be trusted). But this is far too weak a mechanism to sustain a system of rights. If the *only* reason I am doing something is to gain reputation, this means that I will stop doing it the moment these reputation effects are absent. As a result, reputations will not be of much use: everyone will tend to ignore them, knowing that past behavior has no predictive value when it comes to future conduct.[12]

Of course, this is not how things work in the real world. In the real world, people make credible commitments—both promises and threats—all the time. What this argument does show, however, is that in a hypothetical world in which individuals are motivated entirely by rational self-interest, one cannot get the foundations for a market economy in place. Some type of non-self-interested action is required in order to get the basic system of rights going. Individuals need to be able to commit themselves, credibly, to respecting the rights of others. Appealing to the threat of punishment as a way of explaining this commitment is circular, since the ability to make credible threats presupposes some form of commitment.

Yet once one takes away the possibility of threats in the state of nature, the "pure" libertarian project collapses. From John Locke in the seventeenth century to Robert Nozick in the twentieth, libertarians have appealed to individual enforcement as the frontline mechanism for the defense of individual rights. They have failed to realize that presupposing punishment is as good as presupposing universal brotherly love. While positing either one can solve a lot of social-engineering problems, neither can be the result of self-interest alone. As a result, there is no such thing as "spontaneous order" in human society. The invisible hand of the market cannot do all the work; some type of conscious guidance is also required, to get the invisible hand going in the first place.

$$ \$ \ \$ \ \$ $$

So we need to have a state; the market cannot do everything. In particular, the market cannot arise spontaneously: it must be created, and its fundamental rules must be enforced, by the state.[13] People have tried to square this circle in hundreds of different ways, but no matter how you run the numbers, the results always come back the same: You can't get a market economy out of self-interest alone. What is required—and what self-interest cannot provide—is an honest enforcement agency to impose Hume's three "fundamental laws": to protect private property, to ensure the voluntariness of exchange, and to enforce contracts. This enforcement agency must remain neutral among the rival parties; its services cannot simply be available to the highest bidder. In order for its threats to be credible, the enforcement agency must be motivated by some principled commitment to ensuring respect for the law.

This was the first major concession forced upon libertarians, and there is some satisfaction in observing that it results from nothing more than a consistent application of economic tools of analysis. As a result, "pure" libertarianism is practically extinct as a political doctrine. Moderate libertarians, like Nozick, accept the need for an enforcement agency. They believe that government should take the form of a "minimal" state, doing what is necessary to create the institutional preconditions for the market and nothing more. (One can find echoes of this libertarian minimal state in modern conservative doctrines that treat criminal justice, national defense, and the enforcement of contracts as pretty much the only desirable functions of government.) Unfortunately for libertarianism, once the need for a minimal state is conceded, the first step down a very slippery slope has been taken.

Since imposing punishment is costly, an enforcement agency is going to require resources. Yet it cannot rely upon voluntary contracting or donations in order to secure them, simply because any such system is going to be vulnerable to free rider problems. Even if everyone benefits from having the police around to protect private property or to enforce contracts, each individual would like someone else to pay for these services. Knowing that his or her personal contribution is unlikely to make or break the police force or the judicial system, most people will not voluntarily pay for these services.[14] Thus the state has no choice but to impose taxes so that it can secure the resources that it requires.

Taxes, as we all know, are coercive. They restrict individual liberty. Yet the libertarian is forced to admit that taxation—at least at a certain level—is not only necessary, but desirable (in order to institute the foundations of the free market). How is one to justify overriding the freedom of the individual in this case? Coercion is justified here because it is necessary in order to resolve a collective action problem. Thus it is not freedom in general that is being denied by such taxes, only the freedom to free ride, which is not really a desirable form of freedom in the first place.

It should be noted that the level of taxation required to institute even the most bare-bones system of property rights and commercial exchange is not negligible. Anyone who has ever bought a piece of land and has been through the rigmarole of title searches and so forth knows that meticulous public records are essential for determining who owns what. Indeed, one of the reasons that "possession is nine-tenths of the law" is that it is prohibitively expensive to keep definitive records of who actually owns what. In their book *The Cost of Rights: Why Liberty Depends on Taxes,* Stephen Holmes and Cass Sunstein estimate that in 1997 the United States federal government spent $203 million on property-records management.[15] That was just to keep track of things. Protecting and enforcing those rights cost the federal government more than $6.5 *billion*—and that does not include any of the costs associated with the federal justice system (more than $5 billion), much less "police protection and criminal corrections" in the nation as a whole ($73 billion in 1992).[16]

We have a special term for these types of services when they are offered by government and paid for through taxation. They are called *social programs.* (They are also known as *public goods,* although this is a somewhat loose way of speaking—more on this later.) Here we can see the fundamental problem with the libertarian or conservative vision of a minimal state. It has no principled basis: it is simply a list of social programs that people with certain personal preferences and animosities happen to favor. Once the libertarian makes the crucial concession— that it is legitimate for the state to impose taxes in order to provide goods and services that, because of collective action problems, would not otherwise be provided—it's difficult to explain why there shouldn't be other social programs as well, to resolve other sorts of collective action problems.

Conservatives, we are told, support government spending on "law and order," national defense, maybe highways, and perhaps a few other things. But why just these programs? Why not public housing, public education, public health care, state pension plans, unemployment insurance, environmental legislation, and so on? The basic argument for all of these social programs is that state provision is necessary in order to resolve collective action problems. They are, in this respect, no different than the military or the criminal justice system. Of course, the details of these arguments are all controversial. The point is that the libertarian is now forced to consider arguments for each of these social programs on a case-by-case basis. Sweeping denunciations of government "interference" with the market or with individual liberty are no longer credible. The scope of state action and the appropriate level of taxation cannot be settled at the level of political ideology; they now depend upon the answer to empirical questions concerning the occurrence and severity of collective action problems and the effectiveness of government in resolving them.

$ $ $

Modern libertarians might still have been able to make the case for a minimal state had they stopped with Hume's three fundamental laws. Unfortunately, Hume's laws proved to be manifestly inadequate as a foundation for a robust market economy. Property rights and contract law provided the most rudimentary foundations of nineteenth-century capitalism, but the problem with nineteenth-century capitalism is that it didn't *work* very well. It certainly was not the well-oiled wealth-producing machine that we are familiar with today. Between 1870 and 1900, for instance, the American economy underwent eight complete business cycles and spent almost exactly the same amount of time in recession as it did undergoing growth. Apart from innumerable bank runs, there were five full-scale banking panics during that period (when depositors lost their confidence in the banking system as a whole, and so tried to withdraw *all* deposits from *all* banks simultaneously).[17]

As a result, what legislatures did, over the course of the nineteenth century and well into the twentieth, was an enormous amount of tweaking of the capitalist system. The creation of the United States Federal Reserve System in 1914, for instance, followed by the Federal Deposit Insurance Corporation in 1933, essentially eliminated the old-fashioned bank run. (Indeed, the concept of depositors making a "run" on a bank has become so unfamiliar that many people find the plot line of *Mary Poppins* or the ending of *It's a Wonderful Life* somewhat mysterious.) But deposit insurance is a straightforward example of a government social program. When banks take in deposits, they don't actually lock them up in a vault—they lend the money out to other people. This means that if all the depositors show up at the same time asking for their money back, not only does this drive the bank out of business, it is collectively self-defeating from the standpoint of the depositors, since "calling in" all these loans simultaneously makes it impossible to recover their full value. But rather than deterring depositors, this impending catastrophe simply generates a race to the bottom. It gives each person an incentive to get his money out *first*. This creates a hair-trigger mentality, in which everyone races to withdraw funds at the slightest whiff of uncertainty about the solvency of the bank. In this environment, even an unfounded rumor can generate massive instability in the financial system.

One of the ways that banks tried to avoid this was by doing everything in their power to appear as solid as the Rock of Gibraltar. This is why early bank buildings tended to be rather massive stone edifices with classical pillars and marble foyers. The message these buildings sent to potential depositors was "We're here to stay." Government insurance, however, eliminated the need for this sort of grandstanding, by providing depositors with a guarantee that they would be able to recover their funds no matter what happened to the bank. This guarantee eliminated the collective action problem underlying bank runs and, as a result, eliminated the problem of bank runs among depositors. Of course, the primary beneficiary was not the individual depositors (who almost never require indemnity for bank failure), but rather the banks, which were able to go about their business without having to worry much about this particular type of risk.[18] It also allowed them to save a lot of money on architecture, as witnessed by the fact that bank buildings became a lot flimsier after the Second World War.

This is just one example. If you look at the list of services provided by the government to ensure the smooth functioning of the capitalist economy, or just to make life easier for investors, the range is pretty impressive. Until fairly recently, for instance, it did not strike people as obvious that what we now call "white-collar crime" should be subject to criminal prosecution. Until the late eighteenth century, if you went to the police and said, "Help! My accountant has been cheating me!" the response would have been, "That's a shame. You should consider getting another accountant." The idea that businesspeople should be able to run crying to the government every time they get ripped off is relatively new. (Fraud, or "mere private cheating" as it was then called, was first criminalized in England in 1757.)[19] In the United States, the Lochner-era Supreme Court strongly resisted the criminalization of various types of fraud well into the twentieth century. In their view, market transactions were to be governed not only by the principle of "buyer beware," but also by those of "employer beware," "lender beware," and "supplier beware." If a person failed to be sufficiently vigilant with respect to his own commercial transactions, that was his problem, not society's. It could be dealt with through civil litigation, but it certainly was not an issue that the state needed to concern itself with.

Of course, businesspeople *did* run crying to the government when they got defrauded (just as they ran to the government again in 2008, when the subprime mortgage meltdown began). As a result, the state spends enormous sums essentially protecting the integrity of commercial transactions. The criminalization of white-collar offenses like fraud, embezzlement, bribery, and forgery is basically a social program, in this case one designed to reduce the transaction costs associated with private investment. Yet it is also an incredibly important social program. Without the assurance that public prosecution of these crimes offers, it would be impossible to organize widespread investment, or even to conduct what we now regard as elementary business transactions.

Certain older forms of white-collar crime have, at the same time, been decriminalized. People who defaulted on debts used to get thrown into jail. Many businesspeople found this inconvenient, and so lobbied for a program that would help them to avoid this outcome. We now refer to this as "bankruptcy protection." It is essentially a form of social insurance, taken on by the creditor. The protection for the debtor is paid for in the form of a slightly higher interest rate by everyone who takes out a loan.[20] Limited liability has the same structure. It used to be the case that any investor in a corporation—no matter how small his stake—could be held liable for the entire accumulated debts of the firm. This made it impossible for investors to reduce their risk through diversification. On the contrary, buying just one share in a firm would expose the investor to the potential loss of his entire fortune. Legislatures in various jurisdictions slowly adopted limited liability rules over the course of the nineteenth century, essentially guaranteeing shareholders that they could lose no more than the money they had invested. The premium for this form of social insurance was paid, again, in the form of a slightly higher interest rate on loans.

It is important to emphasize that bankruptcy law and limited liability—both of which involve the discharge of debts—categorically violate several fundamental conservative principles. They interfere with property rights, undermine contractual obligations, erode personal responsibility, and leave "society" to pay the bill for the improvident or foolish conduct of individuals. So what do these policies have going for them? They help to stabilize the capitalist system, reducing volatility in output, and they serve as a major force promoting investment and economic growth. They also enjoy nearly unanimous support among the business class. Corporate bankruptcy protection has been a permanent feature of the American economy since 1898, and no modern economy has ever succeeded without similar provisions.[21] It is difficult to imagine how anything even as simple as a mutual fund could be organized without the principle of limited liability.[22]

More generally, what these programs have in common is that they are all forms of social insurance that benefit people with money to lend. They all involve government-created and government-funded exceptions to the principle of "lender beware!" We might think of them as social programs for capitalists. Naturally, one seldom hears complaints from the business class about this sort of government "interference" in the market. What lenders and investors typically oppose is not social insurance, or even the principle of social insurance, but merely the specific types of social insurance that protect *other* people—especially workers and consumers. (Or, speaking more precisely, forms of social insurance that benefit people in their capacity as workers and consumers, rather than in their capacity as investors.)

As a result, the commitment to "limited government" and "laissez-faire" capitalism turns out to be not so much a principled defense of individual liberty as an arbitrary privileging of the interests of those with money to invest (whom we may refer to, for convenience, as "the wealthy"). The right-wing call for "less government" therefore becomes a call to "keep those programs that benefit the wealthy—scrap everything else." And this simply doesn't qualify as a political philosophy. When spoken in the mouths of the privileged, it's just a fancy way of saying, "More free stuff for me, less for you."

Capitalism is not a spontaneous order. The compositional fallacy, however, makes it tempting to believe that it is. Since it is in everyone's interest to have a system of property rights, or to have the orderly exchange of goods, won't people just naturally tend to organize their affairs in that way? Who needs government to step in? Yet as it turns out, we do need government to step in, even to secure the most basic conditions for a functioning market economy. Two boys trading marbles in the schoolyard may constitute a spontaneous order, but the capitalist economic system is a highly artificial construct, based upon an elaborate set of social programs that have been refined and tweaked over the course of centuries.

CHAPTER 2

INCENTIVES MATTER

... except when they don't

Economists are famous for believing that all human action is motivated by self-interest. This reputation is unfortunate, since technically speaking they don't really believe this. What they do believe is that all human action is *unprincipled,* which is not exactly the same thing. They often articulate this idea by saying that action is governed by incentives. "Most of economics can be summarized in four words," writes Steven "The Armchair Economist" Landsburg: "'People respond to incentives.' The rest is commentary."[1] This turns out to be a hotbed of fallacies. Typically, economists start out defining the term *incentive* so broadly that anything can count as an incentive. But when it comes to explaining particular actions, they turn around and limit their conception of incentives to *external* situational factors (most often, money). As a result, they wind up ignoring fairly significant aspects of how people make decisions, such as the role that principles play in our deliberations.

To illustrate the difference between being unprincipled and acting from self-interest, consider the class of philosophical puzzles known as "trolley problems."[2] In the first version, you are asked to imagine a hypothetical scenario in which you are standing by a railroad track when you see a runaway trolley (that is, a streetcar) approaching. It is heading toward a platform, where five people are waiting to board. All of them are certain to be killed unless something is done to stop the trolley. Luckily, you are standing near a switch, which you can use to divert the trolley onto a side track. The only problem is that a maintenance worker is fixing the track, and he will be killed if you divert the trolley. Should you throw the switch? Most people say yes. After all, one person dying is better than five people dying.

In the second version of the problem, there is no switch, but you are standing next to the maintenance worker. He is rather portly (much more so than you), so if you push him in front of the trolley, his body will get caught under the wheels and cause the trolley to grind to a halt before reaching the five people. (You could hop in front of it yourself, but you're not heavy enough to stop the trolley.) Should you push him? Here most people say no. Even though one person dying is better than five, you can't go around pushing strangers onto train tracks.

The difference between these two responses suggests that morality is not just about consequences; it is also about how you achieve those consequences. The final outcome is the same in both cases—the maintenance worker dies so that the five people waiting on the platform can be saved. Yet most of us do not consider it permissible to use just any means to achieve this end. There are certain principles we must respect, principles that carry deliberative weight that is independent of the consequences they promote.

Some people, however, find this to be irrational. Why should we be willing to push trolleys into people but not people into trolleys? Since the two actions generate the same consequences, why, from the moral point of view, should we treat them any differently? If anything, what the trolley problem reveals is an element of irrationality in our ordinary moral (and legal) reasoning.

People who think that, either way, the maintenance worker should be the one to die are known as *consequentialists,* since they believe that an action should be evaluated strictly in terms of its consequences. It is a minority view, largely because it conflicts with many of our most firmly held moral convictions (like the idea that individuals have rights that ought to be respected come what may). Through a series of accidents of intellectual history, however, consequentialism wound up being a fundamental methodological presupposition among economists.[3] One can see clearly in the case of the trolley, however, that caring only about consequences is not the same thing as acting from self-interest. Pushing portly maintenance workers onto railroad tracks requires a certain bloody-mindedness, but it is nevertheless altruistic, since the goal is to save the five people on the platform. The action is both unprincipled and altruistic.

More generally, what the commitment to consequentialism suggests is that if you want to figure out what people are most likely to do, you should look to the future, not the past. You should consider what they stand to gain and lose from their decision, not what they may have promised or decided in the past. You should look, in other words, at the incentives they face.

$ $ $

The funny thing about this commitment to consequentialism is that philosophers who are sympathetic to the doctrine typically adopt it as a theory of how people *should* reason, in an ideal world, but economists have adopted it as a theory about how people actually *do* reason, in the real world. Since people don't actually reason in such a narrow way, this approach has turned out to be something of a recipe for disappointment, at least when it comes to designing empirically testable research hypotheses.

Of course, there are lots of different ways to weasel out of the empirical difficulties that a commitment to consequentialism inevitably entails. Landsburg, for instance, claims only that people respond to incentives; he does not claim that people respond *only* to incentives. The former claim is trivially true, since an incentive is not really an incentive unless it is something that people respond to. The hope of receiving a free pedicure serves as an "incentive" for my wife to frequent a particular store; me, not so much. If no one wanted a pedicure, then it wouldn't be an incentive. In this sense, no one in their right mind—not even Immanuel Kant—has ever denied that people respond to incentives. The question is whether they respond to *other* concerns as well. In particular, the question is whether they have independent concerns about the character of their actions or the principles that guide their choices.

The other way to avoid the problem is to define incentives so broadly that anything anyone could possibly care about, including moral principles, counts as an incentive. Steven Levitt and Stephen Dubner, for example, in *Freakonomics,* consider incentives to include not just "economic" and "social" but also "moral incentives." Thus any moral qualms we might have about pushing people onto railroad tracks counts as an "incentive." (This is clearly not the usual sense of the term. Imagine a company unveiling a new employee "incentive plan" consisting of the following offer: "If you work really, really hard, then you get to feel good about yourself!") In any case, the semantic drift turns out to be irrelevant, because after discussing "moral incentives" just once (in a story involving bagels), Levitt and Dubner proceed to ignore them throughout the rest of the book.

All this weasely talk means that if you really want to figure out what economists are thinking when they talk about incentives, you can't look at the definitions they offer. You have to look at the concrete examples they choose and the types of behavior that interest them. Levitt, for instance, is interested in cheating. It's the (supposedly absent) unifying theme in his work. All the headline results ("Teachers help their students to cheat!" "Sumo wrestlers intentionally throw matches!" "Real estate agents can't be trusted!") are concerned with people working the angles, often in unexpected ways. In each case, the people Levitt studies are taking advantage of opportunities that arise within the system of external incentives. They are guided by what psychologists refer to as extrinsic motives: money, status, power.

Furthermore, Levitt and Dubner repeatedly draw an invidious contrast between "morality"—described as "the way we would like the world to be"—and "economics"—the study of how the world actually is. The message is pretty clear. Morality is for girls. Economics is for tough guys, who are able to stare the world in the eye and come to terms with the way things are. It's for those who are able to look at a homeless man and notice only his expensive headphones.[4] To imagine that morality counts for anything in the real world is to succumb to wishful thinking. The economist is wise to the game. He knows that people are all in it for themselves. Machiavelli put it best, when he observed that, "in general," people are "ungrateful, fickle, pretenders and dissemblers, evaders of danger, eager for gain."[5]

When push comes to shove, these unflattering assumptions concerning human motivation are about the only thing that make Levitt's work count as "economics." After all, most of it is plain-vanilla statistical analysis, of the sort done by social scientists in a variety of disciplines. The major difference is that social scientists who take morality seriously are called "sociologists," whereas those who think it's all a scam call themselves "economists."

$ $ $

Back for a moment to Landsburg's pithy slogan. "Incentives matter," he claims. "The literature of economics contains tens of thousands of empirical studies verifying this proposition, and not one that convincingly refutes it."[6]

One must wonder what Landsburg thinks would count as refutation. No one has ever doubted that incentives, in the sense of *consequences,* matter. The question is whether they are the *only* thing that matters, or whether they matter as much as economists have traditionally thought they do, or whether the *types* of incentives that economists have traditionally privileged have the explanatory power that has been ascribed to them. Here the answer provided by tens of thousands of empirical studies is a resounding "no, no, and no." Unless one takes the Levitt route and defines "incentives" so broadly as to include everything that anyone could possibly care about, the fact is that people are concerned not only with the consequences of their actions, but also with the principles that govern them (and they care not only about extrinsic incentives, but also about the intrinsic character of their actions).

We know this because social scientists of various stripes, including a small army of economists, have spent an enormous amount of time and effort studying the way that people make decisions in various types of "economic" scenarios and seeing what factors influence these decisions. Collective action problems (or "prisoner's dilemmas") alone have been the subject of literally hundreds of empirical studies—such that the best new research consists of "meta-analysis" (or "studies of the studies"), where an author subjects the data from multiple studies to statistical analysis in order to identify patterns. As it turns out, the most important pattern can easily be detected with the naked eye: People almost never act the way economists say they should.

To see the most dramatic example of this, consider an experimental game known as "the ultimatum game." Two people are given a sum of money, which they are entitled to keep so long as they can agree on how it should be divided up. The catch lies in the decision procedure they must follow. One person is given the entire sum of money, then allowed to make a single, take-it-or-leave-it offer to the second. The second can either accept the proposed division, in which case the money is divided up between them under the agreed terms, or reject it, in which case the money goes back to the experimenters and the two subjects go home empty-handed.

Now, if you were fresh out of an introductory economics course and someone asked you how a "rational agent" would behave in this situation, the answer would be pretty clear. It doesn't really matter how much the first person offers, because the second person basically has a choice between taking the money and getting nothing. Since people generally prefer some money to no money, the person should accept anything. Thus the economically rational thing for the first person to do is to offer the smallest amount possible (for example, one cent). Indeed, no matter how large the sum of money at stake, the offer should always be one cent, and it should always be accepted (since rejecting the offer amounts to simply throwing away money).

Now comes the unsurprising part. In the real world, these sorts of lowball offers are almost never made. And in the odd case where they are made, they are never accepted. In hundreds of iterations of this experiment, in dozens of different countries, no one has ever been able to discover any population of human beings anywhere who behave even approximately the way that "standard" economic theory predicts—which is not to say that people don't behave in all sorts of crazy ways (as any anthropologist would anticipate). In some countries, for example, offers of more than 50% are quite common, *combined with frequent rejection of these offers.*[7] (This is weird, until you discover that these are societies with a traditional "gift economy," where it is normal to reject excessively generous gifts out of a combination of politeness and prudential concern.) In any case, no matter how crazy the pattern of behavior, no one has ever been able to find anything quite as crazy as the pattern predicted by the economist.

So what is an economist to do, faced with this sort of an "anomaly"?[8] One way would be to start loosening up the standard economic model somewhat, in order to increase the range of things that can count as incentives. This is tricky, though. The fact is, the kinds of things that economists have traditionally thought *should* influence people's behavior often don't, and the kinds of things that economists have traditionally thought *shouldn't* influence people's behavior often do.

This is most obvious in the case of collective action problems. For over 40 years now, people have been doing studies showing that experimental subjects in anonymous "one-shot" prisoner's dilemmas have a surprising willingness to cooperate. Consider a typical "public goods" game. Players are put into groups of four, and each player is given $20, which they can deposit into either a "public" or a "private" account. At the end of the round, the public account pays out $1.60 for each dollar that was deposited there, but the money is divided up evenly between the four players regardless of who made the deposit. Any money deposited into the private account, on the other hand, is simply kept by the player who put it there. Thus if all four players put all of their money into their private accounts, they each walk away with $20. Yet if they all put all their money into the public account, they will each get $32. The problem is that each one also has a free rider incentive—you get 40¢ from every dollar that the others put into the public account even if you contribute nothing. So the best individual outcome is if everyone *else* contributes their money to the public account (this gets you $24), while you put all of your own money into the private account (which gets you an additional $20, for a total of $44).

Standard economic theory predicts that no one will contribute anything to the public account. In real life, people usually split their investments—two-thirds to the public account, one-third to the private. When the first round of experimental findings came in, many economists dismissed them on the grounds that the subjects had too little at stake in the decision. "Offer the subjects more serious money," they said, "and you'll start to see rates of cooperation fall." Yet offering subjects more money had *exactly the opposite effect*—subjects were more likely to cooperate when there was cash at stake. (One could always dismiss this finding, on the grounds that still not enough money was being offered. This would be a great strategy for justifying arbitrarily large research grants, but at some point it becomes intellectually obtuse.)

The second move was to appeal to the possibility of reputation effects. It was assumed that repeated interaction between subjects would increase rates of cooperation, by allowing individuals to adopt conditional strategies and develop reputations (as cooperative players). Yet once again, the cure proved worse than the disease. Increasing the number of iterations of the game has the opposite effect, producing a slight decline in average rates of cooperation.

Meanwhile, all sorts of strange things seem to have powerful— and from the economist's perspective, unanticipated—effects upon the outcome.[9] The most significant of these factors is the sort of communication that is permitted within the game. For example, a simple intervention from the experimenter ordering the subjects to cooperate can generate a dramatic increase in levels of cooperation. Allowing experimental subjects to talk to one another results in an equally dramatic improvement. Why would this be, if all people care about are consequences? This kind of communication is what economists call "cheap talk"—it doesn't affect the payoffs, and so it shouldn't have any effect on anyone's decision. But obviously it does.

Perhaps the most revealing experimental "anomaly" came from a study at Stanford University, where one group of subjects was instructed to play a public goods game called "the community game," and another asked to play one called "the Wall Street game."[10] The two problems were in fact identical, but the rates of cooperation in "the community game" were twice as high as in "the Wall Street game." (Cooperation in the former was around the "normal" rate of two-thirds; in the latter it was abnormally low, at about one-third.) Another version of this study, carried out among Israeli air force trainers, showed approximately the same effect. In that study, however, instructors were asked to predict how their trainees (whom they knew quite well) would behave. Interestingly, not only were the instructors wrong (they did no better than chance at predicting the behavior of their trainees), but they also made the mistake of ignoring the effect that the name of the game might have upon rates of cooperation and defection.

In this respect, the trainers fell victim to the same fallacy that has plagued generations of economists. It is, in fact, a general flaw in our everyday social reasoning, which social psychologists refer to as an *extrinsic incentive bias*. Simply put, people have a tendency to overestimate the importance of external incentives in motivating human conduct.[11] In particular, we have a natural tendency to overestimate the influence of power, money, and status in motivating other people's decisions.

This bias has been exhibited in many controlled studies. For example, when asked to rank the importance of different motivations (such as pay, job security, learning new skills, or accomplishing something worthwhile) and then to guess how others rank them, management students consistently rank the extrinsic motives quite low for themselves but guess that others will rank them quite high. In another, rather amusing study, prospective law students taking the LSAT were asked to state their motivations for wanting to study law. Only 12% indicated that financial rewards were a factor in their own decision, yet 63% thought that this was a major factor motivating their peers. There is obviously a self-congratulatory element in all this, yet even when that bias is controlled for, studies show a strong tendency toward an overascription of extrinsic motives to others.[12]

Economists can perhaps, then, be forgiven for overestimating the importance of incentives. In so doing, they are succumbing to an extremely common cognitive bias. Of course, rather than trying to correct this bias, they have chosen to elevate it to the status of a methodological precept, thereby exaggerating it almost beyond recognition. Yet we are all susceptible to such foibles. The best that we can hope for is greater responsiveness to evidence, not least on the part of those who aspire to be called scientists.

$ $ $

None of this is to say that external incentives don't matter. Incentives are hugely, incredibly important. Failure to take incentive effects seriously is the single most important source of public policy failure in the modern welfare state, not to mention the most important source of harebrained thinking on the left. But the fact that incentives are incredibly important—and the fact that people often need to be reminded of this fact—should not be allowed to devolve into hyperbole. To deny that morality, as well as social norms more generally, functions as a genuine constraint on human conduct is to be willfully obtuse. The economics profession's rewarding of this sort of obtuseness, and in some cases raising it to the level of an art form, should not be allowed to obscure the fact that it makes for bad social science and, perhaps more important, for bad public policy prescription.

The economist's enthusiasm for incentives needs to be tempered by two realizations. First, incentives are not the *only* things that matter, and second, incentives are often incredibly complex.

Take an issue like minimum-wage laws. A lot of young hotheads, fresh out of Economics 101, find it crushingly obvious that minimum-wage laws create unemployment. Indeed, they regard it as a truth somewhere between "$2 + 2 = 4$" and "p implies p" on the scale of self-evidence. Confronted by the spectacle of doubt, they find themselves forced to question the very sanity of the doubter. And at first glance, the argument does seem compelling. The introductory economics textbook that I studied, back in my undergraduate days, summed up the entire matter in two crisp sentences: "By raising the wage facing employers, minimum-wage legislation leads to a reduction in the quantity of labor demanded and an increase in the quantity supplied. As a result the actual level of employment falls, and unemployment is generated."[13] ("QED," one is inclined to add.)

This isn't complicated stuff. If the wage goes up, more people will want to work, yet employers will not be able to afford to hire as many of them. The result will be an excess of supply or a shortfall in demand (whichever you prefer to call it—they're both just ways of referring to unemployment). Furthermore, although those who manage to hang on to their jobs will be better off, it will be at the expense of those who lose their jobs or are unable to find work. Thus minimum-wage laws create not only a loss of efficiency, but also a regressive social transfer (or a "labor aristocracy").

This argument is perfectly cogent. In fact it's a scintillating example of what Kant called a "synthetic a priori" judgment (that's when you figure out how things in the world must be, just by thinking about it). But of course, so is the argument that says people should defect in collective action problems, or make lowball offers in ultimatum games. In reality, things are a lot more complicated. And, as any student who sticks around the economics department for long enough may discover (perhaps in a fourth-year seminar), there is a very lively debate among economists about whether an increase in the minimum wage actually produces unemployment.[14] For the moment, at least, no one has succeeded in providing convincing empirical evidence that it does.

By way of comparison, it is useful to compare the debate over the minimum wage with the issue of rent control. By imposing limits on the ability of landlords to increase the rent they charge tenants, rent control has the effect of lowering the price of rental housing. It's easy to see what the Economics 101 analysis of this policy will be—it's a simple fill-in-the-blanks exercise: "By lowering the rent that tenants must pay, rent-control legislation leads to an increase in the quantity of rental housing demanded and a decrease in the quantity supplied. As a result the level of rental vacancy falls and a housing shortage is generated."

Again, this isn't a complicated claim. If the price of rent goes down (or fails to keep pace with inflation), more people will want to rent, fewer will want to own, and fewer still will want to buy or maintain rental housing. The result will be an excess of demand for and a shortfall in supply of rental housing. Those who are already in rent-controlled apartments will do very well for themselves, but at the expense of those who lose their apartments (to condominium conversion, for example) or who cannot find one in the first place.

What's interesting about the case of rent control is that the real world *does* work almost exactly the way that Economics 101 says it should (as anyone who has lived in New York or Montreal can attest). As the (left-wing) economist Assar Lindbeck once put it, apart from generating housing shortages, rent control produces "black markets, privileges for those who happen to have a contract for a rent-controlled apartment, nepotism in the distribution of the available apartments, difficulties in getting apartments for families with children, and, in many places, deterioration of the housing stock. In fact, next to bombing, rent control seems in many cases to be the most efficient technique so far known for destroying cities."[15]

If the evidence is so incontrovertible in this case, why should the minimum-wage issue be any different? The most plausible explanation seems to be that the labor market is incredibly complicated. Not only is it full of distortions and always out of equilibrium, but individuals make decisions about whether to work, how much to work, and where to work based on a dizzying array of factors. For example, the male labor supply behaves quite differently from the female labor supply.[16] (The way women respond to price changes is much closer to the ideal of economic rationality. In particular, women tend to drop out of the labor force when it no longer makes "economic" sense for them to be working. Men, for reasons that are not difficult to imagine, tend to keep on working regardless of how the numbers come out—as a matter of principle, one is inclined to suggest.)

To complicate matters even further, the way employers make use of labor and the type of hiring decisions they make are just as complex. Some economists have argued that minimum-wage laws can increase productivity. One of the first things students are taught in management school is that no business is ever actually sitting on the "production possibilities frontier" (which is a fancy way of saying that there is always slack within any organization). When employers are forced to pay their workers more, they may find better ways to occupy them, in order to cover the increased wage bill. Minimum-wage workers, according to this view, are a chronically underutilized resource, simply because they are so cheap. It's not so hard to squeeze a measly dollar or two of productivity out of someone—many employers just lack the incentive to do so.

An increase in the minimum wage could also have an "efficiency wage" effect, leading to a reduction in shirking. Henry Ford once described his decision to double the wage of his workers as "one of the finest cost-cutting moves we ever made," because of the increase in productivity that it generated.[17] When people feel that they are being treated fairly, or even generously, this typically activates a norm of reciprocity, which can generate greater work effort.[18]

The point is that no simple model of supply and demand for labor is going to capture all these variables. Unlike rent control, which involves a relatively straightforward transaction, the complexity of real-world labor markets is sufficient to confound any simple economic model. Yet people persist in making confident predictions about the consequences of the "laws of economics" based upon wildly oversimplified ideas about how economic actors actually behave.

§ § §

One of the core convictions of economically minded conservatives is the belief that government "tax and transfer" schemes hurt the economy. Income taxes essentially punish those who are the most productive members of society, while the transfer rewards those who are the least productive: the poor, the disabled, the sick, the elderly, and so forth. Again, it appears self-evident that "if you pay people not to work, they won't work." From an Economics 101 perspective, it seems like an open-and-shut case: Generous social transfers should result in lower rates of GDP growth.

If this were true, then it would be a very serious problem for partisans of the welfare state. Imagine two societies—one with a very egalitarian distribution of income, the other highly inegalitarian, where low-income workers earn just half what their counterparts in the more egalitarian society are earning. Suppose further that the inegalitarian society is growing at an annual rate of 5%, while the egalitarian one is growing at a rate of only 0.5%. If patterns of distribution remain steady, within a period of only 16 years low-income workers in the inegalitarian society will be earning more than their counterparts in the egalitarian society; by the time they retire they will be earning four times more.[19]

Thus one cannot simply take it for granted that the welfare state, by engaging in straightforward income redistribution, actually helps the poor. The numbers used above are not "science fiction" figures, but fall well within the scope of growth figures that are realistically attainable in real-world economies. If the welfare state actually does have the negative impact upon growth that economic theory says it should, then there is a serious questions about whether its efforts to redistribute wealth are not in fact harming the long-term prospects of the very individuals that it purports to benefit.

Furthermore, there is no point arguing that welfare-state policies don't have important incentive effects, or that they don't change the decisions people make about how much to work. It is certainly not an accident that in Sweden, on any given day, fully 15% of employees fail to show up for work. Surely it has something to do with the fact that they are all, for one reason or another, absent *with pay*.[20] And that has to have an impact on GDP, doesn't it?

In the short term, obviously, it does. But strangely enough, in the medium-to-long term it doesn't seem to. After all, Sweden is by any measure one of the richest countries on earth, despite the fact that government transfers alone typically exceed 30% of GDP. Like any country, Sweden has had its ups and downs, but there is no evidence that the gods of the free market have exacted the sort of vengeance upon the Swedes that has been heralded by standard economic theory. (It is also important to note that the Swedish welfare state has achieved greater equality of income than was ever achieved under Soviet communism.[21] That's worth repeating for emphasis: Swedish capitalism is more egalitarian than Soviet communism.)

In general, the evidence suggests that a generous welfare state does not harm long-term economic growth. This is true not just for Sweden, but around the world. The economist Peter Lindert, who has assembled a comprehensive survey of the relevant historical evidence, summarizes his findings as follows: "Nine decades of historical experience fail to show that transferring a larger share of GDP from taxpayers to transfer recipients has a negative correlation with either the level or the rate of growth of GDP per person. The average correlation is essentially zero."[22]

But before anyone starts jumping to conclusions, it is important to observe that this lack of a correlation does *not* show that economic theory is false, that incentives don't matter, and that government can do whatever it wants. The lesson to be learned is exactly the opposite. One of the major reasons that big-spending governments tend not to be penalized by the market is that, due to their very bigness, they need to operate more efficiently, and they need to work harder to get the incentives right. "There are good reasons why statistical tests keep coming up with near-zero estimates of the net damage from social programs on economic growth," Lindert writes. "It's not just that the tales of deadweight losses describe peculiarly bad policies. It's also that real-world welfare states benefit from a style of taxing and spending that is in many ways more pro-growth than the policies of most free-market countries."[23]

The United States government, for example, can afford to have a nightmarishly complex income-tax code in part because the tax rates are relatively low, and so the incentive to evade taxation is also low. For the same reason, American states can afford to keep their antiquated retail sales taxes on goods. Again, because the rates are low, the fact that such taxes are relatively easy to evade does not cause too much mischief. But once you start pushing middle tax brackets above 30% or the retail sales tax above 10%, tax evasion starts to become a bigger and bigger problem. It then makes sense to streamline the income-tax system, or switch to a value-added tax, which is more difficult to evade and less costly to enforce.[24] (Value-added taxes allow businesses to deduct the tax paid on inputs from the tax they charge on their sales, which significantly diminishes their incentive to evade the former.) This is precisely what big-spending European welfare states have done. They have also switched the *type* of taxes that they impose, away from ones that have the most deleterious impact on growth (mainly taxes on investment and corporations).[25] Big welfare states, in other words, have smarter taxes and run a tighter ship.

Truth be told, it is sometimes difficult for Americans of any stripe to believe that the government could be counted upon to solve any major social problem.[26] The thought of a bunch of people showing up saying, "We're from the government, and we're here to help you" is more likely to bring laughter than relief to the average American. Many observers were genuinely amazed at the incompetence displayed by federal agencies in response to Hurricane Katrina in 2005, not to mention the estimated $2 billion lost to fraud. Indeed, the performance of the U.S. government here more resembled that of an African kleptocracy than a modern democratic nation. Furthermore, the peculiar way that the legislature works in the United States (particularly with the absence of party discipline) makes it essentially impossible for anyone to implement a coherent policy agenda without finding it corrupted by pork-barrel politics and special interests. But this is an argument for modernizing the institutions of American government, not for abandoning the public sector.[27] One cannot infer that "government" is inefficient just because the American government is inefficient, any more than one can infer that "automakers" are inefficient just because General Motors may happen to be. As the management theorist Henry Mintzberg put it, "Societies get the public services they expect. If people believe that government is bumbling and bureaucratic, then that is what it will be. If, in contrast, they recognize public service for the noble calling that it is, then they will end up with strong government. And no nation today can afford anything but strong government."[28]

The other major factor that must be taken into consideration when assessing the impact of government spending on productivity is the positive incentive effect of social programs. As soon as one starts tracing these out, their enormous complexity immediately becomes apparent. For example, one of the reasons that Sweden has relatively high GDP is that it has very high rates of female labor-force participation. This is in part a consequence of the generosity of welfare-state programs, such as maternity and parental leave, along with active government daycare programs. Conservative social policies, aimed at encouraging women to stay home with their children, typically reduce economic growth, by deterring female labor-force participation. (They also appear to have the perverse consequence of lowering birthrates, as more women, forced to choose between children and career, opt for the latter.)

Family-support welfare policies also appear to have other, more subtle effects, such as increasing female labor productivity.[29] Because subsidized daycare makes it easier, not to mention more economically advantageous, for women to return to their jobs after having children, they are more likely to do so. This in turn makes employers more willing to make costly investments in training female employees across the board. The existence of a "mommy track" in the United States is in part a reflection of the fact that it is inordinately difficult for women with young children to return to paid employment, which gives employers an incentive to sideline female employees who appear to be headed in this direction. This has a negative impact on productivity, even among female employees who plan never to have children.

So what can be said about the economic impact of welfare-state policies? At a general level, not very much. Incentives matter; the problem is just that it is difficult to generalize about the incentives that people face. Social status, for instance, provides an incredibly powerful set of incentives, about which traditional economics has had almost nothing to say.[30] Yet status is associated with pre-tax income. No one really knows or cares what the take-home pay of their co-workers is—what they care about is how their *gross* salary compares. Thus, people have a powerful incentive to maximize their income regardless of what tax rates they are paying.

This is just one more example of how, when dealing with labor supply and workplace organization, an excessive focus upon traditional pecuniary motives winds up obscuring as much as it reveals. The sort of two-step deductive arguments promoted by Economics 101 thinking, while useful heuristics for thinking about public policy issues, provide only the first—not the final—word on any subject.

$ $ $

What economists are really trying to get at when they highlight the importance of incentives is the fact that people aren't stupid. (Or that even if they're stupid, they're not *idiots*.) The commitment to consequentialism is largely a distraction, as is the methodological privileging of extrinsic motives. What really matters is an awareness of the fact that large-scale social patterns are an aggregate effect of individual choices, and that the way individuals choose is highly sensitive to local context and situation. Because of this, changes in the environment (brought about, for example, by public policy) can have unexpected consequences.

There are two very nice experiments that illustrate these principles. Both happen to involve taxicabs. The first is known as the "Munich taxicab experiment." It was conducted in the late '80s when anti-lock braking systems (ABS) were first being introduced. About half of the fleet at one Munich taxi company was equipped with the new brake system, which gave investigators a perfect opportunity to study its effects upon accident rates. What they found, perhaps surprisingly, was that the cars with ABS were slightly more likely to be involved in accidents than those without.

The cars were equipped with "black boxes" that recorded all sorts of information, but just to be on the safe side, investigators also assigned observers to accompany drivers and take notes on their behavior (all done blind—observers did not know whether or not they were in ABS cars, and drivers did not know that the person was there to observe their driving). All this data suggested the same things: drivers had very quickly adapted their behavior in response to the presence of ABS, and this response completely canceled out any benefits provided by the new braking system. Once they realized that their effective stopping distance was shorter, they began tailgating, making sharper turns, driving faster, and generally being more careless. The new "safety equipment," far from making the cars more safe, was actually making them more dangerous, simply because its presence changed their drivers' behavior.

What this experiment helps to remind us is that "the automobile accident rate" is not a naturally given fact, like the boiling point of water. It is a product of choices that people make. Even though it involves "accidents," which are not consciously chosen, it is nevertheless affected by choice, because people freely decide how much caution to exercise in their daily lives and what sort of trade-offs to make between caution and expediency. No one forces you to talk on the phone, blow your nose, or put on lipstick while you're driving—these are all choices. When the technological parameters change, people in turn change their behavior. This can undermine the effectiveness of a lot of paternalistic interventions.

So far this is all grist for the economist's mill. (Further excitement was generated when investigators discovered that the accident rate *did* go down once the company started charging drivers a portion of the repair bill when their car was involved in an accident.)[31] But there is a second experiment, this time involving New York taxicabs, that should strike a note of caution. Investigators were interested in seeing how workers responded to changes in their wage rates.[32] Taxi drivers provide a perfect "natural experiment," because their effective wage varies from day to day, depending upon the weather. On cold or rainy days, passengers are quite plentiful, and so the effective wage is relatively high. On warm, sunny days, drivers have to spend more time "cruising" for rides, and as a result, their effective hourly wage is much lower.

Cabdrivers in New York are also perfectly free to work as long as they like. Standard economic theory suggests that a person will work until such time as the value of the leisure that would be forgone exceeds the value of the wage that could be earned. This in turn implies, quite immediately, that people will work longer when their wage rate is higher. Cabdrivers, however, did the exact opposite. On days when rides were plentiful, and thus their effective wage rate was higher, they tended to quit work early. When rides were more scarce, they worked longer, sometimes well into the night. The economic effects of this "perverse labor-supply response" were significant. Investigators estimated that the average driver could have increased his take-home earnings by 5% simply by working a fixed length of time every day, regardless of conditions. Working longer when the effective wage rate was higher could have generated an increase in earnings of over 15%.[33]

Note that this experiment in no way contradicts the thesis that people are responsive to incentives. On the contrary, the amount that cabdrivers worked was strongly influenced by changes in the wage rate—it's just that the response ran the opposite direction from what standard economic theory would lead one to expect. The reason has to do with the type of mental accounting that drivers were engaged in. Most felt they had to earn enough to cover their fixed costs ($76–$86 for use of the cab for 12 hours), plus a certain amount of take-home income. Thus they set out each day with an earnings target, and once they hit that target they called it quits. On rainy days they hit the target quickly, and so they worked less; on sunny days it took longer, and so they wound up working more.

What are we to conclude from all this? The most obvious lesson is simply that human psychology is infernally complicated. The standard assumptions that economists have been known to make about human rationality and the way that people respond to incentives represent a gross oversimplification. Sometimes this simplified model produces incredibly powerful, highly generalizable results. But sometimes it generates predictions that are totally off base. Increasingly, economists are becoming aware of this—there has been a significant move toward so-called behavioral economics within the profession. This approach, as the name suggests, pays a lot more attention to how people actually behave. Unfortunately, behavioral economists have yet to generate anything with the explanatory and predictive power of "the model" that is taught in Economics 101, and so the latter continues to exercise its intoxicating (and sometimes toxic) influence on the minds of the young.

CHAPTER 3

THE FRICTIONLESS PLANE FALLACY

Why more competition is not always better

In 1956, two young economists named Kelvin Lancaster and Richard Lipsey published a paper in the *Review of Economic Studies* with the unassuming title "The General Theory of Second Best"—and handed the left one of the most powerful arguments against laissez-faire capitalism ever developed. Never heard of it? Well, don't feel bad—you're not alone. It's been "suppressed" by the economics profession. Or at least that's what Lipsey told me once when I interviewed him about it.

When the paper first surfaced, economists went into full-scale damage-control mode. Lipsey estimated that within a decade there were "about 200 articles published trying to refute it."[1] They attacked from different directions. Some of them challenged the math. Some of them argued that the consequences were not as severe as they seemed. Others questioned the originality of the claims. In one scholarly journal, the authors were even denounced as nihilists.

But the panic soon subsided. The right wing discovered that there was, after all, no cause for alarm. It's not that the theorem was unsound—it's just that no one on the left seemed to be reading the *Review of Economic Studies*. So as long as everyone in the know kept quiet, the theory would just slide into intellectual obscurity. And this is more or less what has happened. "They couldn't refute it, so they just decided to ignore it," says Lipsey. The Second Best Theorem is still taught in some economics courses—usually in about third year, in public economics classes. But it has never received any popular uptake, and is almost never mentioned in political debate.

This is unfortunate, since the paper identifies an extremely important fallacy, one that plays a central role in much of popular free-market thinking. One of the most ideologically powerful theoretical results in modern economics is the so-called Invisible Hand Theorem—named after Adam Smith's famous speculation—that a perfectly competitive market is also perfectly efficient. What the Second Best Theorem shows is that even if this is true, it is irrelevant, because if even one of the conditions that are required for perfect efficiency is violated, anywhere in the economy, then all bets are off. There is no reason to think that a "second-best," or *almost* perfectly competitive market, will be more efficient than a third-best, or fourth-best, or even totally uncompetitive market. Thus you cannot take the sort of "general equilibrium" model that is the mainstay of introductory microeconomics classes and use it to generate any sort of presumption in favor of the market as a mechanism for promoting efficiency.

As if that weren't bad enough, the authors went on to show that, in cases where one of the conditions required for perfect efficiency was violated, the only way to achieve as-close-as-possible-to-perfect efficiency would be to go out and violate a few more of the rules required for a perfectly competitive market. To the casual reader, this might give the impression that, in the real world, a government that mucks around in the economy is likely to achieve better outcomes than a government that follows a policy of strict laissez-faire. Of course, nothing is so simple in the real world. But to see where the complications arise, it's necessary to take a somewhat closer look at what Lipsey and Lancaster were able to prove.

$ $ $

When economists talk about "efficiency," they use the word in a somewhat peculiar sense. We are used to speaking about efficiency only with respect to the *means* that people employ. Using a jigsaw is a very inefficient way to cut down a tree, compared to using a chainsaw. But what about the outcome, cutting down the tree? It may be more or less desirable, but it cannot be efficient or inefficient, unless there is some *other* purpose that it is intended to serve, such as acquiring firewood.

Economists, on the other hand, do talk about outcomes as being more or less efficient. According to this sense of the term, an outcome in which it is impossible to improve one person's level of satisfaction without decreasing someone else's is called "efficient" (or, using the more technical term, "Pareto optimal"). On the other hand, a situation in which one person's condition can be improved without worsening anyone else's is "inefficient." (The reason that economists choose to call this "efficiency" is a somewhat complicated story—for our purposes the only thing that's important is to remember that economists use the term in a way that deviates slightly from everyday usage.)[2]

The prisoner's dilemma sketched out in the first chapter contains, in this respect, a paradigm instance of an inefficient outcome. When two trappers decide to adopt the "free rider" strategy of poaching from each other rather than setting their own traps, the resulting outcome is inefficient. Fewer traps get set, fewer animals get caught. Thus it is possible to improve the level of satisfaction of both individuals without lowering anyone else's: both trappers would be better off if they left each other alone and focused on setting traps. The "state of nature," in this respect, is a condition of total inefficiency, caused by a complete failure of cooperation.

There is a very close connection between this notion of efficiency and the availability of trades. Suppose you are distributing candy to kids at a birthday party. Being inexperienced at this sort of thing, you do it all wrong: You divide it up evenly among them, forgetting that some of them are allergic to peanuts, some of them hate raisins, and some of them have weird food sensitivities you've never even heard of. As a result, half the kids wind up with candy that they can't eat. This alone does not make the allocation inefficient. What does make it inefficient is the fact that others *could* eat it if you were to change the distribution. You could take the peanut brittle away from the anaphylactic kid and give it to some other without causing any harm to the first, while creating a certain measure of happiness in the second. The initial allocation was inefficient, in the sense that the peanut brittle was being wasted.

Of course, figuring out exactly who should get what would be a very complicated job. You might decide instead just to let the kids take care of it by themselves. Kids are really good at trading, and they tend to know their own preferences (and dietary restrictions) with respect to candy. So let them exchange. At first there will be a frenzy of activity, but eventually things will settle down, as the kids get rid of stuff they don't want and pick up stuff they do. "Markets will clear," as economists like to say. When there are no more beneficial trades that can occur, the outcome will be perfectly efficient. At this point, you can no longer take anything away from any one kid without making him unhappy, even if you try to compensate him with something taken from another. If it were possible to make both kids happier in this way, then they themselves would have already done it, through a voluntary exchange.

This little thumbnail sketch is pretty close to being a complete statement of the intuition underlying the Invisible Hand Theorem (also known, more grandiosely, as the First Fundamental Theorem of Welfare Economics).[3] In order to get the ideal distribution of candy, perfectly adapted to everyone's preferences, there is no need for any complicated exercise in planning. All you need to do is leave people free to trade. Furthermore, the people involved don't need to be motivated by any concern for the common good. They will exchange items only if it is in their interest to do so. As long as they don't go around stealing, this sort of self-interested behavior is all that is required to produce the most efficient outcome.

People sometimes get excited about the ability of markets to reconcile the individual pursuit of self-interest with the common good in this way. Many even claim to see the hand of God at work. In reality, there is nothing so exceptional about it. There are all sorts of "invisible hands" at work in the institutions that govern our daily lives, many of which have nothing to do with the marketplace. Take the following example (from John Kay).[4] Suppose you are the manager of a supermarket, and you are trying to figure out a way to get as many customers through the checkouts in the shortest time possible. You don't want some cashiers standing around idle while others have huge lineups. How to solve the problem? Do you need some sort of high-tech system to constantly scan the crowds, combined with an optimal queuing algorithm to assign waiting customers to lineups? Instead, why not just let the customers look for themselves and choose their own lines? If they want to get home as quickly as possible, then self-interest alone will lead them to pick the shortest or the fastest-moving line. The overall result will be an ôptimal allocation of shoppers to queues, and no cashiers sitting idle. Do we discern the invisible hand of the supermarket deities at work here? No, it's simply a case in which having each person choose the action that is best for her does nothing to prevent others from choosing the actions that are best for them. As a result, the outcome is one in which everyone does as well as possible, under the circumstances, and no one can improve her outcome without worsening someone else's.

So there is nothing to be alarmed about in the suggestion that a system of voluntary exchange—such as one finds institutionalized in the market economy—might promote the "common good" of increased efficiency. Generally speaking, if two people want to exchange something, there should be a considerable presumption in favor of allowing them to do so. After all, if they did not both expect to be better off as a result of the exchange, then they would not be entering into it. There are, of course, conditions under which this presumption may be defeated (such as when consent is obtained under duress or through fraud, or when the goods in question are regarded as unsuitable objects of exchange).[5] Nevertheless, none of us like it when other people start meddling in our affairs. "Society" therefore has to have some fairly strong arguments lined up before it begins to contemplate prohibiting what Robert Nozick once called "capitalist acts among consenting adults."[6]

There is, however, an important difference between the Invisible Hand Theorem and the quasi-platitudinous observation that trading promotes efficiency. The Invisible Hand Theorem generalizes from the case of individual trade to make a claim about the economy as a whole. No one doubts that *one* voluntary exchange leads to an improvement in efficiency. But the Invisible Hand Theorem claims that when *every* economic transaction is organized as a voluntary exchange, then *all* of the available improvements in efficiency will be exhausted. Hence the suggestion that a perfectly competitive market will generate a perfectly efficient outcome.

This sort of inference sounds eminently plausible but is in fact fraught with peril. Generally speaking, it is a hard-and-fast rule in economics that you cannot generalize from what happens in a particular market to what happens in the economy as a whole. Hasty generalizations of this sort are one of the most common sources of fallacious economic reasoning. Imagine watching a group of children playing musical chairs. From the fact that one child finds a seat when the music stops, it does not follow that every child will be able to find a seat. Nor can one infer that from the fact that a second child, or a third child, finds a seat. In order to figure out what's going to happen, you need to adopt a completely different perspective and start counting up the number of children and of seats. The same thing applies in the case of the economy. The fact that one person manages to find an efficiency-promoting trade does not mean that everyone will be able to. The Invisible Hand Theorem amounts to a proof that a market economy is able to achieve a perfect set of matches—so that trade becomes like a game of musical chairs played with the same number of children as seats.

It was recognized early on that there was an enormous gap between whatever platitudinous intuitions we may have about the benefits of exchange and the defense of a completely laissez-faire economy. This may help to explain why it took economists such a long time to come up with anything resembling a proof of Smith's conjecture. Indeed, it was not until 1956 that Kenneth Arrow and Gerard Debreu's "general equilibrium" model showed how such a proof could be constructed.[7] As it turned out, in order to make the move from talking about individual exchanges to talking about a complete economy organized through exchange, Arrow and Debreu had to adopt a rather dramatic series of idealizations. (For example, they assumed that everyone had perfect information about the goods they were about to purchase, that goods never had to be transported from one location to another, that everyone knew the prices that everyone was charging for everything, now and for the foreseeable future, and so on.) Because of this, they didn't wind up proving anything about how actual economies function or what sorts of results we might expect to obtain in the real world. Instead, they constructed a highly idealized model of how a perfectly competitive economy could function, and then showed that the outcomes produced in such a model would be perfectly efficient.

Of course, the model was not entirely science fiction; it did represent *some* kind of an approximation of the real world. A debate immediately broke out among economists (and other interested parties) about whether the approximation was close enough to justify drawing any sort of "real world" conclusions from its results. But in pursuing the debate on these terms, they overlooked an even more fundamental problem. Everyone assumed that if the *assumptions* of the model mapped onto the real world in some approximate way, then the *results* of the model could also be mapped back in much the same way. This was the error diagnosed by Lipsey and Lancaster. As it turns out, the extent to which the model approximates the real world with respect to competition says *nothing at all* about the extent to which it maps onto the world with respect to efficiency. So even if it were incredibly realistic, it would still be completely useless when it comes to addressing public policy questions.

$ $ $

Suppose you live somewhere in the Midwestern United States, and your dream vacation is to go to Hawaii for a week. You could also go to Las Vegas, but that would be about half as much fun. Unfortunately, you don't have quite enough money to pay for a flight to Hawaii. On the other hand, you could *drive* to Las Vegas, which would cost much less. Now suppose a travel agent offers you the following deal: "You can't afford to fly all the way to Hawaii, but I'm willing to sell you a ticket at a reduced fare that will get you 98% of the way. Granted, it doesn't quite get you to your dream vacation. But isn't getting 98% of your dream vacation better than settling for Las Vegas, which is worth only 50% as much?"

This is obviously a crazy suggestion. Getting 98% of the way to Hawaii puts you somewhere in the Pacific Ocean. So clearly, if you can't get your first-best choice of vacation, your second-best option is to forget about Hawaii and go somewhere else entirely. The fallacy lies in thinking that getting something that is the closest approximation to the best is necessarily better than getting something rather different. Evidence to the contrary shows up quite often in everyday life (if the salad dressing you want isn't available, maybe you'd be better off ordering the soup; if you don't get the raise you want, maybe you should be working somewhere else).

Unfortunately, proponents of laissez-faire capitalism have for decades been peddling arguments that rely upon precisely this sort of fallacy. Let us grant, for the sake of argument, that a perfectly competitive market would be the best of all possible worlds. We know that no market is perfectly competitive. No problem, say the proponents of laissez-faire—all we have to do is make sure that our markets are as competitive

72

as possible, and we can rest assured that the outcome we get will be as close as possible to the ideal. Wrong, said Lipsey and Lancaster. If you believe that, then I have a ticket to Hawaii to sell you . . . or at least one that goes *almost* all the way to Hawaii.

How could such an obvious problem get overlooked? The answer has to do with some confused thinking about the supposedly "scientific" character of economic reasoning, along with one particularly misleading analogy. Anyone can see that the idealizations introduced by Arrow and Debreu in their characterization of perfect competition are fairly extreme. In order for their theoretical results to have any direct bearing on the real world, there must be no economies of scale (which means no advantages to mass production), no possibility of influencing prices through one's supply or demand decisions, no transaction costs (a category that includes everything from lawyer's fees and accounting expenses to transportation costs and unpaid bills), no uncertainty about the future (or, in situations where there is uncertainty, an option to purchase insurance against any eventuality), and no information asymmetries (in particular, customers who know *everything* that the manufacturer knows about the products they are considering purchasing). And most important of all, there must be no "externalities," which is to say, no uncompensated costs or benefits imposed upon others.[8] What this means, in practice, is that there would have to be a "complete" set of property rights: each individual would have to have the right to control every aspect of his or her environment.

Anyone who lives in a big city understands the concept of an externality implicitly. A friend of mine was sitting in his backyard one day when he caught his neighbor—who obviously hadn't noticed him sitting there—tossing a load of garbage over the fence into his yard. "What are you doing?" my friend asked, popping his head up over the fence. "Sorry," said the neighbor. "Accident." Such is life in the city. The point is that, with respect to this sort of garbage, the system of property rights provides each of us with a reasonable level of protection (which is why these sorts of episodes are uncommon). One reason the neighbor was probably so quick to apologize was that he knew, as pretty much everyone does, that you can easily get into trouble for throwing your garbage onto other people's land. With respect to other sorts of "garbage," on the other hand, our property rights offer us no protection. The neighbor can produce foul odors, make loud noises, or install hideous lawn ornaments without infringing upon our property rights, because we have no property rights in the air that we breathe, in our acoustic environment, or in the view out the front window.

To imagine what a "complete" set of property rights would look like, you have to picture everyone walking around in very large, opaque, soundproof, temperature-controlled plastic bubbles. No one is allowed to introduce anything into your bubble—no light, no noise, no liquids or gases, nothing—without your express permission. They're also not allowed to touch your bubble, or even to get in your way. If anyone wants to do any of these things, you have a right to charge them (just as they have a right to charge you for fiddling with *their* bubbles). You can also have personal property outside the bubble, and no one is allowed to touch or use any of that, either. As a result, you cannot be involuntarily subjected to any visual or auditory stimulus, you are not obliged to ingest or inhale anything you don't want, you can amass as many possessions as you like and use them however you like, and you can roam freely without worrying about other people. No more problems with noisy neighbors, secondhand smoke, ugly buildings, traffic jams, litter, sexual harassment, global warming, smelly co-workers, stupid jokes, or not finding a seat on the subway. If people want to ruin your day, now they'll have to pay you for the privilege.

This is the world of perfect capitalism. As anyone can see, it doesn't bear much resemblance to the real world. Not a problem, say the defenders of laissez-faire—there's nothing wrong with using idealizations in the development of scientific theories. We develop a set of laws based upon how things work under ideal conditions. When applying these to the real world, we simply have to keep in mind that things will turn out somewhat differently than predicted, depending upon how closely these ideal conditions are satisfied. Consider Newtonian mechanics. Since the force of gravity is proportional to the mass of the objects attracted, it follows that all the objects we observe falling toward the earth travel at the same speed (as Galileo famously demonstrated). This is why two bullets, one fired from a gun parallel to the ground and the other dropped simultaneously from the same height, will land at exactly the same time. This is an important and useful prediction, especially since it is contrary to most people's natural intuitions.[9] But of course, the two bullets are unlikely to land on the ground at *exactly* the same time. Setting aside the effects of the curvature of the earth, the fact remains that both bullets must travel through the air as they descend. From an aerodynamic standpoint, the fired bullet can be thought of as a spin-stabilized bullet dropped sideways, whereas a casually dropped bullet would tend to be quite chaotic in its descent, tumbling and generally presenting a higher coefficient of drag (in the direction of gravity) than the sideways-falling bullet. The casually dropped bullet would, therefore, probably land later (unless, of course, it were dropped pointing down, in its aerodynamic configuration, and did not tumble or precess—in which case it would land first).

But does this matter? Not really. It's not just that the ideal Newtonian model is "close enough" to the real world to generate useful predictions. It's that the *more closely* the real world resembles the ideal world of Newtonian mechanics, the more closely our observations will satisfy the predictions of the ideal model. If we conducted the bullet experiment on an artificial surface that corrected for the curvature of the earth, it would eliminate one source of imperfection and bring our observations closer to the predictions of ideal theory. If we conducted the experiment in a vacuum, that would eliminate another source of imperfection, and so bring our real-world observations even closer.

Because of this, it is not an objection simply to point to the model being used in a particular body of scientific theory and say, "That's not realistic!" It's often not supposed to be realistic. The point of developing models—simplified representations of some aspect of the real world—is to disaggregate things, so that instead of talking about everything all the time, one can isolate and discuss just some of the forces that are contributing to a particular observed phenomenon. This is often referred to as the "frictionless plane" method, after a set of computations carried out by Galileo to predict the movement of bodies moving down an inclined plane. Galileo ignored friction entirely, which meant that his model did not directly correspond to any actual experimental observations. Nevertheless, it provided an analysis that was close enough for all practical purposes, and provided the first clear statement of the forces that interacted in order to produce the observed motion.

Thus there is nothing wrong in principle with using idealizations like the "frictionless plane" in science, and many economists have defended their approach in these terms. Milton Friedman (father of the infamous "Chicago School") appealed to the analogy of geometry in defending the assumption that everyone faces a fixed (or exogenously determined) set of prices under perfect competition:

> *Of course, competition is an ideal type, like a Euclidean line or point. No one has ever seen a Euclidean line—which has zero width and depth—yet we all find it useful to regard many a Euclidean volume—such as a surveyor's string—as a Euclidean line. Similarly, there is no such thing as "pure" competition. Every producer has some effect, however tiny, on the price of the product he purchases. The important issue for understanding and for policy is whether this effect is significant or can properly be neglected, as the surveyor can neglect the thickness of what he calls the "line."*[10]

Friedman's answer is "yes"—at least most of the time. For instance, even if there is a monopoly in a particular sector, that doesn't mean the competitive model is inapplicable. The firm may still choose to behave *as though* it had competitors, knowing that if it began to do otherwise—and thus began to earn supranormal profits—it would quickly attract "new entrants," that is, new competitors. There is, therefore, room for reasonable debate when it comes to the question of how closely the real world matches the competitive conditions specified in the Invisible Hand Theorem. What the Second Best Theorem shows, however, is that *from the standpoint of public policy* none of this matters. If the real world deviates from the ideal of perfect competition in even one respect, then not only will the first-best outcome be unobtainable, but the best obtainable approximation of perfect competition is almost guaranteed to generate an outcome that is worse than some other, second-best alternative. The frictionless plane argument is in fact a fallacy. Wanting an economy that is *almost* perfectly competitive is like wanting a flight that takes you almost all the way to Hawaii. It's not like in physics or geometry, where the more idealizing conditions you satisfy, the more your real-world outcome will approximate the ideal. With respect to perfect competition, the more conditions you satisfy—short of satisfying them all—the farther away you get from the ideal of perfect efficiency.

The perfectly competitive market is more like the Atkins diet than a frictionless plane. The Atkins diet, one may recall, is the one that recommends eating only fat and protein—scrambled eggs, steak, bacon—but cutting out all carbohydrates. It works by tricking the body into thinking that it's starving, thereby prompting it to start breaking down and consuming its fat reserves. But in order for this to work, you have to really trick your body, and that means *absolutely no carbohydrates*. People who follow a 100% Atkins diet can in fact lose a lot of weight. But one cannot infer from this that following a 99% Atkins diet—eating a lot of fat and protein and just a tiny bit of carbohydrates—will lead to almost as much weight loss. On contrary, it's a recipe for putting on massive amounts of weight. In fact, "almost" following the Atkins diet is far worse than not dieting at all.

$ $ $

It's not difficult to see that the Second Best Theorem is a reeling blow to the right. No one has ever imagined that the presuppositions of the

Invisible Hand Theorem could be satisfied in the real world. There will always be sectors that are uncompetitive or in which firms are able to generate significant negative externalities (such as pollution, noise, or funny smells). This will result in prices in those sectors being out of line with what they should be. No problem, say advocates of laissez-faire. Even if we're unable to come up with the right set of prices in one area, we can make sure that competitive conditions prevail in other sectors, so that prices in *those* areas will be at the right level. What the Second Best Theorem shows is that this policy prescription is, in general, not likely to promote greater efficiency. Once one set of prices is wrong, getting the others right is of no help. Or to put the same point the other way around: In an economy with multiple price distortions, fixing just one of them can make things worse, not better.

Consider how this affects, for example, the debate over international free trade. The primary case for trade liberalization is based on efficiency—which is certainly not a negligible consideration. Many people believe that trade restrictions are a source of enormous waste and that a world in which there were no such restrictions would be more efficient and prosperous than a world in which there are some. This is basically correct. But they then go on to claim that a world in which there were *fewer* trade restrictions would be more efficient than a world in which there are *more*. This is where the red warning lights should go on.

The Second Best Theorem shows that if there is even one trade barrier in place, then it may be impossible for any nation to achieve the second-best outcome without imposing trade barriers or granting subsidies of its own. In fact, interfering with trade may be then the only way to promote efficiency. Most obviously, if prices in one sector are artificially high because of trade restrictions, the best move would be to increase prices artificially in all other sectors, in such a way as to preserve the proper exchange ratios between all goods.

There can also be cases where two market imperfections partially (or completely) cancel one another out, so that fixing one of them makes the other worse. The classic example involves a firm that has a monopoly over the production of a particular good and is curtailing output in order to reap the benefits of high prices. If production of this good also happens to generate a significant amount of pollution, getting rid of the monopoly could wind up being a bad thing. Competition would lower prices, leading to increased production of the good, and hence more pollution. (From this perspective, the OPEC cartel may have done the world a favor by keeping the price of oil artificially high for years. The price of oil should actually be higher than where competitive markets would set it, because of the environmental externalities generated by its consumption.)

This situation suggests that the state may be able to generate efficiency gains by granting monopolies in particular sectors where it has an interest in seeing the volume of production decline (liquor stores, casinos, etc.). This is, of course, exactly what the state currently does. The idea is to create offsetting market imperfections.

In general, however, it would be foolish to recommend these sorts of micromanipulations to either firms or governments, simply because the amount of information that would be required in order to get the intervention just right is staggering (and almost always unobtainable). So while the Second Best Theorem appears to give people who like interfering in markets license to go hog wild, in practice it does no such thing. Just because markets fail to create efficient outcomes doesn't mean that government is in a position to do any better—there is an obligation, on the part of those who favor state intervention, to show that the cure won't be worse than the disease. What the Second Best Theorem does show, however, is that it is impossible to derive useful policy recommendations from general equilibrium models of the economy. The standard tools simply do not tell us what it is best to do in the real world. Each situation—every sector, every market, and every public policy proposal—has to be evaluated on its own merits.

When I spoke to Lipsey, he described the primary consequence of the Second Best Theorem as having been to "impose some humility" upon economists, or at least those who were paying attention. It didn't show that any *particular* policy claims were false. (Lipsey himself, for instance, was one of the most ardent proponents of free trade between Canada and the United States.) It just means that you can't make sweeping pronouncements about the efficiency of markets based upon a single, highly idealized model. Not that this has stopped anyone. Consider the following claim, from a recent textbook on welfare economics and public policy:

> [The Invisible Hand Theorem is] probably the single most
> powerful result in the theory of market economies and is widely
> used by economists who believe that markets are competitive
> and that governments should not intervene in economic activity.
> Milton Friedman and the "Chicago School" are the best known
> defenders of this position. In addition, because of its efficiency
> properties, competitive equilibrium offers a useful standard for
> policy analysis.[11]

This last sentence is shocking. It's the sort of thing that lends credence to Lipsey's claim that his theorem was "suppressed."

Markets are, in general, an invaluable tool for promoting human well-being. It's very easy to forget that whenever two people enter into an economic exchange, it's because they both expect to be better off as a result of this exchange than they would have been without it. But it is false to claim, on this basis, that the more our society relies upon competitive markets to organize the production and distribution of goods and services, the better off we will be. Sometimes moving closer to the ideal of perfect competition will make us better off, but sometimes it won't. Not only does the Invisible Hand Theorem offer no guarantees in this regard, it doesn't even generate a presumption in favor of the market pattern of organization. The argument for market solutions must be made on a case-by-case basis; it cannot be derived from an abstract model of how an ideal economy would function.

CHAPTER 4

TAXES ARE TOO HIGH

The myth of the government as consumer

People hate taxes. This is actually just a special instance of a more general law, which is that people hate paying for stuff. Unfortunately, that's not how everyone sees it. "Death and taxes" are regarded as the two great inevitabilities in life, not "death and other people making you pay for stuff." The fact that taxes get singled out in this way, and are capable of provoking such deep-seated anger and resentment, is something that constantly amazes me.

I remember once standing in line waiting to pick up my car after an oil change. When the woman in front of me was handed her bill, she stopped the mechanic and asked, "How much of that is *taxes?*" When he looked at her blankly, she elaborated a bit, saying, "I just want to know how much those bastards are taking from me." This conversation quickly devolved into everyday chitchat, until the woman announced that she needed to get going, since she was a nurse and couldn't be late for her shift at the hospital. "Wait a minute," I said. "You're a nurse? At a public hospital? That means *you work for the government.*"[1] She didn't seem to know where I was going with this, so I said, "Those 'bastards' are using the money to pay your salary. How can you complain about taxes? That's like Tom Cruise complaining about the price of movie tickets." The mechanic laughed.

Unfortunately, I don't think my little public service intervention did much to change her attitude. People have a visceral distaste for paying taxes and an obvious free rider incentive to avoid doing so. Yet if that were all there was to it, the issue would never get much political traction. People may not like having to obey traffic laws either, but that's not really an argument for abolishing them. What sets the issue of taxation apart is the notion, popularized by generations of economists, that taxes are not just a personal inconvenience to the taxpayer but are also objectively bad for the economy. As a general claim this is simply false (despite the fact that there are specific instances in which it is true). It is, however, a typical consequence of a surprisingly pervasive error that I refer to as the "government as consumer" fallacy.

The picture underlying this fallacy is relatively straightforward. Government services, such as health care, education, national defense, and so on, "cost" us as a society. We are able to pay for them only because of all the wealth that we generate in the private sector, which we transfer to the government in the form of taxes. A government that taxes the economy too heavily stands accused of "killing the goose that lays the golden eggs" by disrupting the mechanism that generates the wealth that it itself relies upon in order to provides its services.

Thus the government gets treated as a *consumer* of wealth, while the private sector is regarded as a *producer*. This is totally confused. The state in fact produces *exactly* the same amount of wealth as the market, which is to say, it produces none at all. *People* produce wealth, and people consume wealth. Institutions, such as the state or the market, neither produce nor consume anything. They simply constitute mechanisms through which people coordinate their production and consumption of wealth. Furthermore, the value of what a person produces has nothing to do with who pays his salary. The services of a security guard make the same contribution to the real wealth of the nation regardless of whether he is called a "police officer" and works for the state or is called a "rent-a-cop" and works for a private security firm.

§ § §

A lot of errors in economic reasoning arise from the tendency to treat economic institutions as though they were people. This shows up often in the way that we think about both corporations and government. A surprisingly large percentage of the population does not understand that "making the government pay" for their problems is equivalent to "making your friends and neighbors pay." (I've always thought it would be helpful, on this front, if newscasters would occasionally substitute the term "us all" for "the government," in headlines like "The court's recent employment equity ruling will cost the government over $10 billion" or, for Americans, "The war in Iraq costs the government more than $200 million every day.") In the same way, many people think that having corporations pay taxes represents some sort of an alternative to having individuals pay taxes (rather than being simply an indirect way of taxing individuals).

Both of these errors can be overcome simply by "following the money" to see where it ultimately comes from, or where it ends up. Yet it is also important to have the right sort of "picture" of what these institutions are and what they do. Management theorists have, in recent decades, taken to referring to the firm as a "nexus of contracts." The goal is to draw attention to the fact that, despite the legal fiction of corporate personhood, the corporation lacks corporeality. The firm is nothing more than a mechanism for organizing a very complex set of transactions between individuals. Furthermore, there are other ways of organizing exactly the same transactions that would not involve the formation of a corporation—although presumably these other ways would be less convenient, which is precisely why people choose to incorporate.

The state should be thought of in exactly the same way, at least with respect to its economic role. The primary difference between the state and the corporation is simply that membership in the former is universal and compulsory, while in the latter it is not. (As we shall see, it is precisely these two features that underlie the state's distinctive capacity to enhance economic efficiency.) Because of this nonvoluntary aspect, it would be misleading to call the state merely a "nexus of contracts," even though that is, in a sense, what it is. For now, let's call it a "nub of transactions."

The state, as people on the right never tire of reminding us, grew spectacularly over the course of the twentieth century. It is instructive to look at how much "social spending" Western governments engaged in at the beginning and at the end of the twentieth century (Table 4.1).[2]

	1900	1995
France	0.57%	26.93%
Germany	0.53%	24.92%
United States	0.55%	13.67%
Canada	0.00%	18.09%

Table 4.1 Spending on welfare, unemployment, pensions, health, and housing, as a percentage of GDP

This sort of change is not just quantitative: it represents a qualitative change in the nature of the state as an institution. In this respect, it is slightly misleading to think of the twenty-first-century state as the same sort of institution as the nineteenth-century state. As far as the economy is concerned, the state went from being a bystander to being the single most important actor. It's as though the referees in a hockey game went out and got sticks, then started asserting the right to seize the puck at any time and shoot it wherever they wanted. Not only would this change the game in pretty fundamental ways, it would raise serious questions about whether these people should still be called "referees."

The standard way of distinguishing this new state-as-economic-behemoth from its precursor institution is to call it "the welfare state." This is not a great term, insofar as it suggests that handing out welfare checks is one of the major functions of modern government, which typically is not the case. The word "welfare" is actually being used in a different sense here, but that's probably not worth the effort of pointing out. A better idea would simply be to rebrand it as something else, like "the public goods state." This term reflects an idea, expressed canonically by Paul Samuelson in a 1954 *Review of Economic Studies* paper, that the reason the state has grown so large is because it is uniquely situated to provide a type of good that markets alone will never deliver, namely, a so-called *public good*.[3] Samuelson defined public goods as ones that were nonexcludable—you couldn't prevent anyone from enjoying them—and nonrival in consumption—one person's consumption did not diminish the quantity or quality of anyone else's. The sort of thing he had in mind was a lighthouse, the services of which were available to all ships in the vicinity without distinction and without any diminution from increased usage.

The important part of Samuelson's argument was the way that it drew attention to the efficiency rationale for the welfare state. Unfortunately, Samuelson's definition of a public good was driven more by modeling concerns than by any realistic description of the sort of goods that governments deliver. There are, in fact, almost no public goods in Samuelson's sense—even something like national defense, which benefits all citizens without distinction and regardless of their numbers, does not qualify, since it benefits only *citizens* (or those who find themselves within the borders of the state). More important, though, Samuelson made it sound as though there were a special and distinct class of goods that by its very nature could only be delivered by the state. In fact, many of the goods provided by government are of exactly the same kind as those provided by the private sector. The question is only how we, as consumers, choose to organize our purchases.

$ $ $

Despite the agreeable homophony between "public good" and "public sector," most of what governments are in the business of providing is not public goods, but rather what economists call *club goods*. This term was introduced by the economist James M. Buchanan to bridge what he described as "the awesome Samuelson gap between the purely private and the purely public good."[4] Every good, Buchanan pointed out, has what might be referred to as an "optimal sharing group." Your toothbrush, for instance, probably has an optimal sharing group of one, making it a good candidate for treatment as a purely private good. But other things are not like this. For instance, it's not a great idea to spend too much money on exercise equipment. While it is convenient to have an elliptical trainer in the basement so you can work out in the privacy of your own home, this very expensive piece of equipment is likely to sit unused 362 days of the year. If your neighbor has an equally unused StairMaster, and someone else a stationary bike, then there are obvious efficiency gains to be had from sharing exercise equipment. One could organize a complicated rotation scheme among neighbors, or one could do what most people do, which is simply to take out a gym membership.

A "gym" is basically an arrangement through which individuals collectively purchase and share a variety of different types of fitness equipment. Such an arrangement is advantageous because use of this equipment is relatively nonrival. The equipment is quite durable, and so is not noticeably eroded in the short term through multiple use. Furthermore, the amount of time that any one person wants to spend using it represents a relatively small fraction of the day, which makes it well suited for sharing. Thus the way that we typically organize consumption is by charging people a flat fee for access to the club, which then gives them "free" access to all the machines within.

There are a couple of things worth noting about this arrangement. The first is that the use of a flat fee for payment can have the unfortunate effect of obscuring the nature of the underlying economic transaction.

For instance, people who join a gym often don't realize that they're paying for everything—the treadmill, the sauna, the swimming pool—regardless of whether they actually use it. They think the fee goes to the club, and the club buys the equipment (along with the services of those who work there). They don't realize that the club is just an intermediary, and that it is really the members, collectively, who are doing the purchasing.

The second important point is that club purchasing often involves a significant reduction of consumer choice. When I go out to buy exercise equipment in the market, I pay for exactly what I want to use, and I don't pay for anything else. When I join a club, the fee structure usually ensures that I have to pay for a share of everything, regardless of whether I use it. This is why people who like to swim usually get a better deal out of gym memberships than anyone else. Since the swimming pool is by far the most expensive item to maintain, there is almost always cross-subsidization among members of clubs that have a pool—an effect that clubs sometime seek to diminish by imposing a surcharge, such as a towel or locker fee, on those who use the pool.

This cross-subsidization among members is clearly one of the disadvantages of many club-purchased goods. It is partially attenuated by the fact that different clubs will arise that offer different mixes of goods, and so consumers can shop around for one that most closely caters to their preferences (for example, someone who doesn't like to swim should not join a club with a pool). Although in theory one could get perfect efficiency here, in practice the amount of variety on display is fairly limited (as anyone who has compared fitness clubs can attest).[5] This shows that the efficiency gains arising from the collective purchase (that is, the formation of an optimal sharing group) are sufficiently great that they outweigh the losses caused by the bundle of goods being less tailored to the needs of the individual consumer.

One can see a similar phenomenon in the case of condominiums. Each building offers its members a mix of "private" amenities (living unit, parking space) and "public" ones (elevators, security, heating). The latter are paid for through flat monthly condo fees, and are essentially available to everyone in the building "for free." Again, each condominium offers a different bundle of public (or club) benefits, with options such as a swimming pool, garbage removal, even concierge service. In some cases, this is because the goods are relatively nonrival, and so can easily be enjoyed by all. In other cases, it's because the goods are relatively nonexcludable, and so everyone must be forced to pay in order to avoid a collective action problem. (This is the case with the security guard at the entrance, whose presence automatically confers a benefit upon everyone in the building.)

$ $ $

Hopefully this all seems quite plausible as an account of how health clubs and condominiums are typically organized. Now suppose someone comes along and says, "How high should condo fees be?" or "How much should a gym membership cost?" The answer, of course, is that *it depends*. The only limit in principle is the amount that people are willing to pay. How much they are willing to pay will be determined entirely by how much they want to consume the type of goods that are best purchased collectively. If the members of a health club want a new sauna, or the residents of a condominium want expanded parking facilities, they should expect an increase in fees in order to finance these purchases.

Does it make sense, when shopping for a condominium, to find the building with the lowest possible fees? Again, it depends. Some people are not particularly interested in having a swimming pool in the building or timely repairs to the elevators, so they might be perfectly happy living in a building with rock-bottom fees. Other people, who happen to have more of a taste for the sort of goods that are best purchased collectively, will want to live in a building with higher fees and more amenities. What matters, in other words, is not the absolute level of fees, but rather the value that one gets for them.

This may seem crushingly obvious, and it usually is in the case of condominium fees. Unfortunately, when it comes to the subject of taxes, people tend to get all confused. In the same way that members of a club pay a fee for admission and then enjoy a certain range of goods "for free" once inside, as citizens of a country we all pay fees and then enjoy certain other goods "for free." In the latter case, we call the fee a "tax," but it has essentially the same structure as a club fee.

The fact that some goods are provided for by the state, financed through taxes, is a reflection of the optimal sharing group for those goods. In some cases, the optimal sharing group is *everyone* (consider national defense, the sewage and water system, highways). In this case, the good is provided by the "club of everyone," which is to say, the state. The police are no different in principle from the security guard at the front desk of a condo. Furthermore, payment for these services—in the form of taxes— is mandatory for the same reason that condo fees are mandatory: The benefits are relatively nonexcludable (which is to say, unreasonably costly to exclude people from).

One of the goods that can often be purchased most efficiently through taxes is insurance. Since the benefits of an insurance scheme come from the pooling of risks, the size of the gain is often proportional to the size of the pool. As a result, it is in our interest in many cases to purchase insurance using the mechanism of universal taxation and public provision. This is basically how the health care system in Canada works. I pay taxes, and what I get in return is a basic health-insurance policy, provided by the state. So if Canadians want to consume more health care or a new subway or better roads, what are their options? The situation is the same as with the condo residents who want a new sauna: If people want to buy more of this stuff (and are willing to buy less of something else), then they should vote to raise taxes and buy more of it. It doesn't necessarily impose a drag on the economy to raise taxes in this way, any more than it imposes a drag on the economy when the residents of a condo association vote to increase their condo fees.

One can see, then, the absurdity of the view that taxes are intrinsically bad, or that lower taxes are necessarily preferable to higher taxes.

The absolute level of taxation is unimportant; what matters is how much individuals want to purchase through the public sector (the "club of everyone"), and how much value the government is able to deliver. This is why low-tax jurisdictions are not necessarily more "competitive" than high-tax jurisdictions (any more than low-fee condominiums are necessarily more attractive places to live than high-fee condominiums). Furthermore, the government does not "consume" the money collected in taxes—this is a fundamental fallacy; it is merely the vehicle through which we organize our spending. In this respect, taxation is basically a form of collective shopping. Needless to say, how much shopping we do collectively, and in what size of groups, is a matter of fundamental indifference from the standpoint of economic prosperity.

There is enormous confusion on this point. Every year, in dozens of countries around the world, right-wing anti-tax groups calculate and then solemnly declare a "Tax Freedom Day," in order to let people know what day they "stop working for the government and start working for themselves." But it would make just as much sense to declare an annual "mortgage freedom day," in order to let homeowners know what day they "stop working for the bank and start working for themselves." It takes the average homeowner at least a couple months of work each year to pay off his or her annual mortgage bill. But who cares? Homeowners are not really "working for the bank"; they're merely financing their own consumption. After all, they're the ones living in the house, not the bank manager. It's the same thing with taxes. You're not really "working for the government" when your kids are going to public school, you're commuting on public roads, and you expect the government to pay your hospital bills when you're old and infirm. You're simply financing your own consumption.

One can find a similar fallacy at work in the widespread belief that tax cuts "stimulate" the economy. This is the same as believing that a legislated reduction in condo fees would stimulate the economy. Naturally, if condo fees go down across the board, it will result in people having more money in their pockets to spend. But it will also result in condo boards having *less* money to spend. The result will simply be a shift away from the sort of goods that are provided on a club basis toward the sort that are provided on a private basis. Tax cuts have the same effect. They just mean less money spent on schools and health care, more spent on cars and homes. Absent some effect on savings, the increased demand that occurs in one sector is necessarily offset by decreased demand in some other. (An exception to the rule occurs when the government has no money, and so has to borrow to make up the shortfall in tax revenue. In this case, the tax cut is not really a tax cut—it's more like a mandatory personal consumption loan taken out by the state for each citizen. Either way, the same effect could be achieved by having the state spend the borrowed money on health care, pollution abatement, highway construction, or any other form of publicly organized consumption.)

There are, of course, certain costs associated with the use of the taxation system as a way of purchasing goods and services. For various reasons, taxes can't be imposed as "flat fees" the way that club fees are usually imposed (Margaret Thatcher tried, in the U.K., but didn't get very far with it). This means that they must be collected in other ways, such as income and consumption taxes, which distort economic incentives and generate all sorts of counterproductive tax-avoidance behavior (such as individuals hiring crafty accountants to discover and exploit tax loopholes). Yet this is not a phenomenon that is unique to taxation. Private markets also have transaction costs, such as exposure to the risk of fraud or the need to hire lawyers to look over contracts. That doesn't mean that no one should hire a lawyer, and it doesn't mean that no one should pay taxes. The underlying problem is that people behave non-cooperatively. As a result, we need to worry about being defrauded or taken advantage of in commercial transactions. We also need to worry about being assaulted and about having our property stolen. In order to decide what's best, we have to weigh the benefits of the contemplated transaction against the costs of organizing it in a particular way. How much does it cost to hire a lawyer versus how much does it cost to get defrauded? How much does it cost to pay taxes (in terms of deadweight losses) versus how much does it cost to live with market failure?

The question, in other words, is simply whether the benefits that come from the formation of an optimal sharing group outweigh the costs that are associated with the particular sharing arrangements adopted. To say, as Milton Friedman once did, that any tax cut is a good tax cut is simply to articulate an arbitrary preference against a particular type of purchasing arrangement. It's like saying that the best condo fee is the lowest condo fee. A lot of first-time buyers do have this attitude, but they usually come to regret it.

$ $ $

One of the things that tend to muddy the waters when it comes to understanding club goods is that we often give things different names when they are purchased collectively and when they are purchased individually. To take a somewhat exotic example, consider the case of the life annuity. This is basically an insurance product that people buy in order to protect themselves against the risk of outliving their savings. Although the precise details are usually complex, the basic idea is that one pays a flat sum up front in return for a fixed periodic payment starting at the age of retirement and continuing until death (for example, one might pay $1,000 now in return for a guaranteed payment of $10 a month from retirement until death).

Why might someone choose to buy an annuity? Statistics can tell us, on average, how long each of us can expect to live, and we can infer from this how much we will need to save for our retirements. But unfortunately, there is a fair degree of variation around this mean. As a result, we all face the risk of either saving too much or, more important, saving too little. For any one individual, it may not make sense to save enough to maintain a comfortable lifestyle until the age of 90, but the fact is, lots of people live that long. One solution, therefore, is to buy an annuity. If you die young, you don't get much out of it, but if you live for a long time, it's guaranteed to keep paying out. When an insurance company sells annuities to hundreds or thousands of customers, the ones who die young are likely to balance out those who live longer, so the total of payments made is likely to be quite close to what one could anticipate simply by looking at mortality tables and average life expectancy.

There is a problem, however, in the market for life annuities. It's known as "adverse selection." Basically, a life annuity is a good deal if you expect to live for a very long time, but a bad deal if you expect to die young. As a result, the only people with an incentive to buy them will be those who, for some reason or another, expect to live for longer than the average. In some cases, the reasons people have will be obvious. Women, for instance, typically have a life expectancy five years longer than men, so the value to them of a life annuity is significantly greater. As a result, any insurer that sets a "unisex" price for life annuities would tend to attract only female customers. This would in turn result in greater-than-expected liabilities.

Women, therefore, have to pay more for life annuities than men do (typically, the same up-front payment purchases a lower periodic payment). Yet there are many other factors affecting life expectancy that are not so easily detectable by insurance companies (for example, whether or not you smoked when you were young). As a result, insurers tend to attract precisely the sort of customers that they least want. In effect, the mere fact that a person is interested in buying a life annuity is cause for suspicion, since it suggests that he expects to live for a long time. This "adverse selection" effect needs to be taken into consideration when setting the price of the annuities. But because of this, many of the "good risks"—people who are likely to die young—will be priced out of the market, since they cannot credibly identify themselves to the insurer as good risks. Annuities will simply be too expensive for it to be worth their while to purchase them.

This problem is somewhat attenuated, however, if people go shopping for annuities as a group. For example, if an employer approaches an insurance company and says, "I'd like to buy life annuities for all my employees," this is inherently less suspicious. After all, since very few companies make employment decisions based upon anticipated longevity, a company's employees are likely to be a fairly representative sample of the population (for each one who lives a very long time, there is likely to be one who dies young). The insurer can therefore sell life annuities to the group at a better rate than it can to individuals. A life annuity is thus the type of good that has an optimal sharing group larger than one: It is best purchased not as a private good, but as a club good.

Unfortunately, when we purchase life annuities as a group through an employer, they are no longer called annuities. Instead, they are called "defined benefit pension schemes." This change in nomenclature creates all sorts of confusion; there is an inclination to regard pension schemes as savings arrangements, rather than as insurance products. Nevertheless, an annuity is essentially what is being purchased: In return for an up-front payment (the "pension contribution"), the employer guarantees a fixed periodic payment from the time of retirement until death.

Of course, if it pays to shop for annuities as a group, then the bigger the group, the better. The benefit, in this case, comes from belonging to a group that can credibly claim to be a representative sample of the population. And of course, the best sample of the population is the population itself. As a result, the optimal sharing group for life annuities is the entire country. No surprise then that the state also "purchases" life annuities for its citizens, in the form of public pensions (the Canada Pension Plan, Social Security in the United States).

The failure to appreciate that what is being provided here is a life annuity creates considerable confusion. In the debates over "privatization" of Social Security in the United States, for instance, people routinely compared the rate of return of money that was saved and invested in the stock market with the rate of return of money paid into Social Security. Yet analyzing the latter in terms of rate of return involved a category error. It amounted to comparing an investment to an insurance policy. In this respect, it is like calculating the rate of return on your car insurance: If you had no accidents, your rate of return looks terrible; if you crashed your new Mercedes in the first month of your policy, the rate of return looks great. The same is true with Social Security: If you live until you're 120, the rate of return is going to be spectacular. But that misses the point. People buy insurance not because they hope to get a payout, but because of the peace of mind that comes from being protected against particular risks. With state pension plans and other annuity products, knowing that you can't outlive your savings serves as the primary source of benefit (among other things, it relieves people of the need to have so many children).

Thus what proponents of "privatization" of Social Security in the United States were recommending was not really privatization of the system. Privatization would involve individuals purchasing life annuities privately, rather than collectively—which would be a transparently bad deal. What they were actually recommending was that individuals stop purchasing insurance entirely, and instead simply save for their own retirements. (Many proponents of "defined contribution" over "defined benefit" pension plans are making the same recommendation.) In other words, their goal was simply to undo a mutually beneficial risk-pooling arrangement, for no particularly good reason other than an ideological hostility to government. No wonder the idea didn't go anywhere.

$ $ $

There is, of course, one big difference between paying fees to a club and paying taxes to the government. It is an almost inevitable consequence of shared consumption that it reduces consumer choice. No condominium is likely to provide exactly the mix of "public" amenities that you most value. No health club is likely to have exactly the equipment that you would have bought for yourself. And yet with clubs the consumer still has *some* choice. Not only can you shop around to find the one that is the best fit, you also have the option of *leaving*, if, say, decisions get made that are too far contrary to your desires. People may hate condo and gym membership fees, but they are not forced to pay them.

In the case of the state, however, this exit option is typically absent (even if you do leave, you may not find any other state willing to take you). Thus the mix of goods you get by virtue of membership is likely to be crudely mismatched to your needs ("Public schools—what do I need those for? I have no kids . . ."). The provision of public goods by the state is not just a case of collective shopping; it is also a case of *compulsory* collective shopping. So while the economic character of the transaction may be the same in the two cases, in the case of the state there is an interference with individual liberty that is felt by many to be a rather keen insult.

What is to be said here? Of course, the observation is correct. You have to pay your taxes, and you have to pay for a wide variety of public goods even if you don't use them. Because of this, state provision should be considered only in cases of egregious market failure, when a one-size-fits-all provision is better than the alternative. This is why the state is often more successful in dealing with relatively homogenous goods, such as insurance, where differences in consumer preference are not all that significant. (Compare this to food or clothing, where the advantages of being able to shop around are obviously much greater.) A more general way of putting it would be to say that the optimal sharing group will tend to be larger for goods where consumer preference is more homogeneous, because the losses caused by "preference mismatch" will tend to be smaller.

All that having been said, it is important to note that the amount of uniformity in the package of benefits offered by government is often overstated. This is particularly true in federal states, where the major functions of the welfare state are often discharged at a more local level and where there are very few internal barriers to mobility. Like different health clubs offering a different mix of fitness equipment, each U.S. state or Canadian province offers a different mix of club goods. If you want subsidized daycare, move to Quebec, not Alberta. If you want state-funded universities, move to California, not South Carolina.

Even in a nonfederal system, every country delivers a large number of public services at the level of the municipality, and municipalities compete with one another for both people and businesses by trying to offer an attractive mix of taxation and public services. If you're willing to make certain idealizing assumptions about geography and mobility, the economist Charles Tiebout has shown that municipal governments are able to achieve the same level of efficiency as private markets.[6] Of course, this all needs to be taken with a grain of salt. What it shows, however, is that people who argue for the superiority of private over public provision on the grounds of choice often overstate the amount of choice that actually exists in private markets, while understating the amount of choice that exists in the public sector.

It is worth observing as well that in most cases, when the welfare state provides a certain good, it does so at a very low level, leaving consumers free to "top up" their entitlements by purchasing more of the good on private markets. This is true in all the major categories of welfare-state expenditure: pensions, education, security, disability insurance, health insurance, communications (such as postal services), and sometimes even transportation networks. Thus it is the poor who suffer most acutely from restrictions on consumer choice—but they are not likely to complain, since the one-size-fits-all package that they receive is of much greater value than anything they would have been able to afford on their own.

Finally, it is important to distinguish those who want to exercise an exit option from those who simply want a free ride. In the case of a gym membership, you are always free to quit if you don't think you're getting your money's worth. But the gym also has the right to kick you out—to exclude you from its benefits—if it doesn't like the way you are behaving. States, on the other hand, cannot kick people out (barring certain exceptional cases). The state health care provider cannot discontinue your policy after you develop diabetes, the way a private insurer can. There is an obvious quid pro quo here: a limited right of exit is coupled with a limited right of exclusion. The latter provides a benefit—in the form of peace of mind—that is often taken for granted.

CHAPTER 5

UNCOMPETITIVE IN EVERYTHING

Why international competitiveness doesn't matter

E ven the most sympathetic observer must admit that over the past few decades, the apostles of neoliberalism, globalization, and free trade have done a terrible job of marketing their brand. The more they try to make people feel better about international trade, the more suspicious everyone becomes. The problem can be traced back to one stock phrase, which they repeat like a mantra: "international competitiveness."[1] What are you going to do when the Bangalore call-center workers come for *your* job? How are you going to compete? The specter of millions of diligent, educated, overachieving Asian workers coming online in the next decade is invoked, like a "scared straight" program, as a remedy for Western decadence. General Motors chairman Rick Wagoner summed up the anxiety perfectly when he complained that the U.S. economy was in danger of becoming "uncompetitive in everything."[2]

There's only one problem with all this: It's not possible for an economy to be uncompetitive in everything, and even if it were possible, it wouldn't matter, because, fundamentally, trade is not a competitive relationship. Competitions have a winner and a loser. Trade, on the other hand, is a cooperative relationship. Both parties benefit—otherwise they wouldn't do it. There is, of course, competition on either side of the exchange, among the sellers and among the buyers, and there are external effects. But there is no competition *between* the sellers and the buyers. In this respect, all competition is domestic competition. We do not compete with China, India, or Mexico when we trade with them, nor do we compete with firms in those countries. If you look at the economics textbooks, the key concept in international trade is not "competitive advantage," but rather "*comparative* advantage." These are entirely different things. Furthermore, comparative advantage is an unintuitive and poorly understood concept, one that—it would seem—cannot be explained too many times. Yet rather than making the case for international trade through reference to its win-win structure, many of international trade's most ardent defenders have inadvertently chosen to undermine the case by framing it as a type of competition. This just reinforces the idea that globalization is a zero-sum game, in which the winners benefit at the expense of the losers.

Why would the apostles of free trade sabotage their own case in this way? Part of it has to do with a simple failure to realize how much this rhetoric feeds into the left-wing critique of globalization. Saying that trade creates both winners and losers is just another way of saying that trade is exploitative, which gives aid and comfort to the old-fashioned Marxist view that there is extraction of "surplus value" in these exchange relations. Furthermore, if trade is competitive, what chance does a poor African nation have against the big bullies of the West? Aren't we supposed to be giving them a helping hand, rather than trying to beat them down?

Apart from this unintended side effect, there is also an intended consequence of the "competitiveness" rhetoric: It serves to advance a domestic right-wing agenda. Some people find it politically expedient to describe us as being in competition with our trade partners, even though it isn't true, because it allows them to push for tax cuts, wage reductions, deregulation, and lax environmental standards. The basis for this rhetoric is usually a false analogy between the competitiveness of countries and the competitiveness of businesses. The *New York Times* columnist Thomas Friedman, for instance—long-time cheerleader for globalization—has probably done more damage to the cause through this sort of rhetoric than have any of its most ardent critics. He makes a point of using the words "company" and "country" interchangeably. "If you are going to deal with a system as complex and brutal as globalization, and prosper within it, you need a strategy for how to choose prosperity for your country or company," he writes.[3] This is in a section of *The Lexus and the Olive Tree* entitled "Does your country's or company's management get it and can you change management if they don't?"

This faulty analogy is used to suggest that government needs to become "leaner," more businesslike, perhaps even be downsized. We must learn to "shoot the wounded," as Friedman puts it. Taxation rates, labor standards, environmental regulations—these are just overhead expenses, all of which must be reduced in order to promote competitiveness. The welfare state is a luxury, a frill, an expensive perk that we're going to have to learn to live without. This isn't a choice, it's an inevitability: "Many of the old corporate and government safety nets will vanish under global competition in the flat world," Friedman writes in his follow-up work, *The World Is Flat*.[4] While he does make an effort to talk about comparative advantage, he keeps slipping back into the rhetoric of competitiveness. We've got to pull up our socks, straighten our ties, and stop taking lunch breaks! We need to get serious, get educated, and get back to work, otherwise we'll be crushed!

In fact, we don't have to do anything of the sort. Countries are not companies, and they shouldn't try to act as though they are. In fact, it's tempting to call this analogy the "Lexus and the olive tree" fallacy, in honor of Friedman's relentless conflation of the two. Companies compete with one another; countries do not. Getting mixed up on this point is a recipe for enormous confusion.

§ § §

International free trade is one of the few economic policy questions that has the capacity to become a major election issue. In Canada, the attempt to implement the Canada-U.S. free trade agreement in 1988 actually forced the government to call a general election (after the Senate refused to pass the necessary legislation). The campaign that ensued was fought almost entirely on this question. Like many Canadians my age, I voted against the government. I did so because I was convinced that the free trade agreement would be a disaster for the country. And the reason I was convinced of this had a lot to do with the fact that I didn't understand basic economics. In this respect, I was in good company. Indeed, most of Canada's left-wing intelligentsia (especially writers and artists) spoke out against the free trade agreement, and in the process managed to reveal a scandalous lack of economic literacy. Scanning through these documents with the benefit of hindsight, it is safe to say that pretty much the entire left-wing establishment in the country did not understand international trade.

As it turned out, we were all completely wrong about the effects of free trade. (It is a useful measure of intellectual honesty to see how many are willing to admit this, two decades later. Of course, that's easy for me to say, since I was only an undergraduate at the time.) Who would have thought that Ontario would soon eclipse Michigan as the largest automobile manufacturing center in North America? (And who would have thought that Canada's universal health care system, an expensive government safety net, would be a crucial variable in the decision of various Japanese manufacturers to locate their operations in Ontario rather than Detroit?)[5] Who would have imagined that there would be street protests in Hollywood among film workers, complaining about the massive relocation of movie and television production to Toronto and Vancouver? (And who would have imagined that the alien worlds in science fiction programs, which had traditionally borne a suspicious resemblance to southern California, would soon start to look like the rain forests of British Columbia?)

People had all sorts of reasons for objecting to the free trade agreement. One of the arguments that showed up again and again involved a version of the so-called *pauper labor fallacy*.[6] John Ralston Saul provided a nice example of this back in 1988: "No European nation could succeed in open competition against a Korea or a Thailand, which both maintain nineteenth-century labour conditions. The countries of the European Economic Community therefore limit that competition to their definition of the word by the use of regulations, which include tariffs."[7] The suggestion was that Canada would be crazy to open its borders up to competition with countries where the cost of doing business is lower across the board. In order to "compete" effectively, a country must have costs of production that are, at least in some cases, absolutely lower—and as a result, a rich nation cannot possibly benefit from trade with a nation of "paupers."

This seductively mistaken argument got even more play when the free trade zone was expanded to include Mexico, and Ross Perot made his famous remark about "a giant sucking sound" coming from south of the U.S. border. The basic idea in both cases was quite simple. Initially it had been thought, how can Canada possibly compete with South Carolina, with its low wage rates and almost nonexistent level of unionization? Now the thought became, how can Canada (and the United States) possibly compete with Mexico, where workers are paid pennies instead of dollars?

In the background here is the following sort of picture: Imagine two bakeries, across the street from each other. One of them is on the rich side of the street, and so pays its workers $10 per hour. The other is on the poor side of the street, and so pays its workers $1 per hour. All other expenses are the same, and both bakeries have access to the same equipment and technology. Workers are not allowed to cross the street, but customers are. So how can the "rich-side" bakery possibly compete with the "poor-side" bakery? It seems obvious that it cannot—everything on sale there is going to cost more. Thus the rich-side bakery will have to either lower wages or pick up sticks and move to the poor side.

Some people find this sort of argument so compelling that they regard it as a decisive refutation of the case for international trade (or, at the very least, they consider it proof that globalization serves the interests of bakery owners, not bakery workers). In fact, it is an example of the pauper labor fallacy. The problem is that it is predicated upon a false analogy between companies and countries. Companies typically compete with one another in order to transact with a third party, namely, their customers. Yet in the case of international trade, *there is no third party*, no outside customers. Countries trade with one another. Of course, Canadian firms compete with firms in Mexico to sell to third parties, but that has nothing to do with the issue of free trade. Putting tariffs on Mexican goods does nothing to make Canadian goods more attractive to people in other countries. What trade barriers do is make it more difficult for people in Canada to trade with people in Mexico, and the question is whether there is any advantage to be had from such a policy.

In order to make the bakery scenario properly analogous, one would have to imagine an arrangement under which the bakeries can trade with one another. For example, suppose that customers on both the rich and the poor side of the street are given vouchers to shop with, which are redeemable for baked goods only on their own side of the street. Customers from the rich side of the street can wander over to the poor-side bakery and try to buy something, but the only thing they have to offer by way of payment is rich-side bakery vouchers. The question is, if you are the poor-side bakery, why would you accept rich-side vouchers as payment? What good are they, since the only place you can exchange them for anything useful is at the other bakery? And since the rich-side bakery is paying its workers 10 times more than you are, wouldn't you be better off just making everything yourself, rather than buying it from the rich side? To put the same idea in somewhat different terms, by accepting rich-side vouchers, which are intrinsically worthless, as payment for its goods, the poor-side bakery is essentially committing itself to buying something at the rich-side bakery. How could that be of benefit to them? Isn't the rich-side bakery "uncompetitive in everything"?

It is here that one can see the flaw in the argument, and an opportunity to rehearse David Ricardo's now somewhat old-fashioned point about comparative advantage. Suppose that workers at the rich-side bakery are particularly skilled at making bagels, while workers over on the poor side are much better working with pastry. This means that the relative cost of a bagel, compared to a tart, will be different on either side of the street (the absolute magnitude of these two prices cannot be compared from one side of the street to the other, since they are each denominated in terms of the "local" voucher). For concreteness, suppose that on the poor-side tarts cost half as much as bagels, while on the rich side tarts cost twice as much. This means that the poor-side bakery could improve its earnings by making a few extra tarts, selling them to customers from the rich side, then using the accumulated vouchers to buy the bagels that it sells to its poor-side customers. If they are able to get one bagel in this way for each tart that they sell, then they will be able to halve the amount of time spent supplying the bagel needs of their customers.

Here is another way of thinking about it. The poor-side bakery has two ways to make bagels. One is to do it in-house. The other is to make tarts, sell them to people from the rich side, then run across the street and buy bagels with the proceeds. Whether or not the second way is better than the first will depend entirely upon how good people on the poor side are at making bagels and tarts, compared to how good people on the rich side are. Thus the benefits of trade arise from the comparative advantages of the trading parties, not from any sort of *competitive* advantage. The fact that the wage rate is higher on the rich side of the street is completely irrelevant.

Of course, poor-side customers might get wind of this, and so instead of buying their bagels on their own side, they might go across to the rich-side bakery and try to buy them directly. The rich-side bakery will be happy to accept their vouchers, because they can use them to run across the street and buy tarts. The exchange is necessarily reversible, because both parties have to benefit in order for it to be worthwhile. Thus the two bakeries have an interest in exchanging with each other: They can offer the same range of products to their customers at lower cost through trade, despite the disparities in their wage rates or overall costs of production.

$ $ $

The introduction of "vouchers" into the example above is not accidental. Much of the confusion over international trade arises from the way money obscures the nature of the underlying transactions. To see how this can happen, consider the following scenario. Suppose the two bakeries get tired of handling two types of vouchers, not to mention running back and forth across the street all the time, and so the poor-side bakery decides to stop accepting rich-side vouchers and to stop making bagels, while the rich-side bakery stops accepting poor-side vouchers and stops making tarts. From this point on, anyone on the rich side who wants tarts will have to buy poor-side vouchers from someone, in order to use them at the poor-side bakery. The way to do this, of course, will be to find someone on the poor side who wants to buy bagels, then exchange vouchers. Thus a currency exchange will develop, with a rate of exchange that reflects the ratio of bagel-to-tart productivity on the two sides of the street. People will buy vouchers from one another, then go to the bakery that specializes in the baked good that each wants to buy.

What is the difference between this scenario and the earlier one? In the first case, the bakeries are exchanging tarts and bagels with each other. In the second case, consumers are exchanging vouchers with one another. Yet the latter characterization is potentially misleading, since the vouchers have no intrinsic value; they are simply a stand-in for the goods that can be purchased with them. What's *really* going on in the second case is the same as in the first: Tarts are being exchanged for bagels. The money illusion threatens to obscure that fact. Whether the two bakeries trade goods or the customers trade vouchers, the underlying economic transaction is the same.

This is important to remember in the case of international trade, because national currencies are basically just vouchers. Euros, as such, can only be spent in the euro zone, and thus represent a voucher for European goods. Holding currency is in this respect much like asking for a refund and getting a store voucher, or getting a gift certificate for Christmas. I can remember on many occasions wandering the aisles of a big-box hardware or clothing store with a gift certificate that I didn't really want, trying to find something, anything, that might be of use to me. The experience is not all that different from looking through the gift shop at an international airport, trying to get rid of some foreign currency before boarding a flight home.

It is tempting to think that when we import goods from abroad, we pay for them with money, just as we do when shopping at the corner store. Yet it is important to remember that our money is worthless, as such, to foreigners. They can't use it to pay their rent, for example, as the owner of the local corner store can. It's only useful to them if they can cash it in on *this* side of the border for something they want (or exchange it with someone *else* who wants to cash it in, on this side of the border, for something). When we import a million dollars' worth of goods from China, the best way to think about the transaction is to imagine a bunch of Chinese people subsequently wandering around the country thinking, "Gee, is there anything here I want? Maple syrup? Wheat?"—much like a shopper wandering through the hardware store with a gift card, thinking, "Do I need a table saw?"

Of course, this isn't realistic, since some Chinese people have probably done their shopping in advance, picking out the items they want *prior* to selling us their goods. Because here's the crucial point: If there isn't anything on this side of the border that someone in China wants, *then they won't accept our money as payment*. We will not be able to import anything from them, because we don't have anything of value that we can use to pay them with. (So if the "uncompetitive in everything" scenario were possible, it wouldn't manifest itself in the form of trade deficits. If no one wanted to buy anything from us, then no one would be willing to sell to us either, because we wouldn't be able to pay them.)

No problem, you say—if they don't want to accept our money as payment, all we have to do is go out on the currency markets and buy some of *their* money, and use that to pay for the imports. But this just pushes the problem back a step. What are we going to use to pay for their money? *Our* money. And why would anyone want to buy our money? They're only going to want it if they can cash it in, on this side of the border, for something that they want.

Of course, the Chinese may not actually want anything from us but may earn our money in order to exchange it for some *other* currency. Again, this just pushes the problem back a step. People holding that other currency will be willing to sell it for ours only if there is something that *they* want in our country. Unless, of course, they can find someone *else* who is willing to buy our money . . . But the buck has to stop somewhere. Imagine a Web site where people who got gift certificates that they didn't really want could get together to exchange them with one another. No matter how complex a web of transactions may develop, the fact remains that the only way you'll be able to get rid of that Ikea gift certificate is if someone, somewhere, wants to buy Ikea merchandise.

Finally, if there is really nobody anywhere who wants anything that we make, then people holding our vouchers will start wanting to unload them, and so may begin to sell them at a discount. Their value will decline until someone, somewhere, starts thinking that our goods are becoming attractive at that price.

Currency is thus an incredibly important mechanism when it comes to regulating international trade. Yet all of these complexities should not be allowed to obscure the fundamental fact that in international trade, all imports are ultimately paid for with exports. This is an immediate consequence of the fact that trade is a system of exchange. China doesn't just give us stuff; they also expect something in return. Of course, they may not demand repayment immediately (and by "repayment," I mean payment in real goods, not paper money). They may choose to park their money in the country for a while, by buying government bonds or some other form of investment. This is what makes it possible for a country to show a trade deficit. When imports exceed exports, it means only that *this year* imports exceeded exports, because foreigners are now holding more of our currency (or debts denominated in our currency) than they were in the past. Eventually, by hook or by crook, they will have to be repaid with exports. After all, they're not stupid. They don't want our money: They want our goods.[8]

So when a factory closes down in the United States and the owners relocate production to China, there is not necessarily any net loss of jobs to Americans. Americans will stop producing whatever it is that this factory used to produce, but they are going to have to start producing more of something else in order to pay the Chinese for the goods that are now being imported. This process may cause all sorts of disruption, and it may exacerbate social inequality within the United States. The people who get the new jobs, created to pay for imports, will almost certainly not be the same people who lost their jobs when the decision was made to offshore production. Thus a narrow argument against trade liberalization, focused upon this precise point, has considerable force. Critics of international trade, however, often just ignore the fact that the loss of jobs caused by offshoring will be offset by an increase in domestic production elsewhere. Jobs do not simply disappear domestically. To say that the country is "exporting jobs rather than goods" cannot be correct. Jobs are reallocated within the economy—if this weren't the case, then we would have no way of paying for the goods that we are hoping to import.

$ $ $

It is worth observing that so far I have not said anything at all about productivity. This is unusual, in that defenders of globalization and international trade often try to console those who worry about losing their jobs by saying, "Don't worry, you'll be fine—you're much more *productive* than those workers in Mexico (or China, or Bangladesh, or wherever)." Moreover, the need to improve productivity in order to maintain competitive advantage is a central theme in the "time to pull up our socks" lecture that people like Thomas Friedman never tire of delivering.

Productivity is a bit like a Rorschach blot—an undefined, nebulous entity upon which individuals can project whatever ideological or political preferences they happen to have. For some, increasing productivity will require massive government spending on education and "innovation." For others, increasing productivity will require huge tax cuts, along with aggressive deregulation of industry. Which side is right? Who knows? This is because productivity growth is what statisticians refer to as a *residuum*. The way they calculate it is by taking the rate of growth of the economy and factoring out anything that has an obvious explanation. If some growth is due to more people working, or to people working longer hours, they factor that out. If some growth is due to increased capital expenditure, such as on new equipment or machinery, they factor that out. What they are left with is a rate of growth that cannot be accounted for by any of these obvious changes in inputs. That's what we call "multifactor" or "total factor" productivity growth.

Of course, people have all sorts of different theories about what causes this sort of growth—better education, technological innovation, better management, less goofing around. But does anyone really know? For the most part, it's speculation. In fact, there's no reason to think that the influences are the same from firm to firm, or from year to year. This is in the nature of the beast, since "productivity" is a term that we use to describe all those factors that contribute to economic growth that are poorly understood or difficult to measure. Because of this, anyone who comes along promoting a particular policy agenda on the grounds that it will enhance productivity should immediately be suspected of selling economic snake oil.

But there is an even more fundamental problem with the appeal to productivity as a way of comforting those who are concerned about international trade. Consider the way Charles "The Naked Economist" Wheelan deploys the argument:

> Why wouldn't a firm relocate to Mexico when the average Mexican factory worker earns a fraction of the wages paid to American workers? The answer is productivity. Can American workers compete against foreign workers who earn half as much or less? Yes, most of us can. We produce more than Mexican workers—much more in many cases—because we are better-educated, because we are healthier, because we have better access to capital and technology and better public infrastructure. Can a Vietnamese peasant with two years of education do your job? Probably not.[9]

Wheelan is an economically sophisticated guy, but what he's saying here is wrong. Or at least, it *sounds like* he's saying something completely wrong. Because what it sounds like he's saying to American workers is, "Even though we're paying you more, that's okay, because most of you produce a lot more, and so our operation is still competitive." In other words, it sounds like he's saying that domestic jobs are safe even though the wage rate being paid is higher, because the "piece rate" being paid (the amount that is paid per unit of output) is in fact lower. This is cold comfort for a number of reasons. First of all, it's very seldom true, and people can sense that. After all, how useless could people in these under-developed countries be? When General Motors moves an assembly plant to Mexico, their workers get the same training and access to exactly the same equipment as workers in the United States. Superior education may help workers in United States churn out a few more cars per hour, but 10 times more? Americans aren't *that* well educated.

The problem with Wheelan's argument is that it encourages the reader to believe that wealthy nations need to have absolute advantage in order to remain competitive (that "we" must "produce more than Mexican workers" in some objective sense). This in turn serves to promote an artificial panic about our need to "stay competitive." After all, if our high wages *depend* upon workers in Mexico being somehow incompetent at car assembly, we can hardly expect them to stay that way for long. This suggests that we need to keep working harder and harder in order to stay ahead of the game, and even to avoid any erosion in our absolute standard of living. And this is completely false.

Productivity is important, but it's only *relative* productivity within a particular national economy that matters. Autoworkers in the U.S. get to keep their jobs (insofar as they *do* get to keep their jobs) because they're highly productive *compared to other Americans,* not compared to Mexicans. In other words, the United States has (or had) comparative advantage in automobile production. More generally, wealthy nations typically have comparative advantage in high-productivity sectors, because of the relative abundance of capital and technology and because of the quality of infrastructure. Poor nations have comparative advantage in sectors that require lots of low-skilled labor. This is why trade often results in a gain in employment in capital-intensive sectors in the wealthy nation combined with a gain in employment in labor-intensive sectors in the poorer nation.[10] It has nothing to do with high-productivity workers "outcompeting" their third-world rivals.

In this respect, American automotive workers are like bagel-makers on the rich side, rather than pastry chefs. (The reason they don't lose their jobs as a result of increased trade with Mexico is that some *other* groups of Americans will. Defenders of globalization tend not to dwell upon this fact.) Americans would be willing to pay Mexicans to build their cars only if it were cheaper to do it that way than it would be to build them domestically. Yet as it turns out, Americans are better at building cars for themselves than they are at producing things that Mexicans happen to want in exchange for cars. The best way to see this is to consider David Friedman's now-famous "Iowa car crop" parable:

> There are two ways for Americans to produce automobiles: they can build them in Detroit, or they can grow them in Iowa. Grow-

ing them in Iowa makes use of a special technology that turns wheat into Toyotas: simply put the wheat onto ships and send them out into the Pacific Ocean. The ships come back a short while later with Toyotas on them. The technology used to turn wheat into Toyotas out in the Pacific is called "Japan," but it could just as easily be a futuristic biofactory floating off the coast of Hawaii. Either way, auto workers in Detroit are in direct competition with farmers in Iowa.[11]

It is helpful to consider, from this perspective, how an increase in corporate tax rates would affect the "competitiveness" of the American economy. Assuming that the tax burden fell equally upon both automobile manufacturers and wheat farmers, the answer is *not at all*. Such a tax would leave relative positions intact, and so would not affect the structure of comparative advantage within the country. Far from making the United States "uncompetitive in everything," it would actually have no effect. What would be the consequence of pumping massive amounts of money into education and training? That depends. It may not benefit the automotive industry. If it results in new proprietary "green revolution" crops, it might shift the advantage in the direction of farmers, leading to increased offshoring of automobile manufacturing or other types of industrial production.

$ $ $

The argument of this chapter has been little more than another attempt to present a digestible version of what Paul Krugman has called "Ricardo's difficult idea."[12] Naturally, Ricardo is not the last word on the subject of international trade. It is important, however, that he be given the first word. His analysis of comparative advantage is the bedrock of modern international trade theory. It is simply not possible to have a proper conversation on the subject unless everyone fully understands this theory, along with all the constraints that it imposes upon our thinking about the subject.

That having been said, there are all sorts of interactions in which the harmonious logic of comparative advantage does not prevail. For example, countries compete against one another fairly directly for foreign direct investment. When Toyota needs to decide whether to build a new manufacturing facility in Ontario, Kentucky, or Baja California, it is not misleading to describe the issue in terms of international competitiveness. It is also important to note that comparative advantage is a trickier concept than it sometimes appears to be. When Ricardo presented his original argument, he used the example of England buying wine from Portugal in exchange for cloth. In this case, the fact that it took less effort to grow grapes in Portugal would seem to be a natural consequence of a more favorable climate. This in turn led to the suggestion that comparative advantage arose from conditions that were largely outside of anyone's control, such as natural resource endowment. While this is sometimes true, often it is not. Knowledge, productive technology, and even organizational forms are not nearly as portable across national borders as they are often made out to be. Portugal remains a major exporter of port wine to this day, not because of climatic advantages, but because of advantages stemming from the knowledge, experience, and tradition that have arisen through centuries of producing this product. There are also significant economies of scale in winemaking that confer an advantage upon the "first mover," as well as firms that have a large domestic market for their products.

Many of the most important sources of comparative advantage are completely overlooked in public policy discussions. For example, the presence of a large number of native (or highly competent) English speakers is a source of enormous advantage in particular sectors, not just in media and publishing, but also in law, financial services, scientific research, software development, and so on.[13] Local and national culture can create advantages in ways that are very poorly understood. (Silicon Valley, as people are fond of pointing out, does not contain any significant silicon deposits, but it does contain a lot of Californians.) Network effects are important—the presence and success of one industry can generate advantages in related fields, often in very indirect ways. The legal system also confers advantages upon particular industries. The production of so-called intellectual property, for example, thrives only in jurisdictions with a legal environment that offers reasonable protection of patents and copyrights.

As a result, comparative advantage is not just something that countries happen to possess; it is also something that they can actively cultivate.[14] In particular, subsidies to a given industry may create an advantage that is purely artificial, but over time they can lead to the creation of genuine comparative advantage, as the appropriate support networks, training systems, and reservoir of local knowledge needed for the industry are formed. This is, for example, what the government of Brazil is counting on with its support for Embraer (backed by the desire to get a slice of the international market for commercial aircraft), and the United Kingdom with its subsidization of the video game industry. Of course, this sort of political interference is unwise in many respects, but it does not rest upon any sort of misunderstanding or fallacy. It is possible for a country to do very well for itself through a well-planned and well-executed industrial strategy (particularly in "winner-take-all markets," where the world only needs one or two suppliers). In this respect, the vocabulary of international competitiveness is again not misleading. If a nation has a particular reason for wanting to be an exporter in a particular sector, it may find itself competing with other nations to build up the right sort of advantages for itself.

The important thing about comparative advantage is that it arises out of the *differences* between nations. Unfortunately, when people on the right come forward with proposals to enhance "competitiveness," they invariably do so in a way that seeks to make countries more *similar.* In particular, the only way they can usually think of to compete against underdeveloped countries is to lower overall costs of production, through wage reductions, tax relief, or deregulation. (The pauper labor fallacy is, in a sense, just as popular on the left as it is on the right. The only real difference is that the left uses it as an argument for restrictions on trade, while the right uses it as an argument for the pauperization of labor.)

One of the priceless tidbits on the Watergate tapes was a conversation between President Nixon, Henry Ford II, and Lee Iacocca on the subject of automotive safety standards. The automotive executives were pressuring Nixon to intervene on their behalf with the Department of Transportation to exempt them from recently imposed federal safety standards. Nixon prefaced the conversation by observing that, in his view, "environmentalists" and "the consumerism people" "aren't really one damn bit interested in safety or clean air. What they're interested in is destroying the system. They're enemies of the system." By contrast, he announced, "I am for the system."

Perhaps encouraged by this, Iacocca argued that automakers should be exempt from safety regulations, on the grounds that "the Japs are in the wings ready to eat us alive." If new safety equipment is required, the Japanese "are going to put whatever is demanded by law in this country on at a buck fifty an hour, and we're, we just cracked seven dollars an hour." Ford echoed these concerns, pointing out that "what we're worried about really, basically, is—this isn't an industry problem—is really the economy of the United States . . . If these payments get so high that people stop buying cars . . . They're gonna buy more foreign cars; you're going to have balance-of-payments problems."[15]

A classic presentation of the pauper labor fallacy. Nixon's response? "Right," he said. "I'm convinced."

What can we conclude from all this? For one thing, we now know that, when they were faced with the formidable challenges posed by the entry of Japanese auto manufacturers into the American economy in the early '70s, neither the American president nor the auto-industry executives had a clear understanding of the logic of international trade. Furthermore, one can see that environmentalists and "consumerism people" can hardly be blamed for worrying that globalization and international trade will result in a "race to the bottom" in environmental regulation, consumer safety protection, and labor standards. They would have a lot less to worry about if our captains of industry weren't constantly using the specter of international trade as a bludgeon in order to demand weaker environmental regulation, exemption from consumer safety regulations, and an erosion of labor standards. International trade, as such, creates no such pressures. Right-wing ideology, unfortunately, does. So as long as business executives are influenced more by ideology than by economics, there will always be reason for concern about globalization, simply on the grounds that it generates pressure for bad public policy.

CHAPTER 6

PERSONAL RESPONSIBILITY

How the right misunderstands moral hazard

One of the things that people on the left have a very hard time understanding about contemporary conservativism is the fact that most people on the right conceive of their political views not merely as an expression of their self-interest, but as a consequence of a broader set of moral commitments. This is true not just in matters of sexual morality, where it is easier to see how a conservative might feel entitled to claim the high ground. People on the right also seem to feel that cutting welfare programs and public services, weakening consumer protection and regulatory oversight, and ignoring the effects of human action on the environment are not just convenient for themselves personally, but morally obligatory. They think that being right-wing makes them—or shows them to be—better people. How could that be?

John Kenneth Galbraith once said that "the modern conservative is engaged in one of man's oldest exercises in moral philosophy; that is, the search for a superior moral justification for selfishness." This is not far off when applied to someone like Ayn Rand, who had a fairly straightforward view along these lines. According to Rand, liberals believe in altruism and, as a result, try to use the power of the state to force the powerful to help the weak. Conservatives believe in individual rights. They support the free market and oppose state power because they reject the idea that people are obliged to help one another. Stay off your land? Sure. Buy you dinner? Forget about it. Thus the choice between left and right was simple: Do you want to be an altruist or an egoist? Rand thought you should want to be an egoist.

This is, needless to say, not the self-understanding of most people on the right today. Most would insist that they are just as altruistic as anyone on the left. What sets them apart, and what makes their political ideology superior, is the fact that they also believe in *personal responsibility*. As President George W. Bush put it in his inaugural address, "America, at its best, is a place where personal responsibility is valued and expected. Encouraging responsibility is not a search for scapegoats, it is a call to conscience. And though it requires sacrifice, it brings a deeper fulfillment."[1]

When conservatives see a person asking for a handout, they don't automatically reach for their wallets. They stop to ask, "How did this person get that way?" and "Why exactly is it my responsibility, as opposed to his responsibility, to pay for his dinner?" Liberals, on the other hand, ignore (or feel *obliged* to ignore) these questions. According to conservatives, ignoring issues of personal responsibility simply encourages people to behave more irresponsibly. Thus liberals, with their "ask no questions, just hand over the money" attitude, wind up eroding the moral foundations of our society, which is why liberalism is seen as a morally decadent system of belief.

There is something to this view. But things are a lot more complicated than they might at first seem. What conservatives are reacting to with their call for personal responsibility is a very general phenomenon that economists refer to as *moral hazard*. This is a term that has its origins in the insurance industry, where it has been observed that people who are fully insured against the effects of "bad luck" happening tend to suffer from the effects of "bad luck" more often. For example, it used to be possible to buy life insurance policies not just on your own life, but on the lives of other people.[2] At some point it was observed that individuals who had recently had large policies taken out on them had a strange habit of suffering very serious accidents. It was concluded, on this basis, that allowing such policies to be taken out was not a very good idea (and they have been banned ever since). But many other types of insurance have similar effects. People with fire insurance are more likely to suffer from fires, people with insurance against theft are more likely to be robbed, people with health insurance are more likely to incur large medical expenses, and so on.

The problem, of course, is that insurance takes things out of the domain of personal responsibility. It takes individual losses and turns them into somebody else's problem. More technically, it allows individuals to externalize the costs of their behavior. As a result, these costs rise, which is what offends the conservative sensibility. And there is nothing wrong with being offended by this. However, moral hazard is a general consequence of pretty much *any* insurance system, or *any* system of mutual aid. We cannot, on this basis, simply junk every insurance system. And it is easy to show that modern, civilized societies—not to mention finely tuned economic systems, such as capitalism—are completely impossible without insurance.

The call for "personal responsibility" is essentially a call for self-insurance as a response to moral hazard. The error in the conservative sensibility lies in thinking that merely pointing out the existence of a moral hazard problem is enough to make the case for a return to "personal responsibility." Self-insurance, however, has both costs and benefits. While moral hazard does involve real costs, these need to be weighed against the massive benefits that are provided through insurance (or systems of mutual aid more generally). Thus the conservative call for personal responsibility often involves a variation on the "count the costs, ignore the benefits" fallacy that so often undermines the value of cost-benefit analysis. Furthermore, conservatives often try to pick and choose, ignoring moral hazard when it comes to insurance systems that they like, while using it as an excuse for not supporting insurance systems that they dislike. In particular, they point to moral hazard effects of government insurance schemes as arguments against them, while ignoring entirely the moral hazard problems created by private insurance schemes.

$ $ $

I once had the pleasure of spending a summer living in Hong Kong. One of the quaint remnants of British naval culture in the former colony is the alert system that they use to communicate the severity of tropical storms. It took me a while to figure out what it meant when I saw TV bulletins announcing that "signal number 3 has been hoisted, with an amber warning." As it turns out, the numbering system indicates the severity of wind, with a color code for the anticipated amount of rainfall. The big excitement came with the approach of Typhoon Yutu, which caused a "signal number 8" to be hoisted, along with a black rainstorm warning. The result was an awesome sight, as the entire city basically ground to a halt. Businesses closed, buses stopped running, people stayed indoors. An eerie quiet descended upon what must be, by any measure, one of the loudest cities on the planet. A good day to stay home.

My wife, however, is a surgeon, and needed to get to work at the hospital. She usually took the bus, but since there were no buses, she decided to take a cab. No one was answering the phone at any of the companies, so she went down to the street to hail one. After she stood for about 20 minutes by the side of the deserted street, a lone taxi came by and picked her up. On the way, she asked him why he was working—wasn't there some law forcing businesses to close and cars to stay off the street? Oh, no, he said, there's no law. It's just that once the number 8 signal is hoisted, *your insurance is void*. If you're willing to take a chance, there's no reason you can't keep driving.

In other words, the fact that the roads had emptied out, that the entire city's transportation network was paralyzed, was not an effect of the typhoon per se. Not only was the storm several hours away, out in the Pacific, in the end it never even hit the city. People were not worried about the wind and the rain—there wasn't any. What paralyzed the city was the sudden withdrawal of insurance coverage from anyone using the roads. Like the lion with a thorn in his foot, here was the Asian tiger laid low by one small change in a relatively obscure sector of the economy.

That's the strange thing about insurance. Alcohol is sometimes described as a "social lubricant." Insurance is like that, except that it's an all-purpose economic lubricant. It systematically reduces the cost of all sorts of economic transactions and activities. This makes it worthwhile to take a variety of risks, and do a variety of things for other people, that simply would not be economically viable without insurance coverage. You may not realize it, but no honest plumber would ever agree to fix your pipes, no grocery store would sell you meat, and no doctor would give you a checkup—or not at anything approaching a reasonable price—unless they had insurance. The value of the transaction is simply too low relative to the damage that might occur if something were to go wrong. (Indeed, Hong Kong cabdrivers typically charge three times the normal rate when they are working without insurance.) Yet the role that insurance plays in making all these transactions possible is largely invisible, and not particularly well understood even by those with a vested interest in its success.

In reality, insurance is a fairly simple arrangement. The nature of the benefits that it provides, however, is subtle, because unlike market exchange, it does not generate a classic "gain from trade." In a standard economic exchange, both parties benefit because they have different preferences. One person wants what the other has more than what he has, and vice versa, and so both are happier after the exchange has been concluded. Insurance, on the other hand, produces mutual benefit through a phenomenon known as the "law of large numbers." It does not depend upon differences in preference—two individuals, identically situated, having identical preferences, can benefit each other by agreeing to "pool" a particular risk that they are both exposed to. A benefit can be produced even if, in the end, nothing is exchanged and no money ever changes hands.

The mechanism at work here is fairly straightforward. While a particular misfortune may be equally likely to strike either of two people, it is less likely to strike *both* of them simultaneously. So if they agree to split the sum of their joint losses, they can each substitute a higher probability of a smaller loss for a lower probability of a larger loss. In cases where both are averse to risk, this can be a source of increased happiness. In order to see how the "large numbers" effect works, consider the case of making repeated tosses of a coin. Although the background probability of tossing heads is the same as that of tossing tails, if you flip the coin 10 times you are actually somewhat unlikely to get exactly five heads and five tails.[3] In fact, if you repeat the exercise of tossing the coin 10 times, the percentage of heads that you get within each sequence of 10 tosses will form what's known as a "normal distribution" (or "bell curve") around the mean of 50% heads.

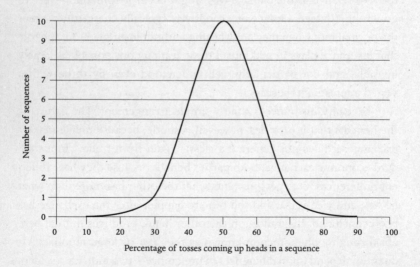

Figure 6.1 Normal distribution with 10 tosses

Now suppose that instead of tossing the coin 10 times per trial, you toss it 100 times. Your chances of getting close to 50% heads increases significantly. (For example, getting six heads out of 10 is quite likely, whereas getting 60 heads out of 100 is far less so.) Visually, this means that the bell curve gets squeezed in around the mean (as shown in Figure 6.2). Technically, this is known as a reduction in the *variance*.

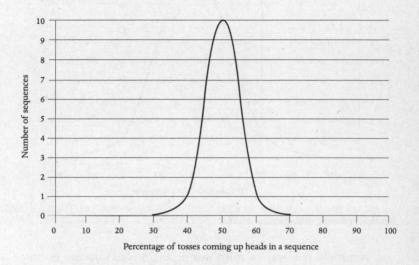

Figure 6.2 Normal distribution with 100 tosses

The same logic that applies to coin tosses applies to human effort as well. Imagine a society in which people depend upon hunting for their subsistence. Each morning, the hunters head out into the bush to find something to eat. Some are likely to catch something, while others are likely to come home empty-handed. Suppose an individual can survive with a failure rate over the course of several days as high as 70%, but beyond that he begins to suffer from malnutrition. This means that even if the average returns to hunting are significantly greater than any of the alternative subsistence strategies, a person needs to worry about the variance as well. If the variability of returns looks something like Figure 6.3, then hunting might not be a very attractive way to earn a living. Average returns are good, but the risk of starving is simply too great.

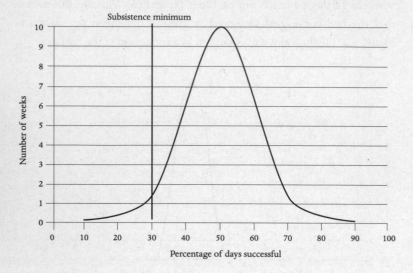

Figure 6.3 Hunting with irregular returns

Naturally, one way to solve this problem is to improve the success rate at hunting (perhaps by inventing better weapons or new strategies). This would shift the curve over to the right, hopefully moving the entire distribution out of the starvation range. But there is another way to solve the problem, one that can be achieved without even changing the average rate of return. Suppose that a group of 10 hunters agree to share with one another, so that those who were lucky and had a good day give some of their catch to those who were unlucky and had a bad day. This is the most primitive form of insurance, or risk-pooling. The result will be a decrease in the variance. In order to end up empty-handed at the end of the day, it would have to be the case that not only you struck out, but that all 10 hunters struck out independently of one another.[4] And even if this happens once, it is highly unlikely to occur again the following day. Thus the effect is the same as that of moving from sequences of 10 to sequences of 100 coin tosses (Figure 6.4).

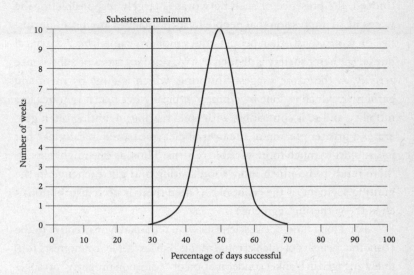

Figure 6.4 Hunting with risk-pooling arrangement

To an observer from on high, it might seem like nothing has changed here—10 hunters still head out into the bush every day and, on average, five of them are unlucky and return empty-handed. There is no more meat available to the group than there ever was. Yet through this simple risk-pooling arrangement, the threat of starvation has now been banished from the community. Here we can see the invisible magic of insurance. (Of course, because each hunter has an obligation to give away some of the catch on days of plenty, the chances of having a block-buster week pretty much disappears. But this is coupled with a matching decline in the probability of starving. Most people are happy to pass up the occasional feast in order to avoid the possibility of famine.)

It is easy to see from this analysis how traditional hunter-gatherer societies, which often get by at something very close to the subsistence level, are far more concerned about risk-pooling than they are about gains from trade. The presence of extensive food-sharing and gift networks in foraging societies is a direct consequence of this. (Indeed, the presence of such networks is largely responsible for the widespread impression that people in such societies are more "altruistic" or "collectivist" than people under modern capitalism.)[5] A typical hunter-gatherer society is divided by two primary types of subsistence activity, as the name suggests: hunting, which is done by men, and gathering, which is done by women (typically because it requires less mobility, and so is compatible with child rearing). Hunting often generates a greater portion of the overall diet (measured in calories), but it is subject to much more variable returns. Thus, as one might expect, there tends to be much more food-sharing and gift exchange in the hunting segment of the economy.[6] (Often there is no redistribution at all in the gathering segment.)

For a long time, social scientists were remarkably inattentive to the economic benefits of such arrangements. For example, economists routinely engaged in blanket condemnation of "common property" arrangements, on the grounds that they generated collective action problems. The story of the "tragedy of the commons" is a good example. According to the received wisdom, the common-field system in England, in which all the peasants in a community were entitled to graze their animals in a shared pasture, led to systematic overgrazing. Since most of the cost of grazing one's own animals on the pasture was borne by other users, the private benefit of grazing always exceeded the private cost, and so everyone kept grazing until the field was destroyed. (The same dynamic has led to the destruction of many common resources, such as the cod fishery on the Grand Banks off the coast of northeastern North America.) The solution typically proposed is, when feasible, to divide up the common property into individual holdings and then limit individuals to the use of their own plots. If the only place to graze your animals is in your own backyard, then the incentive to overgraze disappears, since the full cost is now "internalized," or borne by the individual making the decision.

There is a lot to be said for this analysis. However, it is often suggested that the transition to a private-property regime is an unqualified Pareto improvement. In many cases, particularly agricultural ones, this is not the case, because enclosure also has the effect of "unpooling" various types of risk. If some portion of the land is afflicted by a blight or ruined by hail or eaten by insects, a common-field system automatically divides the loss up among all members of the community. With individual plots of land, on the other hand, some individuals may find themselves with nothing, while others are completely unaffected. Thus private property may increase productivity and improve the incentives for land management, but it will also increase the variability of returns. Whether or not this makes it worthwhile depends upon a large number of factors, particularly environmental ones.[7]

This is not to say that sharing and mutual aid are never based upon purely altruistic sentiment. It is, however, easy to underestimate the extent to which they are based upon rational self-interest, narrowly conceived. Many of the social movements and institutional arrangements that we traditionally think of as "socialist" have a lot more to do with risk-pooling than with equality or distributive justice. And in cases where these movements succeed in generating permanent institutional reform, it is usually because the arrangements they promote involve win-win efficiency gains, not win-lose redistributions of income.

It is interesting to reconsider the history of nineteenth- and twentieth-century "class struggle" in this light. Canadians sometime express puzzlement over the fact that Saskatchewan, which is traditionally the most socialist province in the country, sits right next to Alberta, which is traditionally the most conservative. Yet this is hardly so mysterious when one thinks of socialism in terms of social *insurance*. The left-right political divide coincides near-perfectly with the shift from an economy based almost entirely upon farming, in Saskatchewan, to one based increasingly on ranching (and later oil), in Alberta. Since the growing season on the prairies is barely long enough to support one crop, and rainfall is both low and highly variable, there is a long-standing tradition of mutual aid among farmers. The socialist movement prospered in Saskatchewan primarily because of the risk-pooling arrangements that it helped to create, first in response to price volatility and crop failure, and eventually in response to other shared risks (most important, in health care, through the introduction of "socialized" government insurance).[8] Ranchers, on the other hand, are not affected by very many "exogenous" risks, such as bad weather. Theft is usually their biggest issue, leading to a political emphasis upon property rights, rather than upon solidarity and mutual aid. That's why a rancher is more likely to shoot you if he finds you on his land, whereas a farmer might invite you to stay for dinner.

§ § §

There is, unfortunately, no such thing as a free lunch. Risk-pooling arrangements may generate efficiency gains, through the reduction in variance, but these come at a cost. There are many events that we think of as being outside our control but that, when push comes to shove, we do in fact have the ability to influence. Furthermore, even when we have no control, we usually have some control over how much damage the adverse event may cause. For example, no one wants their house to catch fire, but there are a lot of things we can do to make this less likely to occur (avoid smoking in bed, update the electrical panel, etc.), and many more that can reduce the extent of damage (install automatic sprinklers, keep valuables in a safety deposit box off the premises, etc.). The problem is that all these activities involve some cost to the individual. When people enter into a risk-pooling arrangement (where, for example, all those who own houses that might burn down pay into a common pool, which is then used to compensate those among them whose houses do burn down), the incentive to shoulder such costs declines. Insurance is basically a pool of this sort, where the premiums paid by all policyholders are used to pay out the claims made by those policyholders who suffer a loss. As a result, the number of house fires can be expected to be higher among those who are insured than among those who do not have insurance. This is moral hazard.

One can see quite clearly how moral hazard could arise in the case of the 10 hunters. When each individual eats only his own catch and faces a very real chance of starvation, there's no problem when it comes to work effort. (The workers are appropriately "incentivized," to put it in management-speak.) However, once the food-sharing arrangement has been instituted, the consequences of failing to catch anything are not as dire. Furthermore, if some people are obviously more talented or reliable than others, there may be a temptation to free ride off their efforts. This is why, in traditional hunter-gatherer societies, food-sharing and mutual aid are accompanied by severe stigmatization of laziness (combined with fairly constant harassment of those who try to free ride). Of course, the effects of moral hazard need not be all-or-nothing. It's not as though people will just lie around all day, taking in the sun. The problem may simply be that they put in a little bit less effort, or that they don't concentrate quite as hard, or that they get tired a little bit more quickly. This sort of thing can be very difficult to control, because it's seldom possible for anyone else to know just how much better a person could be doing if he were appropriately motivated. Furthermore, the effects of such "slacking" may not seem like such a big deal, except that when everyone does it, the consequences can be quite dramatic.

If this tendency is not corrected, the average returns to hunting may decline. Starvation may even begin to reappear *as a result of the risk-pooling arrangement.* Although this outcome seems crazy, there are many historical examples of human societies in which it has occurred (including some in the early American colonies).[9] Although we tend to think of poverty as a material circumstance, it is usually the product of social arrangements. In most cases, it is the absence of effective institutions that is to blame. In some cases, however, the problem is that institutions are too effective at generating solidarity (or perhaps too effective when it comes to sharing and not effective enough when it comes to work effort). There comes a point at which it may be better to "unpool" the risk and go back to individual effort. Such a scenario is shown in Figure 6.5, which features the low-variance distribution achieved through sharing, but with the mean shifted to the left as a consequence of moral hazard.

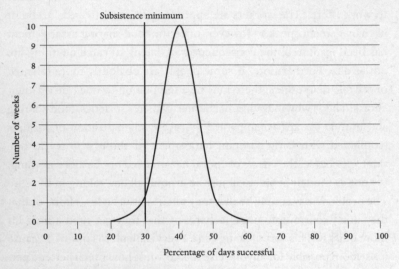

Figure 6.5 Hunting with risk-pooling and moral hazard

More generally, any system of benevolence or mutual aid is likely to be afflicted by moral hazard problems. For example, in an influential article entitled "Famine, Affluence and Morality," the philosopher Peter Singer proposed the following as a reasonable moral judgment: "If I am walking past a shallow pond and see a child drowning in it, I ought to wade in and pull the child out. This will mean getting my clothes muddy, but this is insignificant, while the death of the child would presumably be a very bad thing."[10] One can see this as a specific instance of a more general principle of benevolence, which in its least controversial formulation might go something like this: "If you have the power to prevent something terrible from happening, and can do so at very little cost to yourself, you should do it." Singer concludes, on this basis, that since there are many people starving in the world today who could be saved through a relatively small cash donation, people in the wealthier parts of the world have a moral obligation to do much more than they are currently doing to alleviate global hunger.

It would be difficult to find anyone who didn't agree with the moral intuition here, at least at first glance. Yet if one accepts the principle of benevolence as a basis for action, moral hazard problems are sure to follow. The philosopher David Schmidtz invites us to consider the following scenario:

> *A baby is drowning in the pool beside you. You can save the baby by a process that involves giving the baby's family a hundred dollars. If you do not save the baby, the baby will die. You save the baby. A crowd begins to gather. Seeing what you have done, two onlookers throw their babies into the pool. The babies will drown unless you give each of their families a hundred dollars. More onlookers begin to gather, waiting to see what you do.*[11]

Here you are faced with something of a dilemma. Acting morally seems to be making things worse, not better, because of the way that people are responding to your "moral" choice of action. (Thomas Robert Malthus claimed, many years ago, that "experience has proved, I believe without a single exception, that poverty and misery have always increased in proportion to the quantity of indiscriminate charity.")[12] Yet what does this mean, in practical terms? How many babies do you have to save before you are entitled to say enough is enough?

Surprisingly, many people seem to think that the correct answer in this case is none—not even the first one. In fact, one of the constitutive features of the conservative temperament seems to be a zero-tolerance attitude toward moral hazard. In other words, many people on the right seem to think that the mere presence of moral hazard completely dissolves any sort of prior moral obligation, and even vitiates the gains of risk-pooling. As Schmidtz puts it, "No matter what our intuitions say . . .

the fact remains that no good comes from pouring resources down the sink of an open access commons."[13] The moral hazard problem simply trumps the obligation to contribute to famine relief (or any other form of what Malthus called "indiscriminate charity").

The call for "personal responsibility" is often an expression of this zero-tolerance, "you made your bed, you lie in it" attitude.[14] Indeed, there are many people whose resentment of the "undeserving" has reached such a fever pitch that they are no longer capable of feeling sympathy for the suffering of anyone but small children and animals. (Indeed, there often seems to be some displacement involved, so that as the attitude toward humanity becomes more pinched, the degree of sympathy for animals expands to fill the moral vacuum.) People act irresponsibly, according to this view (say, by throwing their babies into pools), because they know that the cost of their decisions will be borne by others. Continuing to act morally, in this case, is not only asking to be suckered, but doesn't even produce net benefits, because of the incentive effects of the action.

At the other extreme is the view that morality requires us to ignore moral hazard problems entirely. This is perhaps one of the most distinctive and demanding features of Christian morality. Indeed, one of the things that makes Christianity such a difficult religion is the fact the Jesus imposed a categorical prohibition upon the consideration of moral hazard effects (although not in quite these terms). Recall the injunction to "turn the other cheek," the prodigal son, and so on.

The reasonable view, as is typically the case, lies somewhere in between. Moral hazard is a serious problem, but it is not "universal acid," capable of dissolving any sort of moral obligation. The fact that some people cheat on their insurance or start to act irresponsibly once they know that the costs will be borne by someone else does not constitute grounds for tearing up every insurance policy. People do drive more dangerously knowing that they have car insurance. They also tend to inflate their claims after they've had an accident. But that doesn't mean we should get rid of accident insurance. It's a matter of weighing the benefits of the risk-pooling arrangement against the costs that it creates. Moral hazard can seldom be eliminated entirely. The best thing to do, therefore, is usually to manage it, through inspections, deductibles, co-payments, visits from the adjuster, and so on. And sometimes there is a case to be made for just tolerating moral hazard, because the costs that it generates are simply outweighed by the benefits of the risk-pooling arrangement.

$ $ $

There are very few sights capable of undermining American support for welfare programs more quickly than that of a teenage girl, black or Hispanic, bouncing a baby on her knee, explaining in some strange ghetto slang just how *proud* she is to be a mother. As William Galston, one-time adviser to President Bill Clinton, once observed, the American economy may seem like a bit of a casino, but in fact it has a number of very simple rules. Three in particular stand out: finish high school, marry before having a child, and wait until you're at least 20 before having that child. Only 8% of families who follow these rules become poor, whereas 79% of those who fail to do so become poor.[15] Furthermore, even when controlling for income, children born to teenage mothers in the United States do worse on nearly every available measure of social and economic well-being. They are less likely to finish high school and more likely to end up in foster care and, later, in prison. No matter how you slice it, choosing to have a child before the age of 18 is *totally irresponsible.*

The reason that the debate over teen pregnancy gets so heated is that many conservatives regard this sort of irresponsible conduct as a moral hazard effect. Young women choose to get pregnant, according to this view, because they receive a public subsidy for doing so. (To use Schmidtz's image, one is invited to imagine onlookers having babies just so that they can throw them into the pool.) This perception is, of course, heightened by the fact that the closest thing the United States has to a "welfare" system—the Temporary Assistance for Needy Families

program (formerly known as Aid to Families with Dependent Children)—
essentially excludes anyone but parents from receiving support. Furthermore, the pre-Clinton AFDC program used to limit eligibility almost
exclusively to single parents. The result, according to the economist
Robert Moffitt, was "an obvious incentive to delay marriage, increase
rates of marital dissolution, delay remarriage, and have children outside of a marital union."[16] Indeed, it was observed that the dynamics
of AFDC caseload, including entry into and exit from the program, had
almost nothing to do with changes in the labor market and everything
to do with changes in American family structure.[17]

People on the left usually respond to this concern simply by denying that moral hazard is a factor (often based upon the charmingly bour-
geois notion that, since children are so precious, surely no one's decision
to have one could be influenced by monetary factors). If teenagers are
getting pregnant, it must be involuntary, a consequence of their disadvantaged circumstances. And because it is involuntary (after all, who in
their right mind chooses to get pregnant in high school?), there cannot
be any moral hazard. Changing the incentives is not going to change
the behavior. The conservative remedy is thus not only unfair—since
it holds the individual responsible for something over which she has no
control—it is not even likely to be effective.

This "blame it on their circumstances" response has become
almost an automatic reflex for the left. Indeed, much of what it means to
acquire a "progressive" education seems to involve learning how to take
any sort of self-defeating, irresponsible, offensive, or just plain antisocial
behavior and explain it away as the effect of poverty, sexism, racism, or
some shortfall in the achieved level of social justice. The problem with
this defense is that, while it may contain a kernel of truth, it achieves the
desired moral conclusion ("we must help these people") only by denying the agency, or the capacity to engage in rational decision-making, of
the intended beneficiaries. This cedes the moral high ground to the conservative, who is now in a position to argue that liberalism dehumanizes
people, by refusing to hold them accountable for their actions.

There are much better rhetorical strategies available to the left. One option, which often gets overlooked, is to grant that people make choices and to grant that moral hazard effects may occur but to insist upon balancing these costs against the benefits of the broader risk-pooling arrangement. In the case of welfare, these benefits are not insignificant. It is important to remember that the single most serious economic risk that women in our society face is divorce and, in particular, male abandonment of dependent children. Every society invests an enormous amount of moral energy in controlling this sort of behavior (from honor codes to shotgun weddings), yet no society has ever succeeded in extinguishing it entirely. As a result, it remains a serious risk. Furthermore, it is precisely the sort of risk that women could benefit from "pooling" (whereby those who get lucky and don't suffer abandonment compensate those who do). Unfortunately, any such arrangement is beset by huge moral hazard problems.

To see why, one need only consider what would happen if a private insurance company started selling divorce insurance or "becoming a single parent" insurance. First of all, there would be an insuperable adverse selection problem. People who still loved each other wouldn't buy it. People who had secretly, or perhaps not so secretly, begun to loathe each other would. Second, there would be a moral hazard problem. Women are more likely to leave their husbands, and men are more likely to abandon their children, if they think that the consequences will be less drastic. Furthermore, women will be more likely to have children with unreliable men if their subsequent dependency upon that man is reduced. Either way, the private insurance market would fail. (Or to be more precise, it *does* fail: No insurance company sells policies of this sort.)[18]

One might decide that this is just tough luck for women. It just happens to be the case that the single greatest financial risk that they face over the course of their lives is uninsurable. But does this mean that we simply shrug our shoulders and leave women (and children) to self-insure against this eventuality? The social cost of that choice would be enormous (especially given the importance of child rearing for the reproduction of society). As a result, "society" is not willing just to sit idly by and allow women who suffer this fate to be hung out to dry. Furthermore, we are unwilling to allow children to suffer the full brunt of whatever decisions their parents have made. Inadequate or bad insurance would almost certainly be better than no insurance. And this is, of course, precisely what we provide—inadequate, bad insurance, commonly known as "welfare." It is provided at a very low level (much lower than unemployment insurance) precisely because of the incentive problems it creates.

In the United States, welfare takes the rather specific form of "not being able to care for one's children" insurance. In Canada and most of Europe, it is a slightly more catchall program, what one might think of as "screwing up your life" or "general bad luck" insurance. Naturally, you can't offer a very high level of indemnity with this sort of program without creating all sorts of perverse incentives. At the same time, welfare programs serve to alleviate a huge amount of human suffering. They also produce moral hazard. More people are likely to screw up their lives when they know that the consequence of screwing up are not so great. The question is, how many people?

With respect to the AFDC, the version of the U.S. welfare program that had the most obviously perverse incentives, the answer is "not many." An increase in the rates of divorce, single parenthood, and illegitimacy coincided with steady increases in AFDC payments throughout the 1960s and early '70s. However, though real AFDC benefits peaked in 1975, the increase in divorce, single parenthood, and illegitimacy continued unabated. Furthermore, birthrates declined as a whole for all women, regardless of AFDC status. At a more fine-grained level, there was some correlation between AFDC eligibility and various aspects of family structure, in the direction that an analysis of the incentives would lead one to expect. However, as Moffitt observed in an extensive review of the available economic studies, "failure to find strong benefit effects is the most notable characteristic of this literature"—certainly nothing significant enough to register on a demographic level.[19] This is exactly what one would expect in an area like marriage and family, where incentives are extremely complex. Moral hazard is likely to be a factor, and it would be foolish to deny it, but the important point is that acknowledging this one source of inefficiency need not lead to abandoning one's support for the program as a whole. It all depends upon how significant the losses are compared to the overall efficiency gains achieved through the larger risk-pooling arrangement. If you want private property, you're going to have to live with some theft. And if you want insurance, you're going to have to live with some moral hazard.

§ § §

This brings us, finally, to the fallacy underlying the "personal responsibility" crusade of the right. Conservatives blame government handouts for undermining the spirit of self-reliance. This is just a moralizing way of describing a generic problem with insurance systems, where indemnity ("handouts") tends to generate moral hazard ("irresponsibility"). What conservatives fail to realize is that the moral hazard effect in question is a generic feature of any type of insurance system—it has nothing to do with the question of public or private ownership. There is, however, a prior selection effect that gets ignored. Because private insurance markets are so prone to failure in the face of information asymmetries, the type of insurance that is usually prone to moral hazard or adverse selection tends to be feasible only when provided by the "the insurer of last resort": the state. So it doesn't make much sense to blame government for the moral hazard. It's usually because of the moral hazard problem that the government is running the program in the first place.

When criticizing various aspects of the "social safety net," conservatives chronically make the error of drawing an invidious comparison between the moral hazard effects of government insurance and the moral hazards effects of *no insurance at all*. It's no surprise that the latter wins. This is a clear instance of the "add up the costs, ignore the benefits" fallacy. Having no insurance means you don't have to suffer the losses caused by moral hazard, but it also means that you have to suffer the losses of *having no insurance.* Naturally, self-insurance has lower costs; the problem is that it also has no benefits. Thus the only way to make it look good is to consider only the costs and to disregard the forgone benefits.

Unfortunately, the no-insurance option is routinely described in public debate as "privatization," not as "abolition" of the insurance scheme. For it to be real privatization, the comparison would have to be between government provision and private provision of the same type of insurance. Privatizing Social Security, for instance, would mean sending individuals out to buy their own life annuities on the open market, not having them invest in mutual funds. When the comparison is constructed in this way, government provision often comes out looking quite good.

Consider the case of health care. American critics of "socialized" medicine often regard it as a synthetic a priori truth that public provision will generate overconsumption, followed by rationing of care. "If you think health care is expensive now," they say, "wait until you see how much it costs when it's free." If the government started giving away free cheese, people would start eating too much cheese. So why would anyone want to give away free health care?

This line of reasoning, however, contains two obvious errors. First of all, socialized medicine on the single-payer model doesn't mean socialized health *care,* it means socialized health *insurance.* In Canada, for example, health care provision is almost entirely private. (I can assure you, since my wife is a surgeon. Not only is she privately incorporated, I am happy to report that her corporation is quite profitable.) Obviously, the fact that health insurance is provided to all citizens "for free" does not generate overconsumption of *insurance,* since it's provided in the form of a standard, universal benefit. Second, except in the most unusual of cases, Americans don't pay for health care out of pocket. They also participate in various risk-pooling arrangements, ranging from private insurance and health management organizations to government-supplied Medicare and Medicaid. Thus the typical health care consumer faces *exactly* the same incentives at the front end in Canada and the United States. Health care is all "free" at the point of purchase.

Thus the conservative critique of socialized medicine is not actually a critique of public ownership and provision. It is a critique of health insurance in general, both public and private. One can see this in the remedy that conservatives offer for the problems of moral hazard in the health insurance system, namely, health savings accounts.[20] These sorts of proposals are usually based on the assumption that the reason for government involvement in the health care sector is that not everyone can afford it. (This is already a mistake, since the rationale for public health insurance is not distributive justice, but rather market failure. It is only the non-actuarial structure of the premiums in social insurance schemes that is motivated by considerations of distributive justice.) Thus the proposed solution is to give each individual citizen a yearly grant, to be kept in a special savings account. The individual would save or spend this money on health care, as needed. Because individuals would start paying for health care out of pocket, the argument goes, they would lose whatever incentive they may have to overspend.

The problem with these proposals is that they are grotesquely inefficient. Health care spending in our society generally follows what's known as the 80/20 rule: 20% of the population is responsible for roughly 80% of the health care spending. Thus the figure of $2 trillion in annual health care spending in the United States, or $6,700 per person, is slightly misleading.[21] A better aggregate picture would be to imagine one person spending $26,800 per year, along with four others spending only $1,675. So what happens if the government gives everyone $6,700 in a special little account? How much should you save? Well, I guess that depends on whether or not you intend to develop diabetes . . . But of course, you don't know if you are going to get diabetes, just as most other people don't know what *their* future health care needs are going to be. Furthermore, since spending is going to be highly uneven across the population, giving everyone a grant of the same size guarantees that the state will give too much to most people and not enough to virtually everyone who is really going to need it.

But across large population groups, health care spending (not to mention rates of disease) is highly predictable. This means that there is an overwhelming efficiency argument to be made for the pooling of health care savings. This also means that, when you examine any of the more mainstream proposals for health savings accounts, their bark tends to be much worse than their bite. Recognizing that the only rational way to organize the bulk of health care spending is through insurance, what conservatives typically propose is a set of relatively small grants at the front end (perhaps $2,000) coupled with a "catastrophic coverage" insurance mechanism at the back end.[22] When all is said and done, the savings account winds up being just a heavy-handed way of discouraging parents from bringing little Johnny to the emergency room every time he gets the sniffles. It's the back-end insurance mechanism that does all the heavy lifting, covering the cost of all major procedures and accounting for the bulk of health care spending.[23] The same policy objectives could be achieved within a socialized medicine system simply by imposing a small user fee on hospital visits (as they do in Sweden), or in a regular private insurance system by having a large deductible.

So where does all this leave the issue of personal responsibility? Conservatives are not wrong to think that there is a fundamental tension between the old-fashioned ideals of individual liberty, responsibility, and self-reliance and the practices of what European intellectuals like to call the "risk society." Yet they blame the decline of personal responsibility on government, whereas what they should be blaming is the rise of insurance. As François Ewald (perhaps the most original French thinker on the subject of the welfare state) argues, the decisive rupture with the old-fashioned ideal of personal responsibility occurred in the nineteenth century, with the development of actuarial science and the rise of the *private* insurance industry.[24] Government in the twentieth century, in developing the social safety net, was simply borrowing techniques that had been developed in the private sector. "Personal responsibility" was dead long before they got to it.

Whether or not one regards this as a good thing overall, it's important to keep in mind that the development of comprehensive insurance systems coincides with the emergence of capitalism as a relatively stable economic system. Insurance does a lot more than simply keep the taxis on the street in Hong Kong. Every single aspect of our financial and commercial system, every transaction that we engage in, is underwritten at some level by insurance. It truly is the all-purpose economic lubricant. Unfortunately, it also requires us to be somewhat less fastidious when it comes to holding people responsible for their actions. But what can you do? Welcome to the modern world.

$ $ $

To see the limitations of the personal responsibility crusade, one need only consider the case of the subprime mortgage meltdown, which led to the collapse of the investment banking sector in the United States and created economic chaos around the world. The story here was all about moral hazard. Yet the decisions that were made interacted in such complex ways that the desire to find one party who could be held responsible quickly became pointless.

What set the stage for the entire fiasco was the invention of a new type of risk-pooling arrangement. Historically, banks had been very cautious in their lending practices when it came to homeowners. It is not difficult to see why. The "upside" of mortgage loans is not all that great—you get repaid your money with interest, at a fairly modest rate. The downside, however, is enormous. Not only may you never see any of the interest you are owed, but you can lose a substantial portion of the money you have lent out. Equity lenders, on the other hand, such as shareholders, have much greater upside to their investments. If the value of the asset goes up, they get a share of the profits. This is why investors in the stock market are willing to take much bigger risks than traditional banks.

Unfortunately, for the average homeowner, going to the stock market to raise money for a new home purchase is not possible. The only real option is to go to a bank. But because banks are so risk-averse, many people who might actually be able to carry a mortgage are unable to get one.

This seems like the sort of situation where some risk-pooling could be useful. And that's exactly what people did with the creation of collateralized debt obligations, or CDOs. The basic idea was quite simple and, contrary to what one might think, not at all crazy. When you take one single individual with perhaps a patchy credit history and unstable employment, the risk of default on a loan is quite high. But suppose you could take one hundred such individuals? Or a thousand? While some will no doubt default, chances are fairly high that at least half the group will be able to make their payments. If you take the best 10%, say, the chances that they will be able to make their payments would appear to be extremely high.

So what the banks did was package together a large bundle of "subprime" loans—loans made to individuals who would not have qualified for a conventional mortgage—and sell to investors not just the right to collect the revenue stream from all of these loans, but also the right to collect from particular "tranches" of borrowers. This is how they were able to get low-grade loans reclassified as high-quality "investment grade" bonds. When you lend to a thousand people, the chances that more than 900 of them will default seems incredibly remote. (In the same way, the chances that every hunter would come home empty-handed, in Figure 6.4, is close to zero.) Thus the right to collect from the best 10% of the pool would seem to be a very secure investment, even if each particular individual who is being loaned money seems unworthy.

In this way, the banks were able to spin straw into gold. The problem is that they were using a risk-pooling arrangement in order to achieve this, and risk-pooling arrangements have two fundamental vulnerabilities. First, they cannot protect against systemic risk; and second, they generate moral hazard.

Let's start with moral hazard. Now that banks were able to offload the risk of credit default onto investors, and investors were able to convince themselves that the law of large numbers would protect them from individual defaults, the incentive to avoid making bad loans more or less went out the window. The banks—or often private mortgage brokers, working on commission—started lending money to people who had no realistic chance of ever making their payments (such as the now-infamous NINJAs: "no income, no job or assets"). This is a classic moral hazard effect. If you start providing insurance against credit default, you're going to start seeing a lot more credit default.

As though the risk-pooling provided by the CDOs themselves was not enough, several insurance companies started writing policies insuring these CDOs against default. Convinced that the assets could not fail, they set aside little or no money to cover potential losses on these policies (a strategy that was aided and abetted by the U.S. government, which consciously decided not to regulate these contracts). This, of course, added another layer of moral hazard, so that the investors buying up these mortgages became less concerned about who they were buying from or what they were buying—after all, they could always slough off any excess risk onto an insurance company.

It all came tumbling down because investors ignored the Achilles' heel of all risk-pooling arrangements: systemic risk. Consider again the group of 10 hunters who agree to pool their catch in order to ensure that no one faces starvation. When this example was first introduced, I slipped in a little qualification to the effect that the risk-pooling arrangement works only if the probabilities are independent of one another. This means that one hunter's chances of coming home empty-handed must be unrelated to any other hunter's chances of coming home empty-handed. When this occurs, the bad luck will cancel out the good luck, leaving everyone closer to the average. But what if something happens (such as a forest fire) that simultaneously reduces *everyone's* chances of catching some game? When it comes to dealing with this risk, the pooling arrangement is completely useless.

The same thing applies to residential mortgages. In order for the CDO to diminish risk, the chances of one borrower's defaulting must be substantially independent of that of every other. But this is manifestly not the case. The availability of easy credit increased the pool of people crowding into the housing market, leading to enormous inflation in the value of American houses. Furthermore, the structure of mortgage finance throughout most of the United States is subject to rather unusual moral hazard effects, because these loans are "nonrecourse," which means that when a person defaults on his mortgage, the lender can seize the home but cannot go after any of this person's other assets. Because of this, anyone with negative home equity (where the size of the mortgage exceeds the value of the home) has an incentive simply to walk away from it.

With this in mind, it is easy to see how one person's default could have a cascading effect. Many of the loans that were made featured low introductory rates, which began to climb (sometimes quite abruptly) two or three years in. Lots of people bought with no money down and were making payments that did not even cover the interest charges on their loans, much less reduce the principal. As soon as these higher rates kicked in, the NINJAs quickly began to default. When this happened, the banks seized the houses and began to sell them off. But when the banks started selling foreclosed properties, this drove down real estate prices. Prices fell, and many more homeowners found themselves with negative home equity, giving them an incentive to default on *their* mortgages. As a result, the risk of default of *all* the mortgages in CDOs began to increase.

Soon enough, institutions and investors who were holding CDOs began to report huge losses, with some even facing bankruptcy. But no one knew exactly who was holding what, generating some nasty surprises (as when BNP Paribas, the largest bank in France, reported a huge loss due to exposure to U.S. subprime loans). This made banks extremely nervous about lending to one another, which in turn started to freeze up credit markets. At this point, central banks began to step in, discharging their function as "lender of last resort," either propping up banks or else nationalizing them outright. This development, however, had its own moral hazard effects! Once private lenders became convinced that the government would step in and guarantee solvency or buy up bad loans, they became even more averse to making risky loans or even getting rid of bad debt. And so conditions worsened.

Who is to blame for the whole mess? Trying to figure out who acted most "irresponsibly" here is a mug's game. Banks and investors, consumers, government officials, and politicians all acted in ways that made things worse. Who shall we say is responsible? The consumer who bought a house that she could never afford, or the bank who lent her the money? Or the investor whose willingness to assume the loan is what motivated the bank to lend it to her? Or the insurance company whose willingness to underwrite the credit risk is what motivated the investor to assume the loan? Or the government, which didn't bother to make these insurance companies set aside some money to cover such policies?

Take your pick. The point is that *everyone* did something wrong. Unfortunately, when everyone is responsible, that's equivalent to no one being responsible. The solution, therefore, lies in cleaning up the system, in order to eliminate the moral hazards.

PART II
LEFT-WING FALLACIES

In which the wishful thinking and naive moralism of the friends of humanity are sympathetically, and yet unremittingly, subjected to the harsh test of economic plausibility.

CHAPTER 7

THE JUST PRICE FALLACY

*The temptation to fiddle with prices,
and why it should be resisted*

On February 15, 2007, a fire swept through the giant Imperial Oil refinery in Nanticoke, Ontario, forcing the plant to shut down for several weeks. At the same time, a nasty cold snap struck southern Ontario, driving up demand for heating oil while simultaneously freezing up shipping lanes on the Great Lakes, leaving tankers that would have brought in additional fuel stuck in harbor. Meanwhile, a Canadian National rail workers' strike prevented new supplies from coming in by train from neighboring Quebec.

It was, as one industry official observed, "a perfect storm." Within a week, more than 100 gas stations across southern Ontario had run out of fuel. Rumors of "panic buying" among commuters began to surface. Prices at the pumps rose by over 20¢ per liter (75¢ per gallon), but shortages persisted. Into this maelstrom strode Jack Layton, leader of the New Democrats, Canada's foremost social-democratic party.

Striking a blow for the little guy, he roundly condemned the actions of the petroleum companies, saying, "It doesn't seem reasonable to us that there would be increases in prices."[1]

People sometimes claim that the left just doesn't get it when it comes to the market—that, despite the experiences of the twentieth century, it is still peddling a form of anticapitalism that is no longer a viable option in the modern world. Naturally, this is something that moderate, progressive leftists like Layton all heatedly deny. "We love the market," they say, "just so long as it knows its place."

And yet, if you wonder where the concern about anticapitalism comes from, one need look no further than Layton's remark about gas prices. Not *reasonable* that prices should go up? Here's a question, then: Under what conditions would Layton consider it reasonable for the price of anything to go up, *ever*? The function of prices in a market economy is to ration goods in order to achieve a balance of supply and demand. The price of gas went up in February 2007 not because of some capricious, sinister decision by the oil companies, but because *there was not enough gas.* Not to belabor the point, but if oil companies are not allowed to raise gas prices when gas is running out, then there's no point allowing them to set prices at all. We might as well just nationalize the industry and have done with it.

More generally, does it not seem reasonable that people should limit their gasoline purchases in times of shortage, so that those who really need it can be assured of getting some? (For example, I carried an empty 10-liter gas can around in the back of my car for a couple of months that winter. My lawn tractor was out of gas but— since it was the dead of winter—there was no urgent need to refill it. So I waited until prices went down a bit before buying. This is as it should be.) Actually, it doesn't even matter if this seems reasonable or not. The fact is, if you don't find it reasonable that prices should reflect relative scarcity, then fundamentally you don't accept the market economy, because this is about as close to the essence of the market as you can find.

$ $ $

Complaints about "price-gouging" and "profiteering" have been around for a long time. In AD 301, the Roman emperor Diocletian imposed the now-infamous Edict of Maximum Prices, which set limits on the amount that could be charged for over 900 different goods and 150 services.[2] The preamble to the edict explained its purpose—to combat "shameless pricing"—in terms that Layton would no doubt find sympathetic:

> And to the avarice of those who are always eager to turn to their own profit even the blessings of the gods, to seize hold of the abundance of public good fortune; those who in years of need traffic in the services of hucksters, the very ones who drain off huge fortunes which could abundantly satisfy the people, who chase after private gain and pursue their mutilating percent-ages—on their avarice, provincial citizens, regard for common humanity impels us to set a limit.[3]

This is a sentiment that many on the left still share. (That said, Diocletian's edict does go on to prescribe the death penalty for anyone who "should, in his boldness, act against the letter of this statute." Many leftists would probably want to get off the boat at this point—although Diocletian, anticipating such objections, did make a special point of observing that individuals could easily avoid this penalty simply by obeying the law.)

There are two separate issues here that need to be distinguished. Diocletian thought that he was reacting against "profiteering," which occurs when the prices of some things go up because people are taking advantage of conditions in a particular sector of the economy. As it turns out, what he was actually reacting to was inflation, when the price of *everything* goes up. Of course, it is important to be careful when saying this, since it is not literally possible for the price of everything to go up. Prices are essentially ratios: They specify how much some good is worth relative to some others. If you wander into a Polish supermarket and discover that a kilo of carrots is selling for four zlotys, you probably haven't learned very much. It's only once you find out what a pound of potatoes costs, and a chicken, and a pint of beer, that you begin to discover whether carrots are expensive or cheap.

As a result, the price of everything going up is analytically equivalent to the price of nothing going up. It follows that if the price of everything *seems* to be going up, it must be because the price of at least one thing is (inconspicuously) going down. Usually that inconspicuous item with the falling price is hidden in plain sight—money. We tend to overlook money because it's not directly consumed; it simply circulates, thus we forget that it has a price. We think of "four zlotys per kilo" as the price of carrots, expressed in zlotys, while forgetting that it is also the price of zlotys, expressed in carrots.

Sometimes the price of money declines as a consequence of people raising the prices of everything else. This usually occurs thanks to a classic "wage-price spiral," in which the "cost of living" rises, prompting workers to demand pay increases, the costs of which are passed along to consumers in the form of increased prices, which simply generate a demand for further pay increases, and so on. In this case, everyone tries to get ahead of the spiral by asking for more, with results that are collectively self-defeating. This outcome corresponds, implicitly, to a decline in the value of money.

In Diocletian's time, on the other hand, it was possible for money to decline all on its own, through debasement. Since the value of coins in the Roman Empire was derived from their silver content, it was possible to extend one's budget by melting down the currency, mixing it with some "base" metal, then striking new coins with it. It was through this process that the *denarius* went from being pure silver to containing only 2% silver at the end of the third century, at which point Diocletian replaced it with the *argenteus*. The edict on prices was in fact part and parcel of his attempt to bring price stability to the Roman Empire.

One of the most common mistakes people make is to confuse the problem of profiteering with that of general inflation. If the value of money is declining, then people have no choice but to raise prices, just to avoid being ruined. (It is important to remember that workers, by demanding wage increases, are essentially raising the price of labor.) Yet because inflation is a collective action problem, no one actually succeeds in making supranormal profits through these price increases. It seems a bit unfair to blame them for their actions. Yet that mistake is commonly made. For instance, in 2007 President Hugo Chávez of Venezuela decreed a set of maximum prices for a variety of staple goods (and threatened to nationalize any shops found selling beef, milk, and sugar above these rates).[4] He did so during a time at which the rate of consumer price inflation was 18.4% per year. As a result, many supermarkets were simply forced to stop selling staple goods.

Now, whether or not price controls are an effective way of combating inflation, it is important to recognize that this is a fundamentally separate issue from the problem of profiteering. When everyone tries to "profiteer," no one succeeds in doing so. Thus there is no point getting all morally outraged over the "unconscionable" prices that are being charged in an inflationary economy: they are *not actually higher prices*. It's an economic illusion generated by the decline in the value of money.

So if there's one thing that can be said in Layton's defense, it's that he wasn't making the same mistake that has bedeviled economic populists from Diocletian to Chávez. The increase in gas prices that he was condemning was not due to inflation: It represented a genuine increase in the price of gas relative to other commodities. In other words, while driving became more expensive, other options, such as taking the bus, were becoming less expensive (in relative, not nominal, terms).

The moral intuition that Layton was expressing was therefore appropriate in the context. It does seem intuitively unfair that, in times of shortage, people should have "no choice" but to pay extortionary rates for staple goods. A solid majority of people share this moral intuition.[5] In the background is a more general concern that prices, when left to the free play of the market, seem to generate very unjust allocations. Forget about gas prices and suburban commuters—look at the homeless, unable to afford shelter for the night; pensioners on fixed incomes, forced to eat cat food for dinner; single parents threatened by the cold, unable to pay their electricity bill. How can a decent society deny people these essential goods simply because "supply and demand" dictate that the price should be x instead of y? And how can it be right for companies to jack up prices at the first sign of scarcity, thereby imposing the greatest suffering upon those with the least ability to pay?

This is a perfectly reasonable question. It is, however, one that also has a perfectly reasonable answer.

$ $ $

I would hazard to say that anyone who considers himself a member of the left, or even a friend of humanity, finds it unacceptable that some people should be unable to afford food and shelter in a wealthy industrialized society. That much is not in question. There are, however, two importantly different ways of looking at the problem. If some people cannot afford food and shelter, the problem could be that these things are too expensive, or it could be that some people don't have enough money. Similarly, there are two ways of solving the problem: the first by changing the prices, the second by supplementing people's income. Yet for some reason, people have a tendency to overlook the second option. This results in a pattern of reasoning that we might refer to as the "just price" fallacy, whereby prices are directly blamed for injustices that arise in the pattern of distribution, ignoring the effect of endowments.

The almost unanimous preference among economically sophisticated leftists is to let the market set prices in cases where a reasonably competitive market can be organized, and to tackle distributive justice problems from the income side. As the great socialist economist Abba Lerner once put it, the problem with the poor is not the prices that they have to pay, but that they have too little money (hence his realization

THE JUST PRICE FALLACY

that "the solution of poverty lay not with the manipulation of prices but with the distribution of money income"[6]). Yet for some reason, the temptation to pursue distributive justice objectives through the manipulation of prices remains almost irresistible for the left. (Thus Jack Layton and the NDP are not only the chief defenders of cheap gas, in times of shortage, but also of cheap housing, cheap tuition, cheap banking services, cheap anything-that-the-poor-happen-to-consume-some-of.)

Take, for example, electricity prices. Canadians like to make fun of Americans for having a rather unseemly addiction to cheap gasoline, yet they seldom notice that they have an equally unseemly attachment to cheap electricity. In 2004, while Canadian consumers paid an average of 6.8¢ per kilowatt-hour for electricity, Europeans were paying at least twice that (19.8¢ in Germany, 14.2¢ in France, and 13.8¢ in the United Kingdom).[7] Even in the United States, the average price to consumers was 9¢. Yet at the same time that Canadians were wallowing in cheap power, they were being bombarded with government ads encouraging them to conserve electricity, and the country was divided by an agonizing debate over whether (and how) to meet its obligations under the Kyoto accord on climate change.

The answer to both problems was crushingly obvious: Raise the price of electricity. In the United States, comparisons between states show that an increase in the price of electricity by 1¢ per kilowatt-hour above the national average is associated with a 7% decrease in electricity consumption.[8] Raising prices in Canada wouldn't have been difficult to do, since prices throughout most of the country were being kept low through government subsidy. In other words, all that governments needed to do was stop giving away free power. (The best way to think of a subsidy, in this case, is as an offer of the form "buy four kilowatt-hours, get the fifth for free!") Yet anyone who suggested this was immediately shouted down by the left, with the complaint that an increase in electricity prices would hurt low-income families.

Let's say this is true, and that a 30% increase in electricity prices (that is, to American levels) would seriously hurt the poorest segment of the population—and by "hurt" I mean cause real deprivation, not just prompt them to change their behavior. In this context, it is important to remember that being poor in Canada is not quite the same thing as being poor in Malawi. In 2005, households in the lower-income quintile of the population in Canada spent an average of $663 per year, or 3% of their income, on electricity.[9] They also spent an average of $344 per year on cable or satellite television services, and an additional $165 on home entertainment expenses such as audio and video equipment, DVD players, camcorders, and video rental. This doesn't mean that they're living the high life, but it does mean that there is some discretionary use of electricity going on, even in poorer households.

But let us suppose, for the sake of argument, that this lower-income segment of the population is in completely dire straits when it comes to electricity. They are already doing the best that they can—turning off the television whenever they leave the room, hanging their clothes out to dry, and turning down their thermostat by a couple of degrees even when they're at home. An increase in electricity prices would leave them unable to pay their bill without cutting back on some other essential expenditure, such as food or rent. Let us grant all this, and let us suppose that electricity prices are kept low in order to avoid this outcome.

Now think for a moment about what sort of sums are involved. About half of the typical electricity bill represents transmission cost, which would be unaffected by an increase in rates. Thus even a 30% increase in prices would raise the average poor family's bill by only $100 a year, assuming no change in behavior. Since a "quintile" in Canada constitutes about 2.5 million households, the practice of keeping electricity prices low is therefore delivering a benefit worth just under $250 million to this low-income group. This may seem like a lot of money, but it's small potatoes in the scheme of things (by comparison, the Canada Child Tax Benefit transfers over $8.5 *billion* to low-income families with children).

Yet in order to achieve this relatively small subsidy to low-income households, the government is giving *everyone* in the society cheap electricity. It's difficult to imagine a more catastrophically inefficient social policy. Not only does it lead to widespread overconsumption, with disastrous environmental consequences, but the whole policy is extremely regressive with respect to income. Of course, poor people spend a greater *percentage* of their income on electricity, but even then the differences are not as great as one might think. The middle-income quintile spends an average of $1,117 per year (2.4% of income), while the upper quintile spends $1,522 per year (1.1% of income). This means that the $250 million annual gift being bestowed upon the poor is coupled with a $408 million gift to the middle class and a $556 million gift to the richest 20% of the population. Needless to say, a welfare program that required giving $2 to a rich person for every $1 directed to a poor person would hardly be regarded as progressive (despite the fact that, when expressed as a percentage of income, the poor person is receiving "more"). Yet this is essentially how the electricity subsidy works.[10]

In other words, fiddling with the price of electricity is a terrible way of addressing the underlying problem of distributive justice, simply because the benefits of low prices are available to everyone, not just those who are in need. (In the same way, rent-control regimes make lower prices available to everyone, including those who could easily afford to buy their own home.) Compounding the problem is the fact that these sorts of price manipulations generate perverse effects with respect to supply and demand. If electricity is cheap, people will use more of it than, strictly speaking, they need to. Trying to promote conservation, in this context, is like putting a Weight Watchers booth at the end of an all-you-can-eat buffet.[11] (A far more effective approach to portion control has been adopted by many health-food restaurants, where you can choose whatever you like from the buffet, but your plate is weighed on the way out and you are charged by the ounce. Anyone who doubts that pricing systems have a powerful effect on behavior should try eating at a place like this.)

It would be much better—from the standpoint of both equality and efficiency—to charge people the true cost of electricity (by which I mean the market price plus a "green tax" that reflects the environmental externalities), then provide the poor with an income supplement to defray whatever hardship such a change may impose. Not only does this solve the problem of distributive justice, it does so without a perverse incentive to waste electricity. Fiddling with prices has nothing to recommend it. As Lerner put it, "If a redistribution of income is desired it is best brought about by a direct transfer of money income. The sacrifice of the optimum allocation of goods is not economically necessary."[12]

$ $ $

There are a variety of different principles that a society can use to decide what the appropriate price of a good should be. The issue has been the subject of intense controversy throughout Western history.[13] Aristotle argued that a "just price" should be determined by equalizing the benefit going to either party to the exchange.[14] Augustine thought that the desire "to buy cheap and sell dear" was a vice, and that the price should be determined by the intrinsic value of the object.[15] John Duns Scotus argued that prices should be determined on a "cost plus" basis (and thus that supply-side considerations should predominate). The Renaissance "Salamanca School," on the other hand, focused more on the demand side, arguing that goods should be priced in accordance with the extent to which they are "esteemed."[16]

The view that came to predominate, however, is that prices should be determined by the *relative scarcity* of goods. (The scarcity in question is relative because the adequacy of any given quantity of a good is a function of how much people want it: Scarcity is determined by the relation between supply and demand.) It is this concept of scarcity pricing that Layton was tacitly rejecting, by demanding that gas prices remain low during a time of shortage. Now it happens to be a feature of the market economy that competition generates scarcity pricing. However, the appeal of the basic principle extends far beyond whatever affection one may have for the market. One of the great insights of the "socialist calculation" debate of the early twentieth century was the realization that *any* economic system, capitalist or socialist, would want to use scarcity pricing if it hoped to avoid wasting vast quantities of resources and labor.

Unfortunately, people sometimes treat the whole supply and demand business—the problem of scarcity—as merely a capitalist preoccupation. Socialism, on the other hand, will coincide with the move into a "post-scarcity" economy. This is completely wrongheaded. It is important to remember that, in most wealthy nations, the service sector is several times larger than the manufacturing sector. There is a certain sort of environmental perspective that encourages us to think about consumption in terms of natural resources and energy. This is misleading, since most of what we consume are not material goods, but rather *other people's time*. And as long as other people's time is limited, there will always be scarcity. Furthermore, in sectors like health care, there is obviously no limit on how much can be spent and on how much people would be willing to spend (in order, for example, to extend their lives by a few weeks or months). Thus scarcity pricing is an independently attractive moral ideal, one that is accepted both by defenders of capitalism and economically sophisticated socialists.[17]

Oskar Lange—the other great socialist economist of the twentieth century—once wrote that the central attraction of capitalism, when properly institutionalized, is that "competition forces entrepreneurs to act exactly as they would have to act were they managers of production in a socialist system."[18] This is a nice way of putting it. When oil companies raise their prices in response to gasoline shortages, don't think of them as greedy—think of them as *simulating the behavior of managers in an ideal socialist economy*. Unfortunately, the moral intuition here eludes many people (not just Jack Layton). Why would socialist planners react this way? What's so special about balancing supply and demand?

The best way of seeing the answer to this question is to observe that the point at which total supply is equal to total demand is the point at which the price paid by the individual consumer properly reflects the "social cost" of consumption. Whenever someone consumes a good (say, a cup of coffee), this can be thought of as creating a benefit for that individual, combined with a loss for the rest of society (all the time and trouble it took to produce that cup of coffee, now gone). Paying for things is our way of compensating all the people who have been inconvenienced by our consumption. (Next time you buy a cup of coffee at Starbucks, imagine yourself saying to the barista, "I'm sorry that you had to serve me coffee when you could have been doing other things. And please communicate my apologies to the others as well: the owner, the landlord, the shipping company, the Colombian peasants. Here's $1.75 for all the trouble. Please divide it among yourselves.")

"Social cost" represents the level of renunciation, or forgone consumption, imposed upon the rest of society by each individual's own consumption. This is a fairly abstract notion, since it's not just that the good could have been consumed by someone else, but that the labor and resources that went into making that good could have been used to produce something else, which then could have been consumed by someone else. (So when I drink a cup of coffee, I am not only taking away that cup of coffee from all those who might like to have drunk it, but taking away vegetables from those who might like to have used the land to grow food, clothing from those who might like to have employed the agricultural workers in a garment factory, and so on.)

How much inconvenience a person imposes upon others when drinking a cup of coffee depends upon two things: first, how much the rest of us want coffee, and second, how much trouble it will be to produce more (or, in more technical terms, what the demand and supply curves for coffee look like). If the price of coffee tracks changes in supply and demand, then it will tend to reflect this level of hardship.[19] If the rest of us really want coffee, then we will be prepared to pay more for it, and so the price will rise. Coffee will become more "dear" (as the British would say), reflecting the fact that the person who drinks it is denying the rest of us something that we really want. Thus the coffee-drinker had better really want it in order to justify depriving us of it. His willingness to pay the higher price is precisely what ensures that he does, in fact, really want it.

Similarly, if coffee is plentiful and relatively easy to produce, then it doesn't matter that much if one more cup gets drunk; but if coffee starts to require more resources to produce, or if the resources come into high demand in some other sector, we may want to cut back on coffee production and invest our efforts elsewhere. In this case as well, coffee will become more "dear," as a reflection of the fact that the resources might be better used producing something *else* that people want. If the willingness to pay is there, it suggests that coffee production is still worth the time and effort required. If not, then maybe some of us should be switching to tea.

The general principle here is quite simple: Whatever deprivations are imposed upon society by an individual's act of consumption should be *warranted* by the satisfaction that the individual gets from the item consumed. People who would be just as happy drinking tea as they are coffee should not be drinking coffee if the social cost associated with the latter is greater. One way of achieving this is to peer into people's heads and try to figure out how much they really like coffee and tea, then look at the production side to see what is involved in making the stuff. A much more practical way is to figure out a price level at which the total quantity of each good that people are willing to buy is identical to the total quantity that people are willing to sell. These are referred to as the "market-clearing" prices. (A competitive market is one way, but only one way, of getting to these prices.)

To see how this price level uniquely satisfies the moral constraint (that social cost must be warranted), one need only consider what happens when the price of any one good deviates from it. If the price is lower, it means that the individual consumer gains, but not as much as some other consumer *could* gain by taking the resources that were used to produce this good and using them to produce some other good; the social cost of this particular act of consumption is not warranted. If the price is higher, it means that the individual consumer does not gain as much as he should be able to, given the relatively slight cost that his consumption imposes upon society. Of course, one price being too high is analytically equivalent to every other price being too low, so this just means that the social cost of everyone *else's* consumption is unwarranted, given the gains that they enjoy.

This is all just a highly discursive way of saying that when prices deviate from market-clearing levels, the resulting pattern of production and consumption is Pareto inefficient. And this just means that you could shift production and consumption out of some sectors and into others in a way that didn't worsen anyone's condition and yet made some people better off. The only problem is that when it is expressed in this way, many people seem to miss the force of the underlying moral intuition. Lerner once observed that, to him, it seemed "obvious that socialist societies must be just as concerned with economic efficiency as capitalist societies,"[20] and thus that prices in the economy should be aimed at market-clearing levels, regardless of whether that economy was socialist or capitalist. Yet many people never understood his reasoning. And so it is necessary to show, in some detail, why setting prices at these levels is the only practical way of ensuring that the costs that individuals impose upon society through their consumption are in any way justified by the benefits that they derive. Failing to respect this constraint generates totally unnecessary material deprivation. And that translates into needless suffering when a society is poor, and perhaps needless frustration as the overall level of affluence increases.

Naturally, the system of prices would enjoy greater moral authority if the initial distribution of income were equal. That way, everyone would exercise exactly the same level of influence when it came to determining where resources were "needed" the most. But this is a problem in the distribution of income. Scarcity pricing does not make things worse; on the contrary, it can be thought of as a system for making the best out of the existing situation. We need to learn to partition our moral intuitions: We want our economic system to be both efficient and fair. The function of the price system, however, is to deliver efficiency. Delivering fairness is the function of our income policies (and thus, primarily, of the taxation system). So long as the price system is working more or less the way it is supposed to—responding to changes in supply and demand in a way that reflects relative scarcity—we should refrain from making any judgments of fairness or unfairness with respect to the prices that emerge. Whatever distributive justice intuitions we have should be applied to the distribution of income, and to income alone.[21]

§ § §

We have now seen two good reasons not to pursue social justice objectives by fiddling with prices: It's ineffective, from the standpoint of distributive justice, and it creates inefficiency, in the form of wasteful misallocation of resources. There is also an important political reason to avoid doing it: The resulting price distortion generates a perverse response on the market—landlords fail to provide enough rental housing, consumers use too much electricity, and so on. This in turn often tempts politicians to treat the symptoms rather than the disease. "Treatment" in this case usually means coercive measures aimed at prohibiting certain forms of perfectly legitimate market behavior. The resulting body of regulation is often intrusive, costly, and completely ineffective—precisely the sort of regulation that risks giving all regulation a bad name.

The temptation here is all too human. For example, after years of strict rent control a severe housing shortage developed in Montreal. People began to find themselves competing against 20 or 30 other prospective tenants to get an apartment. In most cities in North America, middle-class kids start to settle down by their late twenties—they finish university, get a real job, start to make serious money, and start shopping for a house. In Montreal, they do everything on this list except the last. Renting is such a good deal that there is simply no incentive to buy. As a result, single mothers on welfare find themselves competing against corporate lawyers and freelance film producers to get into an apartment.[22] Needless to say, the welfare mothers tend to lose out in these competitions.

The contraction of supply caused by the price distortion, combined with the increase in demand, led the rent-control regime to harm precisely those whom it was intended to assist. But what to do? Eliminating rent control looks like capitulation in the face of "economic blackmail" by the landlords. Instead the provincial government in Quebec began musing about the possibility of denying landlords the right to ask prospective tenants about their financial status (or adding income to the list of prohibited grounds for discrimination).

One can see a similar temptation in the case of electricity. The best example is the campaign to ban the incandescent lightbulb. Since compact fluorescent bulbs use a lot less electricity than old-fashioned incandescent bulbs (the latter use four or five times more electricity to produce a lumen of light), somewhere, somehow, someone got the strange idea that instead of relying upon the price of electricity to do the work, governments should encourage conservation by banning incandescent lightbulbs. They also managed to persuade the government of Australia that this was a good idea, a decision that led to copycat legislation in other jurisdictions, including Canada and the United Kingdom.

One might think that in Canada in particular the stupidity of the idea would be so obvious as to exempt it from serious discussion. After all, the energy that is "wasted" by incandescent bulbs does not magically disappear into the ether but escapes into the home in the form of heat. In a country where people run their furnaces eight or nine months out of the year, this makes incandescent bulbs 100% energy-efficient most of time—from the standpoint of the whole home. (For the same reason, there is little to be said for tankless water heaters in Canada. It's really only when air-conditioning is on that the escaping heat generates a serious waste of energy.)

It is also important to keep in mind the basic principle that people aren't stupid. What environmentalists want to target is electricity usage, but what they are choosing to target instead is lightbulb purchasing. It's easy for consumers to drive a wedge between the two. I've been a big fan of compact fluorescent bulbs for years. But as a result of switching to them, there are now certain lights that I leave on 24 hours a day, simply because they use so little electricity. (I'm also a big fan of low-E, argon-filled windows. But as a result of that technology, I was able to replace the small windows in my back room with gigantic panoramic windows—a change that probably left the total energy loss from my house unaffected by the upgrade.)

A similar problem arises with the attempt to limit fuel consumption by imposing a surtax on "gas-guzzling" vehicles. There's nothing wrong with *buying* a Hummer; it's *driving* a Hummer that's antisocial. The way to target that is by raising the gasoline tax, not by imposing a surcharge on the vehicle. The same is true for hybrids. I bought a Toyota hybrid in 2005 and received a fairly generous tax subsidy from the government for my purchase. Yet it pains me to report that, as a result of buying a hybrid, I now drive more than I otherwise would. The psychological mechanism is fairly simple: Being an environmentalist, I don't drive very often, and when I do I feel guilty. Driving a hybrid makes me feel less guilty. Ergo, I drive more. I'm not proud of it, but that's how it works.

Apart from being useless and ineffective, there is an even more fundamental problem with the "ban the bulb" campaign. It represents an intrusive use of state power that is extremely offensive to liberal-democratic principles. The argument for this involves a rather subtle point of political philosophy, but it is worth rehearsing, because it bears quite directly upon the importance of using the price system to address environmental issues.

One of the major characteristics of modern pluralistic societies, especially multicultural ones, is that people radically disagree with one another about how best to live their lives. Different people have different goals, projects, and values. Centuries of experience have also shown that it is best, by and large, if the government keeps its nose out of these sorts of lifestyle questions. It is appropriate for the state to impose limits on the extent to which individuals are allowed to annoy one another in their pursuit of the good life, but it is not a good idea for the state to take sides in these debates or to promote one particular lifestyle at the expense of others. This is why, for example, the state does not actively discourage people from becoming Jehovah's Witnesses, despite the conflicts generated by the refusal to accept blood transfusions among adherents of this faith.

Many philosophers have argued that in order to treat citizens with "equal concern and respect,"[23] the state must avoid adopting policies that are based upon the supposed intrinsic merits of particular lifestyles. Naturally, anything that is excessively dangerous or antisocial can be prohibited, but when it comes to issues over which reasonable individuals can and do disagree, it is best for the state to remain neutral. Yet while we don't want the government getting involved in the details of these decisions, the state does have an important role to play in ensuring that individuals, when they make these decisions, pay sufficient regard to the way that their choices affect others. In particular, individuals must be willing to moderate their demands and expectations in recognition of the fact that not everyone can get everything they want all at the same time.

Consider how this applies to the case of electricity. Everyone needs electricity, but different people want it for different things. Some people want air-conditioning, others want to surf the Internet, others want to blow-dry their hair. It's crazy to think that any society could ever sort out the relative merits of these different desires. The best that we can do is to let individuals make their own decisions about how to use it, subject only to a general budget constraint reflecting the fact that the amount of electricity is limited, and that every kilowatt-hour used by one person is a kilowatt-hour that cannot be used by someone else. The easiest way of doing this is to set a price reflecting the general availability of electricity, and then force individuals to pay for what they consume.

In order to keep separate issues separate, imagine that a society decides to divide up its available supplies of electricity equally among all individuals. A decision is made about how much electrical power society should produce (given general needs, the effort involved in generation and transmission, environmental impact, etc.). The society then creates a set of vouchers that it distributes to citizens, entitling each one to an equal per capita share of this power. Let's call this society Voucher World. Now here is the central question: Is it possible to make the case for banning incandescent lightbulbs in Voucher World? The answer—at least if we intend to respect neutrality—is no. People use electricity for all sorts of different things. Some of them seem absolutely trivial to us, and yet are deeply meaningful to those who choose them. (Think of the debates over outdoor Christmas lights.)

The important thing about Voucher World is that people are responsible for the effects of their own choices. If you want to use electricity to blow-dry, straighten, or curl your hair, then that means you will have less electricity available to do other things, such as cook dinner, watch television, or surf the Internet. Some people may not be willing to make these sacrifices, and so may choose to get a "wash and wear" haircut. Others may be willing to, and so will accept economies in other areas in order to finance their hair-care regimen. The important point is this: As long as each individual is using no more than his own personal allotment of electricity, it should be no one else's business what he chooses to do with it. Indeed, a society that dictates how individuals should and should not be using electricity fails to treat its members with equal concern and respect, since it will inevitably privilege the lifestyle preferences of some at the expense of others. Violations of neutrality of this sort are not only an affront to liberty—they are offensive to equality as well.

The case with lightbulbs is exactly the same. Like many people, I am rather particular about lighting. The problem with compact fluorescent bulbs is that they generate spiky emissions across the visible spectrum of light and have a poor color-rendering index. (Put qualitatively: The light is the wrong color and makes things look bad.) I strongly prefer the lighting generated by incandescent bulbs in some applications, and have even spent extra for a "full-spectrum" incandescent for my reading lamp. This may be persnickety, but that's just the way I am. Some people are audiophiles, some people are fussy about food, I'm fussy about light.

On the other hand, I'm not much of a fan of air-conditioning. I don't like what it does to the feel of the air, so I leave it off as much as I can. As a result, even though I waste a certain amount of electricity when it comes to lighting, I save an enormous amount of electricity when it comes to cooling. So how would someone with my preferences fare in Voucher World? Quite well. Since air-conditioners typically consume more power than all other appliances in a household combined, I wouldn't have much trouble finding room for a few incandescent bulbs in my overall electricity budget.

From these reflections, it seems to me easy to see that banning incandescent lightbulbs in Voucher World would be not only intrusive, but manifestly unfair to some individuals. Lots of people use electricity to indulge all sorts of bizarre and idiosyncratic tastes (like leaving their air-conditioner on when they're not home). So why pick on people who happen to like incandescent light? As long as they're paying their own way—forgoing some *other* use of electricity in order to indulge their particular tastes—then whatever decision they make about what appliances to use generates no harm for anyone else. The full cost of their specific consumption decisions are "internalized."

The question then is whether there are any morally salient differences between Voucher World and our own society such that banning incandescent lightbulbs would be politically offensive there but not here. The answer, I would argue, is no. In both cases, electricity consumption is subject to a budget constraint that reflects social cost. An individual who wants to have a bit more of one thing is forced to give up something else. The fact that I like power-guzzling lightbulbs leaves me with less money to spend on other things. Because I'm spending money, and not a dedicated voucher, I don't necessarily have to pay for my lightbulbs by cutting back my electricity consumption elsewhere, but I do have to cut back my consumption of *something*. I might decide to eat less pizza. The general point is the same: My income is essentially a voucher, giving me the right to use up a certain quantity of socially produced goods and services. As long as the prices I am paying reflect the real trade-offs that are involved in our society's capacity to produce these goods and services, then the particular way in which I choose to allocate my income should be my decision, and my decision alone. If I think it's worthwhile paying four or five times the price to get higher-quality light, then the energy used in its production is not wasted: It is being used to satisfy my preference—the social cost is warranted by the benefit I receive.

There are two morally significant differences between Voucher World and our own, but neither of them affects this conclusion. The first is that we are not all assigned an equal share of society's electricity production. Rather than receiving a voucher, we pay for electricity with ordinary money, and the distribution of wealth in our society is unequal. The rich are able to waste a lot more electricity, and indulge many more idiosyncratic tastes, than the poor. Yet though this may be true, it has nothing to do with lightbulbs. It is, if anything, simply an argument for a more equal distribution of income. The second difference is that the price of electricity does not reflect its true social cost, because of various environmental externalities. As a result, we produce too much electricity relative to people's actual needs and preferences. Yet again, this is not an argument for banning incandescent lightbulbs, but simply an argument in favor of true cost pricing of electricity (elimination of subsidies, imposition of a carbon tax, etc.).

So no matter how you run the argument, banning incandescent lightbulbs is an obnoxious and unworthy policy. It should not be excused on the grounds that it's just a "small step," or that it signals a willingness to accept change in order to improve the environment. It is an ineffective policy, one that violates a fundamental principle of equality. It also damages the environmental movement, by suggesting that environmentalists really are just busybodies who want the government to ban all lifestyles they happen to disapprove of.

$ $ $

So far all we've discussed are cases in which the left wants prices to be lowered, in order to give poor consumers a break. By now the limitations of this strategy have become apparent. But there is also an important set of cases in which the left wants to see prices raised, in order to give poor *producers* a break. The most high-profile instances of this involve international trade, since the poverty of producers is more apparent when we buy goods from underdeveloped countries. This is the issue at the heart of the "fair trade" movement.

It is important at the outset to distinguish several different ideas that are often bundled together under the rubric of "fair trade." There are those who simply want "ethical" supply-chain management (environmental standards, freedom from repression in the workplace, etc.), along with reduction in first-world tariff barriers and subsidies. Joseph Stiglitz and Andrew Charlton's book *Fair Trade for All* is representative of this tendency.[24] The concept of fairness here involves eliminating the disadvantages that producers from underdeveloped countries have typically encountered when trying to participate in the world trading system. There is also a desire to protect producers who maintain decent working conditions and responsible environmental practices from "unfair" competition from unscrupulous producers within their own countries. More generally, there is a desire to shield fledgling producers from the "sharp practices" that prevail in more advanced market economies, as well as to protect them from some of the effects of price volatility. This is all well and good.

There is another strand in the fair trade movement, however, that is somewhat more dubious. According to this view, consumers in developed nations, being so wealthy, have a moral obligation to pay more than the market rate for goods that are imported from underdeveloped ones. It is then suggested that *rather than giving to charity,* or contributing to "development" programs, people should pay above-market prices for goods that are imported from the underdeveloped world. This idea was popularized through the Body Shop's somewhat sanctimonious "Trade Not Aid" campaign, launched in 1991.

Actually, a lot of people think that what Africa needs is more trade and less aid (including some on the left, like Stiglitz and Charlton, and some on the right, like the Cato Institute). What the Body Shop meant, though, was not trade at "exploitative" market prices, but rather trade at prices that would be "topped up" in the interests of global distributive justice. Call this an eleemosynary pricing policy. What is important to recognize is that this campaign represents a precise inversion of Lerner's recommendation. Rather than leaving the prices alone and redistributing income, "Trade Not Aid"–type campaigns reject income redistribution in favor of price manipulation.

For many people, the concept of eleemosynary pricing is most commonly associated with "fair trade" coffee. While this sort of coffee has been around for a long time, the movement gained considerable momentum during the "coffee crisis" of 2001, when excess supply in world markets led to a catastrophic decline in the wholesale price of coffee beans. Fair trade coffee was promoted, first and foremost, as a solution to the problems caused in impoverished countries by the declining price.[25] Yet, strangely, no one denied that the root of the problem was that far too much coffee was being produced. Oxfam calculated that in 2001 the total world supply of coffee was 115 million (132-pound) bags per year, whereas total demand was in the neighborhood of 105 million bags. The glut was caused not only by an increase in production, but also by a precipitous decline in coffee consumption in the developed world. (Despite what the proliferation of cafés might suggest, annual coffee consumption in the United States had declined from 36 gallons per person in 1970 to only 17 gallons in 2000.)[26] The low price of coffee was thus caused not by market failure, but by the scarcity pricing mechanism functioning exactly as it was supposed to.

The glut also coincided with the growing popularity of premium coffee in the United States, dispensed through chains like Starbucks, which charged about as much for a fancy cup of coffee as many consumers had been accustomed to paying for lunch. For a while, Starbucks thought it could fight the fair trade fad by pointing out that its coffee was expensive because the company was paying its domestic employees above-market wages—in particular, providing them with health care benefits. But ultimately, the optics of charging $3 for a latte while the person who grew the coffee beans received only a penny or two proved impossible to overcome. Starbucks relented—and quickly became the world's largest purveyor of fair trade coffee.

The fair trade literature is full of heartrending tales of coffee producers being shamelessly exploited by landlords, roasters, middlemen, and multinationals. But there are some facts that can't be changed. If the world is producing 10 million bags more coffee than anyone needs or wants, the proper solution is to stop producing so much coffee. (It is important to remember that all the land and labor being used to cultivate coffee beans for nonexistent Western consumers could have been used to produce things that real people actually do need, such as *food.*) Yet because of the "sunk cost" involved in planting the bushes and seeing them to maturity, too many coffee producers were holding out, hoping that others would drop out of the market before they did.

In a classic case of treating the symptoms rather than the disease, Oxfam and other fair trade enthusiasts suggested that Western consumers should respond to the glut by paying producers higher prices for their coffee. This is a tragically inept proposal. Not only is it the wrong thing to do (in the sense that it won't solve the problem), but it's the opposite of the right thing to do (in the sense that it will exacerbate precisely the problem that it is intended to resolve).

Oxfam's very high-profile report on the subject, released in 2002, quoted Pablo Dubois, head of operations of the International Coffee Organization, saying, "The Fair Trade movement has clearly shown that producers can be paid double today's disastrously low prices without affecting the consumer's willingness to buy a good-quality product."[27] This is all well and good, but completely irrelevant. The question is whether producers can be paid twice the market rate for their goods and still be persuaded to cut back on *production*. Something tells me this will be more difficult.

It is to Oxfam's credit, however, that it was forthright in acknowledging the consequences of the policies that it was recommending (unlike many purveyors of fair trade coffee beans) [28] Oxfam recognized that fair trade pricing would do nothing to address the underlying problem, which was the excess supply of coffee. And so the flip side of Oxfam's eleemosynary pricing policy was a commitment to destroying existing stocks of coffee beans. They recommended that "governments and companies" purchase about 5 million bags of coffee (at an estimated cost of $100 million) and destroy them.

Here we can see the consequences of "Trade Not Aid" in their full glory. Rather than simply giving money to poor people and leaving them alone to grow something that someone actually needs, we're going to pay them to grow stuff that we don't even want, then turn around and destroy it. Isn't it nice to be so rich? Next time you buy a cup of fair trade coffee, don't think of the price premium as a surcharge paid to the producer—think of it as your contribution to the cost of destroying surplus coffee beans. I can imagine the marketing pitch now: "Fair Trade: For every pound of coffee you buy, we'll take another pound and throw it in the ocean!"

The Body Shop encountered a very similar problem with the original "Trade Not Aid" campaign (which is one reason the company dropped it shortly thereafter). Part of the initiative involved purchasing shea butter in Africa at above-market rates. The Body Shop agreed to buy 6.3 tons of unrefined shea butter from cooperative producers in 10 villages in northern Ghana. The base price agreed to was £1.25 per kilogram, about 50% higher than the local rate (to account for the fact that the butter had to meet both European health and safety requirements and the company's own quality standards). But the company decided also to add an additional £.79 per kilogram to the price paid, which the harvesters could invest in local schools or development projects of their choice. This was intended to change the trade relationship into one of "empowerment rather than exploitation."[29]

John Stackhouse, traveling in the area some years later, reported on the rather disastrous consequences of this initiative. In a tragic case of life imitating Economics 101, news of the Body Shop's order created a "shea-nut rush" followed by an entirely predictable glut. Farmers stopped growing all sorts of crops in order to get a slice of the shea-nut action: "In the first season, the northern villages, which normally produced about two tonnes of shea butter a year, churned out twenty tonnes, nearly four times what The Body Shop wanted . . . Making matters worse, The Body Shop, after discovering it had overestimated the international market for shea-related products, quickly scaled back its orders for the next season."[30] Offering to pay above-market rates sends the message to producers that "the world needs more shea butter." Unfortunately, the world did *not* need more shea butter, and so most of the extra production stimulated by this price signal simply went to waste.

It's always painful when the left gives right-wing economists reason to say "I told you so," but this seems like a rather clear-cut case. Eleemosynary pricing not only generates a transfer of wealth, but also changes incentives in a way that can have perverse yet entirely foreseeable consequences. In such cases, the overall humanitarian objectives could be much better achieved through lump-sum transfers (such as charitable giving), which certainly have their problems but at least have the advantage of leaving the price mechanism undisturbed.

$ $ $

Even when we can all agree about what the right outcome is, we often find it simply too heart-wrenching or difficult to carry out the actions necessary to bring that outcome about. No one seriously denies that the appropriate level of supply of a particular good or service is determined by the level of demand, or that prices should reflect relative scarcity. If there's too much coffee relative to the amount that people want to drink, then prices must decline and production must be curtailed. And if there's not enough gasoline relative to what people want to consume, then prices must rise and *consumption* must be curtailed. There simply is no other way to organize an economic system, whether it be capitalist or socialist.

As a result, there is a terrible irony in Jack Layton's pronouncement on the subject of gasoline prices. As Lange observed, the best feature of capitalism is that competition forces private firms to act exactly as they would if they were governed directly by the decisions of socialist planners. Historically, however, the way that capitalism simulates socialist planning has been far more successful than any actual socialist system. The primary reason is that "socialist planners" cannot be trusted to make the hard decisions that socialist planners are supposed to make. In part, this is because a true socialist organization of the economy leaves the price system far more open to political interference than the market does. Generally speaking, one of the major reasons for wanting to keep the state out of the economy as much as possible is that politicians can't resist dabbling around in it, in ways that are extremely detrimental in the aggregate or in the long term. This is why, even in the case of government monopolies, such as the central bank, a strict separation must be imposed between politicians and managers.

In other words, the fact that politicians insist upon behaving the way that Layton was behaving in calling for lower gasoline prices is one of the primary arguments for keeping the state out of the economy. Layton was unknowingly exhibiting the behavioral tendency that has served as the primary impediment to the development of a feasible socialist organization of the economy. To put the same point more polemically: It's because of people like him that socialism doesn't work.

CHAPTER 8

THE "PSYCHOPATHIC" PURSUIT OF PROFIT

Why making money is not so bad after all

Here's a question that some of the bright minds at the University of Chicago have been pondering of late: Why are there no for-profit charities?[1] Actually, the answer to that question is a bit too obvious, since tax law basically forces charitable organizations to incorporate as nonprofits (not only so that the organization can avoid paying a variety of corporate taxes, but so that individuals can claim deductions for their gifts). Thus the more precise question is, why do we force charities to be nonprofit organizations? Why not permit *for-profit* charities? What if some entrepreneur came along, looked at the administrative overhead ratios of existing charities, and promised that his for-profit charity could deliver the same level of assistance more efficiently? Suppose he offered a money-back guarantee, promising he could get 10% more of any given donation into the hands of the intended beneficiary than any other leading charitable organization? The only catch would be that once this 10% guarantee was met, any extra money would go to the owners of the charity in the form of profit.

If the purpose of the charitable donation is to benefit the needy, wouldn't this arrangement be an attractive one for many donors? Why get hung up on the organizational form of the institution that delivers the benefit? Of course, it would be *better* if the money that went to the owners, in the form of profit, went to the needy instead. But if the insertion of a profit motive is able to supply superior incentives, such that for-profit charities *as a matter of fact* deliver a higher level of benefit than nonprofit charities, then this is nothing but an abstract hypothetical. If our real-world choice is between inefficient nonprofits and efficient for-profits, why should we shun the latter, or begrudge those who are able to deliver this superior performance their slice of the pie?

Yet of course people do get hung up on questions of organizational form. It seems obvious that—with the possible exception of a few economists[2]—few people would give money to a for-profit charity. There's just something about the idea of making a profit from helping the needy that seems wrong. Oskar Schindler spent himself into bankruptcy during the Second World War in order to protect the Jewish workers at his factories from extermination by the Nazi regime. History might not have looked so kindly upon him had he chosen to save 200 fewer in order to maintain a reasonable rate of profit. It would be something of a paltry defense to say that, while he may have saved only 900 instead of a possible 1,100, he nevertheless saved more than any *other* German industrialist, and so we should not begrudge him his reasonable reward.

As this example shows, the tendency to regard profit as a source of moral pollution is in some cases perfectly legitimate. Some people, however, suffer from a rather hypertrophied version of this intuition. They think that any sort of profit is indefensible, and so the capitalist system as a whole is morally prohibited *ab initio* (that is, from the get-go). A more common view holds that it is immoral to make a profit from any transaction that can be plausibly described as satisfying a human "need." This gives rise to the popular "communitarian" theory of the welfare state, according to which the central rationale for public provision of certain goods and services is not that the private sector fails to provide them, but that it would be morally odious for the private sector to do so. (For example, people argue against the privatization of water services, not on the obvious grounds that distribution is a natural monopoly, but on the dubious grounds that water is "essential to life." It is never really explained why water in pipes possesses this sacred quality, such that it must be delivered by government, while water in bottles does not.)[3]

Joel Bakan's book (and film) *The Corporation* (subtitled *The Pathological Pursuit of Profit and Power*) represents a particularly clear expression of this tendency. Bakan argues that the corporation is essentially an institutional construct "designed to valorize self-interest and invalidate moral concern."[4] These are characteristics that, were they to be found in a person, would lead to diagnosis of psychopathology. Since "the corporation, like the psychopathic personality it resembles, is programmed to exploit others for a profit," we are best advised to keep it out of sensitive areas.[5] This explains the rise of the welfare state: "Essential public interests, and social domains believed to be too precious, vulnerable, or morally sacred to subject to corporate exploitation, were inscribed by law and public policy within protective boundaries . . . Institutions essential to human health and survival (such as water utilities and health and welfare services), human progress and development (such as schools, universities, and cultural institutions), and public safety (such as police, courts, prisons, and firefighters) were deliberately placed beyond the corporation's exploitative grasp."[6]

The sentiment here may be right, but the economic analysis is completely wrong. Unfortunately, it's an analysis that is actually used, in many cases, to guide public policy.[7] It is, therefore, worth putting the moralizing tone on ice for a bit in order to analyze more carefully the evils that are supposedly perpetrated in the name of profit.

$ $ $

There are two very widespread errors that need to be set aside before even considering the role that profit plays in the capitalist economy. The first involves a straightforward confusion of "profit" with "self-interest." Bakan confuses them systematically. A standard business corporation does indeed try to produce "profits." Yet maximizing profit seldom coincides with the self-interest of any particular individual working for the firm, even its top managers. The profits in question take the form of dividends paid out to shareholders. The separation of ownership and control in a large firm, however, means that these shareholders typically have no involvement in the day-to-day operations of the firm, while the managers who actually run things seldom have a meaningful ownership stake.[8] Despite all the hype about "performance pay," large corporations face enormous difficulties imposing adequate discipline upon managers. Stock options, for instance, which were touted as a magic bullet for getting managers to act and think like owners, in many cases had the opposite effect—they simply created new opportunities for the exploitation of shareholders by management.

In this context, it is important to note that the wave of "ethics scandals" that hit the corporate world in the early twenty-first century (misleadingly described, since it was actually a crime spree) all involved the betrayal of shareholders by management. The problem at Enron, for instance, was not that the firm engaged in "dubious, though highly profitable, practices," as Bakan claims.[9] The problem is that there *were no profits*. The "dubious practices" at Enron, which eventually led to its collapse, all involved ways of concealing this fact from investors so that they would keep pouring in the money (and so that banks would keep lending). At the time of its bankruptcy, Enron had almost $38 billion in debt yet only $13 billion showing on its books. (This is why the case remains so fascinating to so many people. Unlike the other scandals, which involved fairly pedestrian acts of theft and concealment, Enron was much more like a pyramid scheme, but pulled off in broad daylight, right in the teeth of a supposedly sophisticated investment community.)

Gordon Gekko's famous "Greed is good" speech, which is often mentioned in the same breath as Adam Smith's "invisible hand," is widely misunderstood in this regard. It is not actually a paean to the virtues of the free market. It's about firing greedy, parasitical managers. Gekko's argument was simply that his own greed had a more useful social dimension than that of management. The central problem in many large, publicly traded corporations is that ownership becomes extremely diffuse. This creates a collective action problem among shareholders: Since each one owns such a small stake in the firm, and since participating actively in governance involves large fixed costs, nobody has much of an incentive to mind the shop. As a result, managers can get away with all sorts of things, ranging from excessive pay packages to outright graft (none of which, it should be noted, maximizes the profits of the firm). In the movie *Wall Street*, Gekko is a corporate raider whose central service to humanity consists of buying up companies (thereby consolidating ownership) and firing their unproductive managers. Ironically, the takeover craze of the '80s faded in part because of the realization by many corporate raiders that their actions were somewhat too altruistic. Tender offers typically generated a substantial return for the old shareholders, combined with highly uncertain returns for the new owners, and then only in the long term.[10] Furthermore, raiders were often no more successful at installing good managers than their predecessors had been.

It is because of the difficulties that owners experience trying to control management that the law explicitly imposes a *moral* obligation upon senior managers to advance the interests of the firm. It does so by imposing a fiduciary duty upon them (similar to the duties imposed upon doctors toward their patients, or lawyers toward their clients).

This fiduciary duty includes both an open-ended "duty of loyalty" and a "duty of care," and these place serious restrictions on the way managers must conduct themselves in both their professional role and their personal capacity.[11] The reason these sorts of obligations are necessary is that managers in the private sector are not directly exposed to the "sharp" incentives of the market. They are insulated by several different layers (such as the board of directors), both from the market and from the owners of the firm (which is how they are able to draw gigantic salaries that are largely unrelated to performance).[12] As a result—since they have all sorts of ways of circumventing or undermining direct control—it can be difficult to get them to do what they're told.

In this respect, private-sector managers are not all that different from managers in the public sector. They act from a combination of motives, sometimes pursuing their own interests, sometimes doing as they're told. Because of this, it is highly misleading to think of private corporations as acting out of "self-interest" and state-owned enterprises as acting "altruistically." Self-interest and altruism are not the issue, since all managers act out of a combination of self-interested and altruistic motives (or, more specifically, out of some combination of internal factors, such as loyalty to the organization, and extrinsic incentives, such as performance pay, opportunities for promotion, and so on). Maximizing profit, for the manager of a private firm, is typically an altruistic act, since the benefit flows almost entirely to other people. It is terribly misleading, therefore, to confuse organizational objectives with the sort of incentives that *individuals* have when they act, and to judge them morally on that basis.

The second major error lies in the widespread impression that "society" gives corporations carte blanche to go out and maximize profits. In fact, society allows corporations to act in a profit-maximizing fashion only in cases where a *competitive* market can be organized. Where a competitive market cannot be organized, government regulation explicitly prohibits firms from maximizing profits, almost without exception.

This is why private companies that enjoy a natural monopoly—such as electricity distribution or cable television—have to ask the government for permission every time they want to raise their prices. The reason firms are encouraged to maximize profit in a competitive market is that when multiple firms are competing with one another, the attempt to maximize profit generates among firms a collective action problem that pushes the level of profit down to zero.[13]

In other words, to claim that society requires corporations to maximize profits is like saying that society encourages hockey players to commit common assault. There is an element of truth to it, insofar as society does encourage hockey players to run into one another at high speeds, to threaten one another, and occasionally to punch each other in the face. But it needs to be mentioned that this sort of behavior is encouraged *only in the context of a hockey game.* We don't let hockey players act this way in the mall, or with their families. Similarly, we encourage corporations to maximize profits only in one, very particular context: that of the competitive market, which is a very carefully staged competition. And just as physical contact is not the objective of the hockey game, merely the means employed, so too the maximization of profit is not the objective of the market economy. The proof of the latter claim lies in the observation that, in the ideal world of the perfectly competitive market, *there are no profits.*

This is the biggest problem with *The Corporation*'s indictment of the modern business enterprise. One might think that with all the fuss that's been made over the years about the "invisible hand," Bakan would at least deign to *mention* that the pursuit of profit on the part of corporations is subject to the constraint of competition. We don't allow monopolies to maximize profits, and we don't allow corporations to form cartels. Of course, many people on the left pooh-pooh the idea that firms actually compete with one another (often striking a note of world-weary cynicism). John Kenneth Galbraith gave a stamp of approval to this line of thinking, arguing that firms would stop competing with one another on price just as soon as they realized that it

was not in their collective interest to do so.[14] He thereby underestimated the seriousness of the collective action problem that is imposed
upon corporations by the market. Whenever firms collude to raise
prices, demand declines, which means that the market will not clear.
This results, in practice, in two things: first, there will be a reservoir of
customers willing to pay good money for the product, at a price where
it would still be profitable to sell to them; and second, some firms will
have excess inventory just sitting around, or will have unused productive capacity. In this context, the temptation to "cheat" the cartel and
sell to this reservoir of customers on the side at a lower price will often
be overwhelming. But of course, this is a classic free rider strategy—it
generates profits for the firm that is doing it, but only by lowering the
profitability of the industry as a whole. If everyone acts this way, then
the cartel falls apart and profits are bid down to zero.

This is why the competitive market, as beatified by economists, is often described in the business world as "commodity hell."[15]
A *commodity,* in this sense of the term, is a good that is extremely
homogeneous, such as wheat, milk, or coal. As a result of this lack
of differentiation, the only real way for producers to compete is on
price, which then eats away all profits. According to *Fortune* magazine, "In commodity hell, everyone looks the same. Your products
look the same, your margins look the same, and—wait a minute,
where did those margins go?"[16] Corporations respond to this threat
by trying to differentiate their products from those of their competitors, through quality and innovation or, when that fails, through the
appearance of quality and innovation (the latter strategy is known as
"branding"). The goal is to avoid having to compete head-to-head on
price. The important point, however, is that the drive toward product
differentiation would not be so great if the collective action problem
underlying price competition were not so severe, and so effective at
driving profits down to zero.

It is worth noting, by the way, that just because corporations
try to avoid commodity hell does not mean that they succeed. For

example, despite enormous efforts on the part of oil companies, no one has ever really succeeded in branding gasoline. PetroCanada may spend millions trying to convince Canadians that they need to buy specially blended "winter gas," but the fact remains that if a Shell or Esso station across the street is selling gas for even a penny less per liter, no one will be filling up with "winter gas." Most consumers remain resolutely unconvinced that there are any significant differences in quality between the major providers. Of course, after filling up with cheap gas, they may blow their savings inside by buying a bottle of Dasani or Aquafina water, which for some inexplicable reason they are willing to pay three times more than gasoline for even though it's nothing but glorified tap water. (One might pause for a moment to savor the thought of marketing managers at the oil companies being driven mad by this phenomenon.) The fact that all companies tend to charge the same price for gas, whereas the price of bottled water varies enormously from brand to brand, is a reflection of the fact that the market for gasoline is one of the inner circles of "commodity hell."

$ $ $

The other major source of unproductive ambiguity in the debate over the moral status of profit is a confusion between "making money" and "making a profit." American juries sometimes award eye-poppingly large compensation packages in civil suits filed against corporations, on the grounds that these companies make so much money, they can afford it. But of course, the fact that companies earn large amounts of revenue doesn't mean that the money is just sitting around, waiting to be confiscated. Most revenue that is earned is used to cover costs, such as paying employees, purchasing materials, servicing loans, and paying rent. What we call "profit" is the residual—the amount that is left over after all the firm's contractual obligations have been met.

Thus it is somewhat odd to say that "corporations exist solely to maximize returns to their shareholders,"[17] or that profit is their sole objective. Naturally, a standard business corporation aspires to make a profit. But it also aspires to stay in business, which means making payroll, retaining customers, paying suppliers, covering the interest on its bank loans, and meeting a host of other contractual obligations, all of which must be satisfied in order for the firm to avoid bankruptcy. Paying out profits to shareholders is actually the most expendable item on the list, and the one area where the firm can default without legal consequence. Microsoft, for instance, paid no dividends at all to shareholders between 1986 and 2004—so obviously its predatory behavior (including significant violations of law in both the United States and Europe) cannot be blamed upon a thirst for profits. (One of the most elementary errors that people on the left make is to take some type of obnoxious corporate behavior and blame it on the profit motive without checking to see if the firm actually pays out any profit to its investors.)

Generally speaking, every corporation brings together four different classes of individuals, distinguished from one another by the contribution that they make to the operations of the firm. Every firm purchases certain "inputs," or raw materials, which it then transforms in such a way as to provide an "output," or good. Thus we have *suppliers* on the one side, who provide the inputs, and *customers* on the other, who purchase the outputs. A firm also has certain fixed expenses, such as the building in which it operates, the computers or equipment that its employees use, and so on. This is traditionally referred to as "capital," which is supplied by *lenders*. And finally there are the *workers*—those who contribute the labor that makes it all happen. One very useful way of thinking of the firm is therefore as a nexus of contracts between the individuals who supply these four different types of input (as in Figure 8.1). This reflects the fact that the firm typically has contracts with all these constituencies, which specify in some detail exactly what each group will provide and what the firm will owe in return.

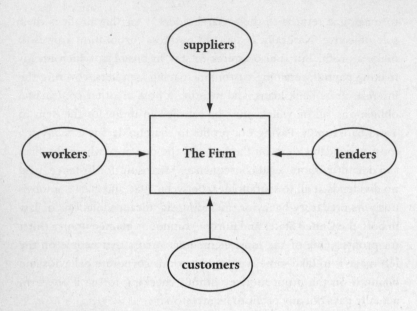

Figure 8.1 The firm as nexus of contracts

The question of who "owns" the firm is actually not as straight-forward as one might think, since many of the rights that we normally associate with private property are absent in the case of corporations. The fact that I own several shares in my local bank does not give me any entitlement to access their premises, use their computers, or tell their managers what to do. Indeed, the only reason shareholders of the bank are regarded as owners is that they are the residual claimants and that they exercise formal control over the organization, through their power to elect members to its board of directors. It is useful to compare this relation with other types of property, such as home ownership. People with large mortgages often joke about how "the bank" owns their house. Strictly speaking, though, this is not true. The difference between the credit extended by the bank and the homeowner's equity is that the latter confers a *residual claim*. The bank and the homeowner have put their money together and made an investment. The value of the home may go up, or it may go down. But the bank has advanced its capital on fixed terms. On the one hand, this means that the bank is owed repayment even if the value of the home declines (and if things go sour, so that the house needs to be sold, the bank will be first in line to be repaid). On the other hand, it means that the bank gets no more than the fixed rate of return, even if the house skyrockets in value. After the loan is repaid, any gains or losses constitute the residuum, which goes to the individual with the equity stake, that is, the "owner." Naturally, since the owner is bearing all the risk, it is natural that the owner will also want to exercise control over the asset and look after its day-to-day upkeep.

In principle, there is no reason that the firm needs to have any "owners," in this sense of the term, since all of the necessary inputs can be acquired through market contracting, and residual earnings can simply be reinvested. This, combined with a self-perpetuating board of directors, is in fact how nonprofit organizations function. In the more standard run of cases, however, ownership is assumed by one of the firm's constituency groups. But again, there is no reason that those who supply capital (such as shareholders) need be that group. Although the majority of corporations are owned in this way, the law typically permits any one of the four constituency groups to take control. When workers, suppliers, or customers own the firm, it is usually referred to as a *cooperative*. A surprising number of the firms that we deal with in day-to-day life are in fact cooperatives, although most of us don't realize it. Both Visa and MasterCard, for instance, are supply cooperatives (owned by the lending agencies who supply the credit). True Value Hardware is also a supply cooperative. Many farmers are organized into cooperatives, such as the Saskatchewan Wheat Pool before 1994, or various well-known dairy cooperatives, such as Land O'Lakes. Customer-owned firms are common in the agricultural sector, while somewhat less common in the retail sector (with outdoor equipment retailers REI and MEC—Mountain Equipment Co-op—being noteworthy exceptions, not to mention the ubiquitous organic and bulk food co-ops). It's worth remembering as well that every condominium is essentially a consumer-owned corporation, as are standard "mutual" insurance firms. Finally, many taxi companies and travel agencies are worker cooperatives, as is the standard law firm.

The key to understanding the shareholder-owned corporation is to see that it is no different in principle from any of these other cooperative arrangements. As the Yale law professor Henry Hansmann has observed, the standard business corporation is essentially a "lenders' co-op."[18] Hansmann explains this through an extremely helpful comparison between a dairy cooperative and a shareholder-owner firm. Many dairy cooperatives own factories, which take in milk as the primary input and produce butter, cheese, or yogurt to sell to customers. A typical farmer-owned cooperative will purchase milk from its members at a fixed price that is well below the market rate, in order to ensure that the firm stays in the black. At the end of the year, all "positive net earnings" (that is, profits) will be paid out to the suppliers in the form of a dividend, proportional to the amount of milk that each one has supplied to the firm. Similarly, control of the board of directors is often exercised through voting rights that are based upon the amount of milk contributed. Thus "ownership rights are held by virtue of, and proportional to, one's sale of milk to the firm."[19] If the firm needs to raise capital, it can simply go to the bank and obtain it on a contractual terms. (The firm also has the option of buying milk on the side, under contract, from farmers who are not members and who are awarded no rights of control.)

Now consider how a standard business corporation works. Anyone who buys new shares in a corporation is essentially lending money to the firm. And like the dairy farmers selling milk to the cooperative at below-market rates, the amount that shareholders "charge" the firm for this loan is below the market rate—in fact, the interest rate is zero. This makes it easier for the company to stay in the black. At the end of the year, all "positive net earnings" (the profits) will be paid out to these lenders in the form of a dividend, proportional to the number of shares owned. Shareholders also exercise control of the board of directors, through voting rights that are proportional to the amount of money supplied to the firm. In other words, the corporation functions in almost exactly the same way as the dairy cooperative, except that it treats money rather than milk as the currency that confers ownership rights. Similarly, the firm is free to secure additional money through contractual relations, which is why companies are typically financed through both equity (money owed to owner-lenders) and debt (money owed to contract-lenders).

This analysis makes it clear just how misleading it is to say that the standard business corporation is interested only in making profits. In order to remain viable, the firm needs to satisfy its obligations to *all* its constituency groups, and obligations toward residual claimants are, by definition, last on the list. Creditors can force a firm into bankruptcy if they are not paid, while shareholders cannot. In certain respects, shareholders are completely expendable. If you think of "capitalists" as the people who contribute capital, then one can quite easily conceive of a market economy in which capitalists don't actually own the means of production. Every firm in the economy could be organized as a worker, supplier, or consumer cooperative. The stock market could be closed down, leaving lenders with no option but to deposit their money in banks, which would then make these funds available to the various cooperatives on strictly contractual terms. One would then have capitalism without the capitalists—and all this could be done without significantly changing the existing body of law. There are, however, various reasons why this would not be a good idea. To see why, we need only look at our own economy, and how the shareholder-owner, equity-financed business corporation remains the most popular way of organizing production.

§ § §

Here's a question that causes proponents of worker co-ops some measure of discomfort: Given that there are no legal barriers to the creation of workers' cooperatives, and that they enjoy massive tax advantages in many jurisdictions, why are there not more of them? Furthermore, why are supplier and consumer cooperatives not more common? In Canada and the United States, standard business corporations pay a "profit" tax on all net earnings *prior* to paying out dividends to shareholders. With cooperatives, on the other hand, dividends are paid out of pretax earnings—in other words, payment to the owners (the "members") counts as an expense, not an element of profit. This allows cooperatives the discretion to reduce their profit to zero every year and never pay any tax. Their earnings are taxed only once, as personal income in the hands of the owners. Profits going to shareholders, on the other hand, are singled out for double taxation—once in the hands of the corporation, and again as income in the hands of the owners. Given that this is the case, why do people still find it advantageous to organize companies as shareholder-owned firms? Why don't corporations all convert to cooperatives (which shareholders could then lend money to, using the tax saving as a source of higher returns)?

This is an interesting question—and, needless to say, also the subject of considerable debate. It is certainly the case that, in some respects, the existing institutions of capitalism stack the deck against cooperatives. Banks, for example, are not especially forthcoming when it comes to lending money to cooperatives. They often look at debt-to-equity ratios as a way of judging the riskiness of a loan, so firms with no equity have difficulty persuading banks to lend to them. Firms that raise money from shareholders also have assets that can be used as collateral for a loan. Because of the prohibition on slavery contracts, however, workers are unable to put their "human capital" up as collateral. Perhaps for this reason, worker cooperatives are far more common in non-capital-intensive sectors of the economy. Law firms and travel agencies, for example, require very little in the way of material assets. Other industries have much higher levels of "capital intensity." Consider the case of utilities, which in Canada have over $3 million in fixed assets per worker, or mining and petroleum extraction, with $1.8 million per worker.[20] In these cases, one could not expect the workers to collectively "own" these assets, nor is it easy to imagine circumstances under which they could obtain them on credit.

There is, however, one very striking feature that successful cooperatives all share. As Hansmann observes, cooperatives are most successful when the type of "input" provided by the owners is extremely homogeneous.[21] Supply cooperatives are most successful when the input is a single commodity, such as milk. Condominiums—which are consumer cooperatives—are most successful when tenants occupy similar units and share similar lifestyles. Worker cooperatives are most successful when there is a single class of workers, each doing approximately the same job. Problems arise, on the other hand, when different people start providing different goods or services to the firm, simply because this creates divisions within the class of owners. If a dairy cooperative takes both milk and eggs as input, it immediately politicizes a whole range of questions, creating controversies and factions where previously none existed. How much of the advertising budget should be used to promote butter? Should new investments be made to enhance the productivity of the cheese operation? How many quarts of milk is equivalent to a dozen eggs when it comes to dividing up revenue or assigning voting rights? In a milk-only cooperative, people may disagree over all sorts of questions, but it reflects mere differences of opinion—there is no underlying conflict of interest. A farmer who supplies only eggs, however, has very different interests from one who supplies only milk. (As a result, many cooperatives prefer to purchase "extra" inputs on contractual terms, rather than expanding the class of owners.)

Exactly the same situation prevails in worker cooperatives. When everyone is doing the same job and has approximately the same level of skill, it is relatively easy to decide how compensation is to be arranged. Since everyone is contributing roughly the same thing to the firm, responsibilities and entitlements can be divided up in a fairly mechanical way. Even then, it's hardly trivial: Should everyone earn the same income, or should the firm recognize seniority or superior productivity? Should the firm increase wages, or put the money into the pension fund, or invest in new equipment? Conflicts between younger and older workers often represent the major fault line. But when people start doing different jobs, things become even more complicated, and more serious conflicts can arise. Not only is it difficult to compare what people are contributing, but everyone has a natural tendency to think that their own job is more important than anyone else's. Thus all the broader social conflicts that go on about wages—skilled vs. unskilled, white-collar vs. blue-collar, dangerous vs. safe—get reproduced within the firm, as debates between the firm's many owners. One starts to see "politics"—in the pejorative sense of the word—within the firm. This not only has direct costs, in the form of time and energy spent fighting, it also creates the potential for collective action problems among the owners, as a result of the partiality of individual interests.

The experience of United Airlines, which has to date been the largest employee-owned corporation in North America, provides a cautionary example. In 1994, facing bankruptcy, United shareholders agreed to give employees 55% ownership of the firm, in return for $4.88 billion in wage concessions. Yet very little changed at the firm, and in 2002 United finally filed for bankruptcy protection. The problem was that, with over 85,000 employees, there was little change in the incentives that each employee faced with respect to work effort, or in employees' attitudes toward the firm. Part of this was due to the fact that the pilots, mechanics, and ground crew remained members of three separate unions, each of which continued to bargain aggressively with the firm for wage increases. In particular, the mechanics' union resisted, until it was too late, wage cuts that would have allowed the firm to stave off bankruptcy. Many members proudly adopted the slogan "Full Pay to the Last Day!" In other words, the mechanics' union used the threat of driving the firm into bankruptcy as a strategy for pressuring the other two employee unions into wage concessions. The potential for collective action problems here is obvious.

This sort of infighting is one of the direct costs of employee ownership. There is also an indirect cost associated with having an internally heterogeneous ownership group. Every sufficiently large organization develops a separation of ownership and control, and so needs the services of professional managers. Worker cooperatives, in particular, often choose to hire managers on contractual terms, rather than bringing them in as worker-owners, precisely because they want to avoid troublesome internal hierarchies within the class of owners. Yet once managers are brought in, the problem of controlling these managers—ensuring that they actually serve the interests of owners, rather than just their own—begins to loom large. This in turn creates "agency costs," which are either losses that occur as a result of malfeasance by the agent (in this case the manager) or else additional costs incurred as a result of the need to engage in costly supervision. Every firm has agency costs, but internal conflict among the owners has the potential to exacerbate those costs quite dramatically.

Our natural tendency is to think that, in a bureaucracy, people are simply told what to do, and that they then go out and do it. We are particularly inclined toward this view when we think about cooperatives or government, where we expect more public-spiritedness on the part of employees. Unfortunately, this optimism is not really borne out by the evidence. All large organizations succeed, to varying degrees, in motivating loyalty on the part of their workers, but this means that they also all *fail* to varying degrees. Simply ordering managers to act in the interests of workers or customers or, as we have seen, shareholders is almost never entirely effective. This is also true in the case of government, when civil servants are ordered to act in the interests of "the public." Just telling them to do so does not guarantee that they will actually do so. It is always necessary to have some incentive system in place as well. (As we've seen, incentives aren't everything, but they're not nothing either.)

The problem with organizations that are owned by multiple interest groups (or "principals") is that they are often less effective at imposing discipline upon managers, and so suffer from higher agency costs. In particular, managers perform best when given a single task, along with a single criterion for the measurement of success. Anything more complicated makes accountability extremely difficult. A manager told to achieve several conflicting objectives can easily explain away the failure to meet one as a consequence of having pursued some other. This makes it impossible for the principals to lay down any unambiguous performance criteria for the evaluation of management, which in turn leads to very serious agency problems. As long as the manager is determining how the various objectives should be balanced, assigning managers multiple objectives is in many respects equivalent to giving them a "get out of jail free" card—an automatic ticket to escape accountability for their own professional failings. These difficulties are compounded by the fact that internal conflicts among the owners creates the opportunity for managers themselves to "play politics," pitting one group against the other, in order to evade responsibility.

Of course, if every firm in the economy required only milk as input, a society of supply cooperatives might be feasible. The same is true if labor inputs were all roughly the same, or if consumers had approximately the same needs. Unfortunately, most firms require a very complicated mix of inputs and labor types. Yet there is one input that stands out as being extremely homogeneous, in exactly the right way—money. With money, it is extremely easy to say how much each person has put in and how much each one is taking out. Investors then all tend to have the same interests when it comes to the behavior of the firm. There are, of course, many small differences between investors. Some are traders, looking to make a quick profit, while others are in it for the long haul. Some are looking for growth, others want dividends. Some are even "ethical" investors, willing to sacrifice a certain measure of profit in return for assurances that it was earned in a respectable manner. And indeed, all of these divisions can serve as a source of agency costs. (In fact, the willingness of many investors simply to sell a stock rather than get involved in governance issues is one of the tendencies that managers have been able to exploit for personal gain.) Nevertheless, it is difficult for managers to play "divide and conquer" with respect to shareholders, simply because there are no obvious points of division.[22] And even in cases where they don't have a perfectly united front, the divisions among shareholders pale compared to the differences within other constituency groups. This means that the agency costs associated with shareholder ownership—even though they can become quite massive, as the corporate scandals of the "Enron era" show—tend to be low relative to any other organizational form. (File that away under "sad but true.")

What does this mean in practice? Quite simply, it means that internal fighting within a cooperative often becomes so corrosive, or the place becomes so badly run, that it becomes in *everyone's interest* to hand ownership over to a group of relative outsiders, who will be able to make business decisions in a more impartial manner and to impose them more effectively. That group is the shareholders. Don't believe it? Well, the proof is in the pudding. Go out and start a worker's cooperative—see if you can do better than everyone else who's tried. After all, *no one's stopping you.* You'll even get a big tax break from the government.

§ § §

In the decades immediately following the Second World War, many firms in Western Europe were either nationalized or created under state ownership, not because of natural monopoly or market failure in the private sector, but out of a desire on the part of governments to have these enterprises serve the broader public interest. In Canada, similarly, the government at various times owned an airline, a railroad, and an oil company, not to mention numerous mining operations. The government was also (and, in some cases, continues to be) involved in shipbuilding, aerospace, forestry, oil and gas exploration, nuclear-reactor building, agricultural land ownership, interurban bus service, and automobile insurance. These state-owned enterprises competed directly against privately owned firms, either domestically or in international markets. The reason that the state was involved in these sectors followed primarily from the thought that, while privately owned firms pursued strictly private interests, public ownership would be able to ensure that these enterprises served the public interest. Thus managers in these firms were instructed not just to provide a reasonable return on the capital invested, but to pursue other, "social" objectives, such as maintaining employment or promoting regional development. Of course, this story played out not only in Canada but in just about every industrial democracy in the twentieth century—in many cases to an even greater extent.

But something strange happened on the road to democratic socialism. Not only did many of these corporations fail to promote the public interest in any meaningful way, many of them did a worse job than regulated firms in the private sector. In France, state oil companies freely speculated against the national currency, refused to suspend deliveries to foreign customers in times of shortage, and engaged in predatory pricing policies toward domestic customers.[23] In the United States, state-owned firms have been among the most vociferous opponents of enhanced pollution controls, and state-owned nuclear reactors are among the least safe.[24] Of course, these are rather dramatic examples. The more common problem was simply that these companies lost staggering amounts of money.[25] The losses were enough, in several cases, to push states like France to the brink of insolvency, and to prompt currency devaluations. The reason that so much money was lost has a lot to do with a lack of accountability.[26]

We tend to think of these problems as the primary rationale for the privatization of many state-owned enterprises during the neoconservative backlash of the '80s. But this is incorrect. The "public interest" mandate of state-owned enterprises was abandoned by socialist, liberal, and conservative governments alike long before that wave of privatization. The heady days of the '60s, when public enterprises were encouraged to pursue all sorts of social objectives, were followed by a long period of "commercialization," primarily during the '70s, in which those same enterprises were instructed to abandon or curtail these activities and to restructure their operations in accordance with more traditional business principles.[27] In fact, the managers of public firms in competitive industries were often instructed simply to maximize profits. In Canada, for instance, a 1974 government directive instructed the Canadian National Railroad to be profitable, and a new director was appointed with an explicit mandate to implement the necessary changes.[28] In 1978, the Air Canada Act instructed the airline (with somewhat comical understatement) to run its operation with "due regard to sound business principles and, in particular, the contemplation of profit."[29] Both these decisions were made by the left of-center Liberal government of Pierre Trudeau, long before there was any discussion of privatization.

Similar stories unfolded in France and Spain, where socialist parties imposed "commercializing" reforms upon the state sector. In fact, one of the reasons that it was so easy for subsequent right-wing governments to privatize state firms is that in most countries those firms had already been restructured in such a way that their behavior was no different from that of private enterprises. In cases where state-owned enterprises operated in competitive sectors, commercialization relieved them of their social-responsibility mandate, and thus eliminated the primary reason for holding them in the public sector. Even now, competitive firms that have remained in the public sector usually behave no differently than privately owned firms. As Joseph Stiglitz has observed, by 1994 there was essentially no difference in the behavior of Texaco (private), Petrofina (public), and BP (mixed).[30]

The most widely accepted explanation for this extraordinarily perverse outcome is that, during the heyday of public-sector ownership, government simply lost control of the managers of these companies— or else never had it to begin with. There was no way to evaluate managerial performance, and so no way to supply appropriate incentives. As a 1967 government report on public enterprises in France put it, "Unless we can clearly distinguish the potential for profit specific to a particular economic activity from the costs imposed by the public interest constraints, there are no standards for these enterprises: no criteria of good management, no incentive to improve management, and no penalty for bad management."[31]

This is what gave rise to one of the major sources of disillusionment of the twentieth century. Public enterprises, run by managers who were officially committed to the public interest, often did a worse job of promoting the public interest than private enterprises, run by managers who disavowed any concern for the public good. Yet when looked at from an agency cost perspective, this is perhaps not so surprising. As Charles Lindblom has observed, the mere fact that public-sector managers are committed to pursuing the public *interest* does not entail any promise of public *control*.[32] In particular, it does not prevent managers from defining the public interest in a way that is contrary to the wishes of the public. Ironically, public control is often easier to exercise over private, profit-oriented firms, simply because these organizations respond to a single, easy-to-manipulate incentive.[33] If you want private corporations to reduce pollution, make them pay for their discharges. But how do you get state-owned enterprises to reduce pollution? Write a memo to the managers? What happens if they say no? Should you fire them? Most are already doing you a favor by agreeing to work at public-sector salaries when they could be earning several times more in the private sector. Furthermore, what do you do when someone from Finance or the Treasury calls to complain about the effects on government revenue of the new pollution-abatement measures, or an elected representative calls to complain about the layoffs that have just been announced in her jurisdiction? And what are the chances that your own managers are the ones behind these complaints, having leaked the relevant information to the interested parties?

People sometimes talk as through corporations control everything. This is truthy, but not actually true. Corporations do have a lamentable tendency to ignore laws that inconvenience them, but then so do people. On the other hand, when governments succeed in getting the incentives to stick, corporations respond in highly predictable ways, which in turn makes them easy to manipulate. Thinking that profit is the root of all evil and that society could be improved by persuading corporations to take a more active interest in the public good ignores the extent to which we, as a society, already succeed in coaxing social benefits out of privately owned enterprises. And we are able to do that precisely because the state has such a high level of control over them—both indirect, through the creation of competitive markets, and direct, through regulation and taxation. As Lindblom observes, "Seals are easily trained because they have an appetite for fish."[34] Corporations are also relatively easy to control, because they have an appetite for money. To extend the metaphor, trying to get corporations to care about the public interest, rather than simply maximizing profit, is like trying to persuade the seal that he should love jumping through hoops, rather than eating fish. It's much easier just to give him a fish whenever he succeeds in jumping through the hoop.

There are two major reasons that people get hung up on the issue of profit. The first is that they equate profit with self-interest, and so assume that nonprofit organizations, such as the government, are somehow more likely to behave altruistically. The true story is a lot more complicated.

The second is that they fail to see that standard business corporations are just a special type of cooperative, and that all cooperatives serve the interests of their owners. If the owners are the customers (as in the case of a consumer cooperative), then the organization tries to get them a better deal on the merchandise they consume. If it is a workers' cooperative, then the organization tries to give the workers a better deal on their terms of employment. And if it is a lenders' cooperative, the organization tries to get those lenders a better deal on the loans that they have made. In each case, management works for only one of the firm's four constituency groups. Thus there is no morally relevant difference in the character of these organization—not such that the shareholder-owned firm deserves to be called "psychopathic."

CHAPTER 9

CAPITALISM IS DOOMED

*Why "the system" is unlikely to collapse
(despite appearances to the contrary)*

One of the most cherished bits of wishful thinking on the part of the radical left has always been the thought that it might not be necessary to go out and overthrow the system—the system might do us all a favor and collapse of its own accord. Karl Marx obviously did a lot to encourage this view, with his claim that capitalism contained "inherent contradictions" that would someday reach fruition and usher in an era of revolutionary transformation.

The high-water mark of this sort of optimism in the West was no doubt reached during the Great Depression, when over 25% of the workforce in the United States and Canada was unemployed, and GDP shrank by over 35% in a period of just five years (1929–1933). In my home province of Saskatchewan, two-thirds of the population became dependent upon food aid. (When I was young, I can recall, some older people had no qualms about eating grasshoppers, this having been a normal part of their diet during the Depression years.)

During the '30s, it was extremely difficult to convince anyone that capitalism was viable in the long term as an economic system: Plain facts seemed to contradict that very assessment. Furthermore, the way the Depression ended (the Second World War) didn't do much to bolster anyone's confidence.

By the end of the twentieth century, it was starting to look as though the problem had been licked. People were getting used to the idea that capitalism might be here to stay. With the subprime mortgage crisis in the United States, however, and the contagion that spread through the global banking system, capitalism began to look vulnerable once again. Yet this time around, there were some differences. Governments, although beleaguered, seemed to have *some* idea what to do. Particularly in Canada, where the last official recession ended during the second quarter of 1991, people found it difficult to imagine that a panic on financial markets would actually translate into mass unemployment and social unrest. In 2008, when the crisis began to unfold, Canada had enjoyed uninterrupted growth for over 17 years, combined with at least a decade of low unemployment, stable public finances, and broad-based tax reductions. In this context, it was difficult for anyone to summon up anything more than bemused complacency when it came to questioning the long-term stability of capitalism and the welfare state.

While the subprime mortgage crisis was clearly a big deal, the fact remains that upheavals on this scale used to be a lot more common. In the nineteenth century, it was reasonable to expect a big crash at least two or three times per decade. The fact that we've now got that down to two or three crashes per *century* is a remarkable achievement. How did this (relative) stability come about? Basically, Western governments got much better at managing the economy (with, of course, the exception of the United States, where free market ideology was responsible for some rather dramatic omissions). The turning point occurred with the publication of John Maynard Keynes's *General Theory of Employment, Interest and Money*, which essentially "cracked the code of crisis economics."[1] Keynes showed that the semi-regular occurrence of recessions, depressions, and even crises did not reflect a deep problem with the structure of capitalism, but was actually caused by something more like a glitch in the system. As Paul Krugman put it, "Because Keynes saw the causes of mass unemployment as narrow and technical, he argued that the problem's solution could also be narrow and technical."[2] Keynes's diagnosis of the problem—that recessions were caused by problems in the supply of money—was taken up and expanded upon most influentially by Milton Friedman, and thus became very much the received view on the right. The left, on the other hand, embraced Keynes's central policy prescription—that governments should spend a lot of money during recessions—yet rejected his underlying diagnosis of the problem, out of deference to the old-fashioned Marxist crisis theory. This has been a huge mistake, one that is responsible, in part, for the fact that most people on the left still don't understand what recessions are, or what causes them. As a result, they continue to believe that capitalism is doomed, despite the lack of either empirical or theoretical support for this view. Most of this is based upon an error known as the *overproduction fallacy*, which continues to dominate left-wing thinking on the subject of crisis economics.

$ $ $

What is a recession? Perhaps more important, why does our economic system experience periodic bouts of unemployment and negative growth? Why would an economy that is chugging along just fine suddenly go into reverse, start producing less, and begin shedding jobs?

Perhaps the best place to start is to describe the phenomenon. What a recession *looks like* is a general failure of demand. One day sales are great; the next day they start to slacken. Customers seem to disappear. Across the economy, inventories begin to accumulate. Companies are still producing, or still have the capacity, but no one wants to buy. As a result, firms start to lay off workers. Yet this only makes things worse. With workers having no more paychecks to spend, demand begins to slacken even further. Companies lay off more workers. At this point the economy enters into a vicious spiral, creating mass unemployment. It bottoms out only when enough factories have closed and enough wealth has been destroyed that demand is once again able to "catch up" with supply. The economy begins to take its first, gingerly steps toward recovery. Eventually, companies start to rehire workers, demand begins to recover, and growth resumes.

What could explain this apparent shortfall in demand? The most obvious hypothesis is that this apparent shortfall in demand is exactly what it appears to be, namely, a shortfall in demand. The economy, according to this view, is in a state of "overproduction" (or as they used to say back in the nineteenth century, "universal glut")[3]—too many sellers, not enough buyers.

One merely needs to state this thesis, however, to see that it can't be straightforwardly correct. (Indeed, it has been referred to as the "overproduction fallacy" for over a century.)[4] This is because the supply of commodities and the demand for commodities are the same thing, seen from two different perspectives. As John Stuart Mill put it, back in 1848, it cannot be the case that consumers lack the "means of payment" to purchase all that has been produced:

> Those who think so, cannot have considered what it is which constitutes the means of payment for commodities. It is, simply, commodities. Each person's means of paying for the productions of other people consists of those which he himself possesses. All sellers are inevitably, and by the meaning of the word, buyers. Could we suddenly double the productive powers of the country, we should double the supply of commodities in every market; but we should, by the same stroke, double the purchasing power.[5]

The underlying principle here is known as Say's Law (after the early French economist Jean-Baptiste Say). Simply put, it is that goods constitute the demand for goods. Supply creates its own demand, because supply *is* demand. The economy is, fundamentally, a system of exchange, which means that the seller of one good is simply the buyer of some other good. Thus general overproduction is, in general, impossible *unless it is possible to identify some exception to the rule.*

In a pure barter economy there are no such exceptions. It is possible to have too much of one commodity, relative to the level of demand for that particular commodity—this just means that there is some other thing that people would rather buy (and so the price of the former will fall, and that of the latter will rise). But the idea that there might be too much of *everything* makes no sense. Relative to what? It can't be relative to total income, since total income and total production always add up to the same amount.

Things get more complicated, however, in an advanced market economy. Here, the fact that goods are exchanged for other goods is obscured by the fact that we accept money as a means of payment. Furthermore, money does not behave like other commodities—it is not consumed, but rather gets passed along to someone else. Thus economists for a very long time suspected that recessions might have something to do with the fact that we use money to mediate exchanges (or that the behavior of money might be the source of an exception to Say's Law).

The first suggestion to come along was that *savings* might be responsible for gluts. What happens if people accept cash in return for goods but then turn around and save the money, rather than spending it? Doesn't this create a situation in which a person is selling something but not buying anything in return? And couldn't this result in a greater quantity of supply than demand?

Possibly. But this intuition turns out to be a minefield of economic fallacies.[6] Perhaps the most common mistake made by the economically unsophisticated is to imagine that money deposited in banks is somehow removed from circulation. To take just one example, Thomas Homer-Dixon suggests that in order to maintain demand, it is important that consumers spend their income, "rather than put it in a bank or under a mattress."[7] But putting money in a bank is not even vaguely analogous to putting it under a mattress. Banks don't actually take the money that is deposited and put it in a vault somewhere down in the basement. They turn around and they lend it to someone else. This person either spends it or puts it in another bank, which turns around and lends it to someone *else.* The only reason this process doesn't continue indefinitely is that banks have to put aside a certain percentage of each deposit in order to make sure they have enough cash on hand to cover withdrawals. Saving money is not really *saving*—it is really just giving it to someone else to spend (usually on investment goods).

This is why the amount of "money" that people have (for example, if you add up the value of everyone's savings and checking accounts) is about an order of magnitude larger than the amount of physical bills and coins in circulation. (The discovery that banks were doing this scandalized many people in the early twentieth century, including Major Clifford Hugh Douglas, who founded the somewhat nutty "social credit" movement based upon a fallacious understanding of the relationship between savings and credit.)

When thinking about the impact of savings on total demand, it is best to imagine each individual dividing his income not between consumption and savings, but rather between "money that is spent by me" and "money that is lent to someone else." Early proponents of the overproduction thesis, like Malthus, saw that savings alone were not going to cause any shortfall in demand.[8] Malthus rested his case, therefore, upon the claim that banks would run out of people to lend to, simply because investment opportunities would be subject to diminishing returns. He failed to respond to the claim that if banks wound up with too much money on their hands, they could easily get rid of it simply by lowering the interest rate that they charged. This "classical" view, articulated by David Ricardo, "conquered England as thoroughly as the Spanish Inquisition conquered Spain."[9] It became standard to assume that the interest rate, which functions essentially as the price of money, would react to changes in supply and demand just like any other scarcity price, and so would bring the markets for savings and investment into equilibrium.[10]

Money shouldn't make any difference: Total supply should still equal total demand.

§ § §

So putting money in the bank is not the same thing as putting it under a mattress. But what if people actually *do* put their money under mattresses? Doesn't this create a situation in which people are selling but not spending, and doesn't this have the potential to create an imbalance of supply and demand?

In a sense, yes. But it's hard to see how this could be a problem. Sticking money under a mattress is always going to be a somewhat marginal activity, since it involves forgoing the returns that could be achieved by investing it. People will want to keep a certain amount of cash on hand in order to conduct routine transactions, and a few odd-balls (or criminals) will want to hoard large stocks of it. It is, however, fairly easy for the government to anticipate, in the aggregate, how much money will be required, and simply print enough of it to go around.

So again, in a fairly static situation, the inclination to hoard money doesn't really change anything. Classical orthodoxy again prevails. Keynes's great insight, however, was that a *change* in this propensity to hold money could be enormously disruptive. The important thing about money is that it serves not only as means of payment, but also as a store of value. Thus the amount of money that businesses and individuals want to hold on to is determined not only by the amount of cash they need on hand to cover their transactions, but also by their expectations about the future. In particular, if they expect prices to fall, they may want to hold on to their money, rather than spend it right away, simply because it will be worth more in the future. Threats to the currency or to the banking system can have the same effect.

What does it look like if there is a sudden increase in the demand for money? What it *looks like* is a decrease in demand for everything else. (Which is to say, it looks like overproduction, or "universal glut.")

Just as inflation appears to be an increase in the price of all goods but amounts to just a decrease in the value of money, a recession appears to be a decrease in the demand for all goods but is really just an increase in the demand for money. Furthermore, if there is not enough money to satisfy this demand, people begin to hoard it. They will then refuse to engage in ordinary economic transactions, not because these transactions are disadvantageous, but because they regard holding on to their money as more advantageous. In other words, when money starts to seem intrinsically valuable, rather than just instrumentally valuable, it can have the effect of seizing up the entire economy.

The dynamic at work here is best illustrated by the Great Capitol Hill Baby Sitting Co-op Crisis (after a famous, only semi-satirical article published in the *Journal of Money, Credit, and Banking* in 1977). A babysitting co-op is usually organized by parents who want to exchange child-care services with one another. People earn credit by babysitting for other members of the co-op. They can then "spend" this credit by hiring babysitting for themselves. Some co-ops use a complicated bookkeeping method, keeping a ledger that records how much credit there is in each individual's account. An easier way is simply to issue "scrip," or coupons that can be exchanged for babysitting services. Provide one hour of babysitting and you get "paid" with a coupon, which can in turn be used to purchase one hour of babysitting from any other co-op member.

Anyone can see that members of the co-op will want to keep a certain number of coupons on hand so that they have the option of purchasing babysitting on short notice. (If you receive an invitation on Tuesday to go out Friday evening, you don't want to be stuck having to earn the necessary coupons on Wednesday and Thursday.) Keynes called this desire to have scrip on hand the individual's "liquidity preference." In order to get a system like this up and running, you have to issue enough scrip to satisfy this preference. In the Capitol Hill Baby Sitting Co-op, members were all issued 20 free coupons at start-up (with an obligation to repay 20 coupons on exit).

Everything went along swimmingly for a while. Yet gradually, the co-op began to experience a slackening of demand. There were all sorts of people willing to babysit, but no one wanted to hire them. The members tried implementing all sorts of rules and regulations, forcing people to babysit at least once a week, but nothing seemed to improve the situation. Eventually the realization began to dawn upon the members: The babysitting co-op was experiencing a recession.

How is this possible? One might think that, in this system, the supply of babysitting is always equal to the demand, since the only way to purchase an hour of babysitting is to provide an hour of babysitting. And if someone wants to work as a babysitter, it's presumably not just for fun, but rather because she would like, in turn, to hire a babysitter. So how could there be a shortfall in demand? How could there be unemployment?

Keynes's observation was that a recession like this can be due to a change in liquidity preference. Suppose that during the year people are happy to hold, on average, 20 coupons to purchase babysitting on short notice. Yet as summer vacation approaches, and more opportunities to go out begin to present themselves, people will start to anticipate a greater need to hire babysitting. The number of coupons that the average person will want to keep on hand may increase, say, from 20 to 30. How do you increase the number of coupons you're holding? You do it by increasing the amount of babysitting that you *provide* to others and/ or decreasing the amount of babysitting that you *purchase* from others. If everyone does this, however, the result is an increase in the supply of willing babysitters combined with a dramatic shortfall in demand. People want to work, but no one wants to hire—in other words, there is unemployment. It is a recession.

Is there actually a shortfall of demand here? Not really. Once the scrip is introduced, there are actually two "commodities" in the economy, babysitting and coupons. The problem is that coupons serve not only as a means of payment for babysitting, but as an independent object of demand. If there is no demand for scrip as such, the supply of babysitting translates directly into demand for babysitting. But if people start wanting coupons for their own sake, the supply of babysitting gets divided up between demand for coupons and demand for babysitting (since supplying babysitting is the only way to buy either babysitting or coupons). This then *looks like* a case of oversupply, or "universal glut," simply because of the tendency to ignore demand for scrip.

How does one cure this ailment? In the case of the babysitting co-op, the solution is simple—print more coupons, until they return to having a purely instrumental value. The problem is not that people don't want to hire babysitters; the problem is that people want to increase their stockpile of coupons. So if you simply print up a bunch of new coupons and give 10 to each member, the problem will instantly disappear. This is, more or less, how the Capitol Hill Baby Sitting Co-op solved their problem. Once the members had 30 coupons on hand, the desire to hoard coupons dissipated, and as a result, they became willing to start hiring babysitters again. This in turn meant that anyone wanting to earn more coupons was able to do so. The system of exchange became "unblocked," and the pattern of mutually beneficial exchange resumed.

Keynes's revolutionary, and to many people unbelievable, claim was that recessions in the real world have essentially the same structure. Ultimately they are a monetary phenomenon, caused by a "glitch" in the circulation of currency in the economy. They are not the result of "inherent contradictions" in the capitalist system. As Krugman put it, "To many people it seems obvious that massive economic slumps must have deep roots. To them, Keynes's argument that they are essentially no more than a problem of mixed signals, which can be cured by printing a bit more money, seems unbelievable."[11] Yet the empirical evidence has all been on Keynes's side.

For example, during the Golden Age of laissez-faire capitalism, recessions were often preceded by bank failures. Because banks lend out most of the money that they receive, they cannot actually repay more than a small fraction of depositors at a time. As we have seen, this has the potential to spark a bank run—a collective action problem in which depositors, convinced that the bank is going to fail, try to get their money out before the bank does, yet, in so doing, essentially guarantee that the bank will fail.

While this may be tough luck for the bank's customers, it is not necessarily a problem for the economy as a whole. Furthermore, it is not clear why it should cause a recession. Keynes's analysis, however, provides a very simple explanation. It is the way the *other* banks responded that created general problems. As soon as one bank failed, all the other banks immediately tried to increase their cash reserves in order to protect themselves against the impact of copycat withdrawals and the possibility of a generalized bank panic. Furthermore, customers would get antsy about making deposits, and so would begin holding on to their money. The result was often a huge overnight shift in liquidity preference, with everyone suddenly wanting to hold as much physical currency as possible. This led to a systemic slackening of economic activity in all other sectors, as people became loathe to engage in transactions, preferring to hold on to their money.

As was mentioned in the first chapter, public deposit insurance, one of the most important social programs for capitalists, essentially eliminated the problem of runs on ordinary commercial banks. (This is one of the reasons why the financial crisis of 2008 occurred in what some called the "parallel" banking sector—financial institutions that were operating outside the scope of government regulatory programs, including federal deposit insurance.) Stabilizing the banks had significant stabilizing effects on the business cycle (a fact that Marxian "crisis" theory is unable to explain). Recessions became less common and less severe, simply because one of the primary sources of volatility in the demand for money had been eliminated.

In retrospect, it seems clear that Keynes presented his observations as somewhat more revolutionary than they in fact were. In particular, he claimed to have "refuted" Say's Law, whereas what he actually discovered was something more like an exception to it. If you talk about the demand for all goods in the economy *except money*, then it is possible to have an excess of supply. But that's merely equivalent to saying that there is excess demand for money. It doesn't mean that supply and demand aren't the same thing, or that goods aren't ultimately exchanged for other goods. It just means that money can gum up the works.

Keynes's policy advice was also a lot more dramatic than most contemporary theorists are inclined to accept. The crucial part of Keynes's argument is his demonstration that the movement of interest rates cannot be counted on to automatically adjust the supply and demand for money. This is the basis for his claim that governments should take an active role in managing the economy, first and foremost by controlling monetary policy. (Indeed, one of Krugman's neatest observations is that now that we have enlightened central banking, the market economy behaves much more the way it was supposed to under the "classical" model. The visible hand of "the Fed" now does what the invisible hand of the market was to have done, but as a result, interest rates now regulate savings and investment decisions in more or less the way that the classical model said they *should* have.)

Keynes also tried to show that countries can get stuck in a "liquidity trap," in which simply printing more money will not satisfy the urge to hoard. Under such circumstances, the only way for the government to get the economy going would be to inject more money directly into circulation, in order to "stimulate demand." Hence the recommendation—highly congenial to the left—that the government engage in massive public works projects. Left-wing fans of Keynes, however, have largely chosen to ignore the extremely narrow set of circumstances under which he thought this might be beneficial—certainly not during a period of expansion, and not even during an ordinary recession. Yet misunderstanding of Keynes on this point is responsible for the widespread impression that governments should constantly be spending money—or cutting taxes—in order to "prime the pump" or "stimulate demand." As a matter of fact, demand doesn't need to be stimulated, except perhaps at the bottom of the deepest trough of the deepest depression, when interest rates are as low as they can feasibly go. Luckily (or unluckily, as the case may be), such conditions have not been seen in the West since the 1930s (although, at the time of writing, the U.S. economy seems to be getting rather close).

$ $ $

There is a famous story about former United Auto Workers president Walter Reuther (famous, in part, because Ronald Reagan retold it in an approving tone): "Reuther was touring a highly automated Ford assembly plant when someone said, 'Walter, you're going to have a hard time collecting union dues from all these machines.' And Reuther simply shot back, 'Not as hard a time as you're going to have selling them cars.'"[12] This is a great line. Unfortunately, it's based upon a version of the overproduction fallacy, in this case one that is due to Marx. Whereas Malthus thought it was oversaving that would generate shortfalls in demand, Marx thought it was the introduction of labor-saving technology in the factory that would do so. According to this view (popularized by generations of union wage negotiators), the only way to avoid a recession is for workers to be paid enough that they are able to "buy back the product" they create.[13] Employers who introduce labor-saving technology, according to this view, are engaging in self-defeating behavior. They hope to enhance their profits by introducing machines, yet in so doing, they undermine demand for their own products. This requires a new round of cost-cutting, which further undermines demand and eventually generates a crisis of overproduction.

It's amazing how many people believe this, even though it's based on such an elementary economic fallacy. Consider the following, written by the urban theorist and management professor Richard Florida, in the middle of the 2008 financial crisis. His objective was to show that—despite appearances to the contrary—the crisis was not just financial, but "in reality a much deeper crisis of our underlying economic model and our way of life." Here is how he explained it:

> *The roots of the current crisis are tied to the fundamental nature*
> *of the postwar model of economic development called "Fordism."*
> *That model drew a tight connection between assembly-line mass*
> *production and mass consumption—ultimately fuelled by mas-*
> *sive suburbanization. After introducing the assembly line and*
> *making car production more efficient and cars cheaper, Henry*
> *Ford realized that a bigger market for his cars was needed—so he*
> *boosted workers' wages by introducing the "five-dollar day." But*
> *even that was not enough, and so North America and the world*
> *lapsed into the Great Depression.*[14]

The problem with this argument is that workers are not the only ones who spend money (or, more correctly, labor income is not the only source of earning for households). What was Henry Ford doing with all that money *before* he raised his workers' wages? Money earned by corporations winds up being transferred to one or more of the firm's constituency groups, or else held by the firm and reinvested. If the corporation is able to lower its costs of production through the use of labor-saving technology, the money that would have been paid out in the form of wages simply goes somewhere else. Suppose the firm decides to lower its prices. Then consumers may respond by purchasing more of the good, or they may take the money they save and spend it on something else. Suppose the firm decides to pay off a supplier, or retire a loan, or transfer the earnings to the owners in the form of profit. Again, the money gets spent (or put in the bank, where someone else will spend it). The same is true if the firm keeps it as retained earnings.

In fact, there is no need to do a "follow the money" exercise to ensure that every penny not spent by laid-off workers will be spent by someone else (and thus overall demand will remain constant), because the spending of money is ultimately not what is at issue. Supply constitutes the demand for goods (setting aside some disruption in the monetary sphere); thus the fact that the firm is still able to sell its goods means that total demand remains unchanged.

To see the flaw in the Marxian argument, consider how it would apply to the case of the babysitting co-op. Suppose that one member of the co-op introduces a new piece of labor-saving technology, which allows him to increase his productivity (for example, he buys a TV set, which he can park the kids in front of). Now, instead of babysitting for just one family at a time, he is able to take in the kids from two families simultaneously. As a result, he is able to earn two coupons per hour, rather than just one. Naturally, this innovation leads to some other babysitter's being "laid off," since the demand for babysitting services of these two families now generates employment for only one person, rather than two. The babysitter who was laid off is not earning coupons, so he will not be spending coupons either. Does this not lead to a shortfall in demand?

Of course not—because the coupons that aren't being earned by the laid-off babysitter are simply going to the other, more productive babysitter. These coupons are of no value to him, as such, and so his capacity to earn more is going to translate into greater spending. Assuming no change in liquidity preference (that is, no inclination to hoard), he will then go out twice as much, and so hire twice as much babysitting. Total supply and demand will remain unchanged.

Suppose that this innovation catches on, so that everyone begins to babysit for multiple families simultaneously. This is productivity growth. Members of the co-op are now able to enjoy the same number of hours without their kids, but the number of hours spent with extra kids has been halved. Of course, the quality of those hours (and of the child care) may have declined—that's a separate issue. The important point is simply that productivity growth, whether it be due to technological innovation or to something else, has absolutely no tendency to generate either overproduction or unemployment.

Despite these obvious problems, the Marxian theory of crisis still enjoys enormous popularity on the left. One of the reasons is that many people think it provides an explanation not only for business cycles, but also for the phenomenon of "consumerism." Roughly speaking, the argument is that the capitalist system requires a continuous production of new desires in order to stimulate demand and to make up for the shortfall induced through overproduction. Here is an unusually clear statement of this view, written by Russell Jacoby in *The Nation*:

> As the industrial apparatus becomes more efficient and requires fewer workers, it undercuts itself. After all, the workers themselves are part of the market. If they are unemployed, they buy little or nothing and the commodities go unsold. The specter of overproduction haunts the modern economy, which responds in several ways: by selling goods to new consumers (say, baby formula to breast feeders); by selling more goods to existing consumers (say, bigger television sets to television set owners); and by selling more goods to the government (say, aircraft carriers and Hummers to the military).[15]

There are two straightforward fallacies here. The first is the idea that if unemployed workers buy less than before, commodities will go unsold. This simply does not follow. One need only substitute "babysitting co-op" for "industrial apparatus" in the first sentence to see why. The second involves a confusion—clearly diagnosed by Mill back in 1848—between the "desire to possess" and the "means of payment."[16] If workers are laid off, presumably what they experience is a decline in their ability to *pay for* goods, not any decrease in their desire to possess goods. So why would it be necessary for the system to stimulate any new desires? Furthermore, the problem is not that people lack desires, it's that they lack money, because they lack jobs. How would stimulating new desires in other people do anything to increase effective demand? If people are unemployed, people are unemployed. Tricking them into wanting baby formula or big televisions doesn't provide them with the means of paying for these things.

To see the problem with the "overproduction generates consumerism" argument more clearly, consider how easy it would be to produce a "right-wing" version of it. Let's blame the government for consumerism. "As the government grows larger, and requires greater tax revenues, it undercuts itself. After all, if workers are paying all their money to the government, it means that they can buy less for themselves, and so commodities go unsold. Thus taxation creates a problem of overproduction for the modern economy. Recessions, however, undermine government tax revenue, and so in order to keep the money flowing, government has no choice but to stimulate consumers to want new goods . . ."

This is a silly argument, and to my knowledge no one on the right—not even on Fox News—has ever made it. But one is forced then to ask why left-wing intellectuals, like Jacoby, make arguments that have exactly the same perfectly obvious problem. After all, if individuals are paying taxes rather than spending their own money, it just means that the government is spending it for them. Thus demand for the kinds of things that governments buy (road-paving equipment, mass transit vehicles, health care services) will increase, as demand for the sort of thing that individuals buy (SUVs, pet food, lawnmowers) will decline. From the standpoint of "the economy," it all comes out the same. As we have seen, tax revenue is not consumed—it is spent.

In any case, the idea that people need to be tricked and cajoled into wanting to buy new things is, and always has been, bizarre. The human capacity for wasteful expenditure seems to be completely unbounded. Homer-Dixon worries that unless people have "insatiable material desires," "they may not spend enough money to spur companies to create new jobs for the workers displaced by rising productivity."[17] But who ever said that people have to have insatiable *material* desires? There are a million different ways to spend money. They could just as easily have spiritual desires, which require high levels of personal service in order to satisfy. The capitalist may decide that he needs shiatsu massage therapy, a sweat-lodge experience, or an ecotourism guide—*voilà*, new jobs are created.

In fact, an increase in service-sector employment has been one of the major trends in wealthy nations in the last three decades. Close to 80% of the workforce in the United States is now in the service sector. Yet there is still an enormous amount of room for growth. In the late nineteenth century, a typical upper-class Edwardian household employed a live-in cook, butler, gardener, and governess, not to mention several footmen and kitchen maids. Wealthy families in our society "outsource" almost all of these tasks, with the partial exception of governesses (that is, nannies). They do so in order to reduce costs. Yet if hard-pressed to find some new form of wasteful expenditure, is it so difficult to imagine that they might happily return to the nineteenth-century model?

It is important to remember that the term *employment* is just a fancy way of talking about getting other people to do things for you. People don't generally suffer from any failures of ingenuity when it comes to designing new schemes of employment in this sense. Thus the fact that capitalism suffers from periodic bouts of unemployment has *nothing whatsoever* to do with any incapacity on the part of the public to think up new ways to spend money. One might think this too obvious to require explicit statement, yet people talk themselves into the strangest of views when it comes to finding flaws with the market.

§ § §

No discussion of Keynesian economics would be complete without some mention of its most pernicious ideological consequence, which has been to persuade vast swathes of modern left-wing intellectuals that the creation of jobs represents some sort of a public service that corporations (or, worse, consumers) perform. Generally speaking, work is bad, which is why people seek to avoid it. Absent the specter of mass unemployment, it would seem fairly obvious that being able to achieve the same result with less effort is better than being able to achieve it with more effort. Yet people are constantly drawing conclusions that imply the exact opposite.

For example, people routinely describe a decline in the value of the currency relative to our trading partners as good for the domestic economy, on the grounds it will create jobs in the export sector. Yet the only reason it creates jobs is because it forces us all to work harder in order to purchase the same bundle of imported goods that we used to get for a lot less. Similarly, people on the left have an inexplicable hostility to the growth of part-time employment, as though the ideal world is one in which everyone works as much as possible.

William Greider, the "economics" specialist at *The Nation*, recently provided a choice example of this sort of fallacy. He begins by noting that most job growth in the United States has been provided not by the 10,000 or so publicly traded corporations, but by privately held firms in the small-business sector. During a period in which Fortune 500 companies reduced employment by 4%, privately held firms increased employment by approximately 20%. Greider concludes, on this basis, that "if more American capital flowed into the smaller enterprises and less to the larger ones, the economy would not suffer but benefit."[18]

Greider is committing the elementary error of determining what's good for the economy by looking at how much work we do, as opposed to how much we produce. If Fortune 500 companies are reducing employment, it's not because they're reducing output but because they are shifting toward more capital-intensive forms of production. Greider is essentially recommending that capital be shifted out of more productive sectors into less productive ones, in order to produce more employment. This is backward. Our objective, as Dwight Lee reminds us, should be to create wealth, not jobs:

> This is the point of the apocryphal story of an engineer who, while visiting China, came across a large crew of men building a dam with picks and shovels. When the engineer pointed out to the supervisor that the job could be completed in a few days, rather than many months, if the men were given motorized earthmoving equipment, the supervisor said that such equipment would destroy many jobs. "Oh," the engineer responded, "I thought you were interested in building a dam. If it's more jobs you want, why don't you have your men use spoons instead of shovels."[19]

The fallacy may seem obvious when put in the form of a story like this, but that doesn't stop it from showing up, again and again, in public policy debates. For instance, anyone who has driven through Oregon or New Jersey will have probably noticed the complete absence of self-serve gas stations in these states. Both jurisdictions have laws that pro-hibit motorists from filling up their own tanks. While initially adopted for consumer-protection reasons (gasoline was thought to be too flam-mable to be handled by ordinary citizens—there is no law there against self-serve diesel pumps), the laws have proven impossible to repeal, on the grounds that they "create employment."

One might just as easily lament the passing of the elevator atten-dant or the caboose operator. The crucial thing to remember is that freeing people from these sorts of unproductive occupations makes them available to do more worthwhile things. Rather than having 50 men with shovels digging a ditch, we now send out a single worker with a backhoe. As a result, the 49 remaining men are free to do other, more useful jobs. Far from serving as a source of unemployment, this process of productivity growth constitutes the entire foundation of the prosper-ity of modern economies.

Under ordinary circumstances, "creating jobs" is not something that has to be *done*, it's something that the economy does all by itself. People on the left seem to have a selective consciousness of this fact but fail to apply the underlying principles consistently. For instance, it is widely understood that the idea that immigrants take jobs away from the native-born is based upon an economic fallacy (sometimes known as the "lump of labor" fallacy). While immigrants do increase the supply of labor, Say's Law dictates that they simultaneously increase the demand for goods (because their supply of labor constitutes demand for goods). In order to meet this increase in demand, firms must expand production, which requires more labor. This is why the rate of unemployment in a country has nothing to do with the number of people in the country. (It's also why dying doesn't "free up" a job for some other lucky person.) There is no such thing as "technologically induced" unemployment for the same reason that there is no such thing as "immigration-induced" unemployment. Immigrants may displace particular individuals from particular jobs, just as technology may displace particular individuals from particular jobs, but this does not create any net loss of jobs in the economy as a whole. Again, one need only consider the model of the babysitting co-op to see why this must be so.

There is, however, an exception to all this, which is precisely the one that Keynes identified. *During a recession* the economy does not produce jobs all on its own, because people are unwilling to undertake the transactions that are required to effectively communicate demand. Under these conditions *and only under these conditions,* there may be something to be said for having the state undertake "make-work" projects. (Note that a "make-work" project should not be confused with the provision of a public service. In the latter case, the effort expended is justified by the value of the output produced. In the case of a "make-work" project—such as burying bottles full of banknotes in abandoned mines—the justification lies not in the output produced but in the fiscal stimulus that the payment of the salary generates.) Because of this, promoting "make-work" projects during ordinary periods of economic expansion is simply a waste of money (which is to say, a waste of time, energy, and resources).

$ $ $

The "social credit" movement has been a powerful force throughout the British Commonwealth, right up to the present day.[20] Yet it took only a decade or so for the various right-wing political parties inspired by Major Douglas's writings to abandon the cracker-barrel economic theory that had provided the initial impetus for the movement. Unfortunately, that process doesn't seem to work quite so quickly on the left. In particular, "Chicken Little" economic thinking—where each little hiccup in the economy is taken as a sign of the impending collapse of the entire system—has become so deeply entrenched that anyone who does *not* think the world is on the brink of catastrophe is sometimes greeted with puzzlement and suspicion.

Yet over the course of the twentieth century, it became clear that the economic contradictions of capitalism were not all they were cracked up to be. So "neo-Marxists" began to look instead for "cultural contradictions" in the capitalist system. Most of these theories were centered on the idea that consumerism would undermine the work ethic, leaving workers unwilling to submit themselves to the tyranny of the clock.[21] Yet as the countercultural movements of the '60s and '70s fizzled, these "contradictions" also began to look less threatening.

In recent years, expectations have shifted toward two new possible sources of crisis. The first has been globalization. According to this view, the inherent contradictions of capitalism were for a long time simply externalized, displaced onto non-capitalist societies. If overproduction generates a shortfall of demand at home, the spillover can be absorbed by bringing new people—in India, Africa, or China—into the consumerist fold (ignoring, of course, the question of how these people are supposed to pay for this excess product, if not by selling goods back to us). But once markets become global—when there is no more virgin soil to be plowed under—the limits of this strategy become apparent. The second major crisis theory has a similar structure, but looks instead at the environmental limits of capitalism. The claim is that rich countries have been able to grow only because the cost of this growth has been largely externalized onto the natural environment. Now the limits to growth are being reached, both because we are running out of resources and because there is nowhere left to dump the garbage.

Of course, there is a lot to worry about with the environment, and there is in many cases genuine cause for alarm. Similarly, increased globalization has introduced an element of instability into market institutions, both international and domestic, particularly in the form of currency crises. But it is important to see that none of this threatens the market as a mechanism for coordinating economic activity. There are many problems with modern capitalism, but there are no existential threats.

Take first the case of globalization. One way to understand the issue is simply to think of the problems of globalization as nothing but the problems of nineteenth-century capitalism reappearing on a world scale.[22] The unregulated capitalism of that era was plagued by multiple forms of market failure. The welfare state arose in the twentieth century essentially as a way of plugging these gaps. Now that market exchange has become more international, the same gaps are starting to show up again, on the world stage. The difference, of course, is that this time around we have a much better idea what the solutions should look like (although the question of how to implement them remains thorny).

Take the case of currency instability. Critics of globalization point to the Mexican peso crisis of 1994 or the run on the Thai bhat in 1997 as evidence that the world trade system is nothing but a Trojan horse for the imposition of structural adjustment policies by the International Monetary Fund. But currency instability has an illustrious history that long predates either the IMF or the "Washington consensus." It was actually a hallmark feature of nineteenth-century capitalism. Back then, in the U.S. for instance, banks used to issue their own paper money. Thus there were multiple competing currencies, each backed by the assets of a private bank (much as today, on the international level, there are multiple competing currencies, each backed by a different nation-state). Whenever there was a run on a bank, or even the rumor of a run on a bank, anyone holding that currency would want to dispose of it as quickly as possible. The result would be a sudden and catastrophic devaluation of those banknotes.

How was this problem solved? By central banking on the national level, and, in particular, by having the state exercise an effective monopoly in the market for paper money. This exercise of state power eliminated the problem so completely on the domestic level that most people have forgotten that money risk ever existed (and no longer think of issuing money as a welfare-state social program). As a result, international currency crises are regarded as some new and unexpected consequence of globalized capitalism rather than as an elementary defect in the structure of unregulated capitalism, one that can be resolved through an exercise of administrative power.

This is not to suggest that a single world currency represents the solution to the problem of monetary instability. That would be undesirable and unworkable on many levels. What it does suggest is that the problem of instability is going to be addressed through the development of increasingly powerful international financial institutions, with the ability to impose their will in a more binding fashion upon both governments and private parties, whether we like it or not. Nothing else has ever worked at the national level, so why should we expect anything different at the international level? Globalization of markets is far more likely to produce world government—or international institutions with increasingly statelike powers—than it is the collapse of capitalism.

As for the environment, most of the doom and gloom about impending resource scarcity is based upon straightforward neglect of the way prices automatically ration goods in response to scarcity. Back in 1971, the Club of Rome made the elementary mistake of ignoring the price mechanism in projecting the "limits to growth." It should go without saying that at a price of $8 a barrel, the world would quickly run out of oil. And yet at $100 a barrel, it turns out you can find oil in the damnedest places—like the bottom of the ocean. It should also go without saying that as the world "runs out" of oil, the price will rise.

As far as economic growth is concerned, the thought that environmental sustainability is going to require an end to economic growth is usually based upon a confused or partial understanding of what "economic growth" consists of. Consider Joel Kovel, whose work has been enormously influential in Green Party thinking. In his book *The Enemy of Nature*, he claims that we face a simple choice between "the end of capitalism" and "the end of the world." The problem with capitalism, however, is not capitalism as such (after all, communism was several times worse for the environment). The problem is that capitalist economies are committed to growth. "Since the one underlying feature of all aspects of capital is the relentless pressure to grow, we are obliged to bring down the capitalist system as a whole, and replace it with an ecologically viable alternative, if we want to save our species along with numberless others," Kovel writes.[23]

This idea that growth is somehow a central problem from an environmental perspective has become widespread in Green political thinking. Consider, for example, the following remarks by the Canadian Green Party leader Elizabeth May:

> When a human being grows, at the age of about 18 physical growth levels off, but your development doesn't stop—in fact it may be the beginning of your developing artistic abilities. You might start writing poetry, you develop interests, you develop wisdom. So economic development need not be wedded to perpetual physical growth, because we're up against physical limits in the biosphere. So it becomes a rather psychotic addiction to imagine that every economy has to be linked to economic growth.[24]

This is all fine—except that "economic growth" in wealthy nations stopped measuring anything that vaguely resembles "physical growth" decades ago. GDP does not measure the physical output of goods in the economy (the way, for example, old Soviet plans used to measure output in terms of tons of steel or bushels of wheat). What GDP measures is the volume of transactions that are occurring, and it expresses this in terms of the value of those transactions. Thus, for example, one of the reasons that Sweden has very high GDP per capita is that it has very high rates of female labor-force participation. When a parent returns to work and hires a nanny to look after the kids, GDP increases (since both the parent's and the nanny's income are added to national income accounts). Yet nothing is happening here that should be any cause for alarm to the environmentalist (or that risks bumping up against the limits of the biosphere). A particular service (in this case child rearing) is simply being moved out of the household into the formal economy, at which point it registers as growth.

If anyone is concerned that this example is unrepresentative, it is important to remember that services constitute *most of the economy* in wealthy nations (ranging from 65% to 80%). And even within the class of what are called "goods," most of the value in these goods has no material basis (think software, movies, music). Last year, Americans spent $3 billion on yoga lessons and related paraphernalia. That contributes to growth, but there is nothing unsustainable about this from the standpoint of the biosphere. (I say this as someone who makes a comfortable living selling "wisdom" to people—which presumably has a rather minimal environmental footprint.) More generally, the "energy intensity" of growth in the United States—the amount of energy required to produce a given increase in GDP—is declining by a rate of about 2% per year.[25]

The point is that some growth is ecofriendly, while other growth is not. Since GDP simply measures the value of transactions, what matters, from an environmental perspective, is not whether the sum is rising or falling, but rather the *type* of transactions that are occurring. But since growth measures only the sum, there is simply nothing useful that can be said from an environmental perspective on the question of whether growth as such, or capitalism more generally, is sustainable. There is no doubt that particular technologies and particular practices are unsustainable, but that's a completely separate issue. Furthermore, there is no reason to think that environmental problems are going to constrain economic growth in any global sense. And given that it's electoral suicide to position one's political party in opposition to growth, it might be a good idea to work out the economics of the position more carefully before making the sort of rash claims that May was making.

Meanwhile, there is a perfectly sensible critique of economic growth—in particular, of the way that GDP is used as a proxy for social welfare—which is in danger of being drowned out by all the noise. The problem with GDP is that it only adds up the value of transactions that employ money as a medium of exchange. The cost of environmental externalities is completely ignored (precisely *because* the effects on the environment take the form of externalities). Anyone who treats economic growth as an *overriding* policy objective is therefore guilty of committing a "count the benefits, ignore the costs" fallacy. Furthermore, since consumption is subject to diminishing returns, there is good reason to think that the unhappiness caused by external environmental effects, relative to the welfare gains associated with increased consumption, is likely to become less favorable over time to the cause of increased growth. Thus not only should economic growth not be our sole preoccupation, it should be something that we become less and less concerned about as we become wealthier.

Of course, this is not a revolutionary criticism of the capitalist economy. That's because environmentalism is not a revolutionary doctrine. Most environmental problems are the result of a "glitch" in the system, in the same way that the business cycle is the result of a glitch. This isn't to say that the consequences cannot be catastrophic—the Great Depression was a catastrophe—or that the problem can be easily fixed. It just means that the problem is not a structural feature of the system: One can fruitfully think of ways to fix the glitch while leaving the rest of the system intact. Unfortunately, Marx's crisis theory set a bad precedent for left-wing thinking, by suggesting that these glitches are "fundamental contradictions" and that the capitalist economic system is a brittle structure that might easily come crashing down under the impact of even a slight tremor. There were reasons for believing this in Marx's time, but the last hundred years have shown the reality to be quite different. Although capitalism does have certain vulnerable sectors, which must be carefully regulated and controlled, it is the most decentralized system of cooperation ever devised by man (comparable in many ways to the Internet in its lack of central control structures). To get a sense of how much effort it would require to "abolish" capitalism, consider how much time, energy, and straightforward coercion have been employed trying to abolish the market for various sorts of drugs. Keep in mind that the market for illegal drugs functions almost exactly the way that standard economic theory predicts: Prices respond to supply and demand pressures in the usual way, an advanced division of labor has developed, technological change and product innovation occur in regular cycles and respond in predictable ways to external forces, such as law-enforcement strategies. All this occurs despite the fact that the central contracts are not only legally unenforceable, but legally proscribed—buyers and sellers still manage to find one another, from one side of the earth to the other. Anyone who thinks that the "war on drugs" is futile should be inclined to think that a "war on capitalism" would be equally futile—for exactly the same reason. The question is not whether there is going be a market: Once the genie is out of the bottle, there's no going back. The question is how the market is to be managed, how inclusive and humane the system is to be, and how the benefits and burdens of cooperation are to be distributed.

CHAPTER 10

EQUAL PAY

Why some jobs must suck, in every aspect

In chapter 7, I argued that fiddling with prices is a terrible way of trying to achieve distributive justice. Not only does it lead to waste and misallocation of resources, but it seldom delivers much to those who are its intended beneficiaries. Better to let the market work out a set of scarcity prices, then use progressive taxation as a way of achieving greater equality of distribution. Yet even among those who accept this principle, there is one price that is an extremely tempting target for fiddling. That is the price of labor, better known as *wages*. When Abba Lerner talked about changing the distribution of income, he was talking about using the tax system to achieve transfers between individuals. But it is easy to interpret "changing the distribution of income" to mean "changing the amount that people earn." And because this is such an obvious temptation, the advantages and disadvantages of such a policy merit their own special discussion.

One of the things that has always rankled people about capitalism is the fact that what workers get paid seems to bear no relationship to what they deserve. In particular, a lot of the work that we think of as quite hard—backbreaking, repetitive, and stressful—is very poorly paid. Meanwhile, a lot of jobs that don't seem to involve much exertion at all—to the point where it is unclear why they are even called "jobs"—are extremely well remunerated. I'll be the first to admit, for instance, that I am wildly overpaid. (You can check for yourself, if you don't believe me. Thanks to the Ontario provincial government's Public Sector Salary Disclosure Act, you can look up my salary—along with that of most of my colleagues—on the Internet.) It takes me about 15 minutes to earn what the average worker in Beijing takes home in a day. By the time I've gotten to my office and finished reading the Monday newspaper, I will have earned more money than most people in the world will earn all week. For me to tell some complicated story about how I'm morally entitled to keep all this money because of the massive amounts of "value" that I produce would be ridiculously self-serving. And yet people do try to tell such stories.

There was a time when the dominant view on the right was that the market was a system of "natural justice." They thought that competitive markets could be counted upon to assign to each worker a wage that was precisely equivalent to the value that its earner brought to the organization. This turned out to be not just false, but completely the wrong way of looking at things. The most important determinant of wages is not what you produce, but rather how easily you can be replaced. This doesn't coincide with many people's sense of "natural justice," but there are certain advantages to having wages determined in this way. The best way to defend the system is to grant that it's morally counterintuitive but then point to these other advantages.

People on the left, on the other hand, have all too often fallen prey to what might be called the "social recognition" fallacy—the idea that wage rates are determined by the value that "society" confers upon a particular type of labor. In reality, wage rates aren't even determined by the value that *employers* confer upon a person's work, much less society at large. Unfortunately, the social recognition fallacy has led many people to think that the problem of the "working poor" can be cured by changing the perception that people have of these workers or of the contribution that they make to society. Barbara Ehrenreich's book *Nickel and Dimed* created a small cottage industry of journalists working undercover as low-wage workers in order to report their findings.[1] The moral of the story was pretty much the same in every case: These are good, hardworking people who are woefully underpaid given the backbreaking labor they perform and the humiliations they are forced to endure. This is all true, and worth reminding ourselves of. But what are we supposed to do about it? There are generally two recommendations made, either explicitly or implicitly. First, we should be nicer to them. This seems to me uncontroversial. Second, *we should pay them more.* Here is where the argument (such as it is) runs into trouble.

While it seems natural to think that good people doing hard work should receive a decent salary, the simple fact is that capitalism doesn't work that way. It doesn't work that way domestically, and it doesn't work that way internationally. The resulting distribution of income is, to say the least, morally problematic. The question is what we want to do about it. The general problem is that wages in a market economy, like all other prices, are not just rewards but also incentives. Engaging in an eleemosynary pricing policy for reasons of distributive justice can have perverse incentive effects. Thus the market, as usual, has a frustrating tendency to transform initiatives designed to help people out into ones that leave them worse off than they were before. As a result, antipoverty initiatives need to be a lot more sophisticated than simply paying people more. Often it's better just to give people money (typically through the tax system) than to fiddle around with the wage that they're paid.

s s s

Whenever we talk about wages, it is important to keep in mind a few basic economic facts. First of all, the baseline human condition is one of abject poverty. Most of humanity, throughout most of human history, has lived at or near the subsistence level, with an average life expectancy somewhere around age 30, and constant exposure to the perils of famine, disease, and war.[2] Poverty does not require any sort of special explanation—it's simply what you have in the absence of anything else. Go to any museum of archeology and consider how much effort it used to require to fashion a blade, or a vessel capable of carrying water, or a roof to keep the rain off your head. When contemplating what life must have been like, one is reminded of Friedrich Nietzsche's suggestion (offered as a "consolation for the delicate") that perhaps "at that time pain didn't hurt as much as it does nowadays."[3]

The second important fact is that inequality is not as big a part of the story as it is sometimes made out to be. Social inequality has always afforded some individuals within every society something of a buffer against the uncertainty and hardships that afflict the majority. And when people are extremely poor, the difference between social classes stands out in stark relief. Members of the upper class in England used to be easy to identify, for example, because they were often a good head taller than the average person. This wasn't genetic; it was due to the fact that they were the only ones who had been properly fed since childhood. At the beginning of the nineteenth century, the average 14-year-old upper-class boy entering the Royal Military Academy stood a full 10 inches taller than naval recruits of the same age drawn from the working classes.[4] Thus officers would quite literally "look down upon" enlisted men or "stare down their noses" at them (hence the origin of these expressions).

As it was then in England, so it is today in many underdeveloped countries. Yet despite the enormous differences in standard of living that prevail, not to mention a class system that often seems like little more than organized theft, the fact is that in most poor societies, inequality does not contribute all that much to the deprivations of the ordinary person. Even if you seized all of the wealth being hoarded by the upper class and redistributed it to the people, you wouldn't actually see much of an improvement in the average person's standard of living.[5] Why? Because in a typical underdeveloped country there is just not that much wealth to go around. It may seem like a lot, but usually that's just because it is highly concentrated in the hands of a very few individuals. Once you start dividing it up among thousands, it turns out not to go very far. (You can see this by looking at GDP per capita statistics, which basically tell you how much each person would get if all the wealth in a country were divided up equally.) The fundamental problem in underdeveloped countries is not that the wealth is badly divided, but that there is not enough of it. And so what is needed, first and foremost, is growth. (Indeed, the major harms inflicted upon poor countries by social inequality tend not to be a direct consequence of the pattern of distribution, but rather a product of indirect consequences—such as corruption—that undermine the institutional preconditions needed for broad-based economic growth.)

It is also worth keeping in mind that the relative share of national income going to workers tends to be fairly stable over time. The "income share of employees" in the G7 economies has been between 55% and 58% of GDP since 1970 (in the United States, it has remained between 55% and 60% since the 1950s). Furthermore, the long-term trends that emerge tend not to be the result of "political" factors, such as the success of unions in securing wage increases for their members. While the United States has seen a decline in the labor share of national income since the 1980s, that decline has been even more dramatic in Europe and Japan. The rollback of unionization in the United States over the past three decades is not really a central part of the story (far more important have been long-term changes in the *types* of work people are doing). Also, most industrialized nations have not seen any significant increases in economic inequality in the past decade or two.[6] The United States is quite exceptional in this regard, and is not representative of the dominant trends in capitalist economies.

What really determines the income of the average person in any given country is not how well or how badly "labor" is treated by that country's social and political institutions. It may make a big difference to the quality of life of the average worker, but it is not the most important factor in determining his or her wealth. Distributive shares are important; they just aren't *that* important. What really matters is the average level of labor productivity. This is what, ultimately and in the long run, determines wages. Beijing factory workers are paid badly because the entire country is poor. You can fiddle with wages all you want, but the only way to give them a permanent, stable, sustainable increase in income is to make the entire country more productive. To take just one example, in 1999 the average worker in a Chinese steel mill produced 45 tons of output. Meanwhile, the average worker at South Korea's largest steel manufacturer produced 1,501 tons per year.[7] This statistic says a lot about why workers in China are poor and workers in South Korea are rich—not just in the steel industry, but across the entire economy.

Because of this, if one's goal is to enhance the welfare of the average worker, getting too absorbed by questions of distribution is not really that great a strategy. It would take Herculean effort to increase the labor share of national income by even a percentage point or two. Meanwhile, whatever impact this was having on the wage-distribution front would be completely overshadowed by the effects of economic growth. (Recall that even a mature capitalist economy can grow at a steady annual rate of 2% or 3%: A single year's growth is typically as great as the total magnitude of variation in distributive shares over the course of a decade.) This means that gains on the distribution front can easily be vitiated if the struggle to obtain them depresses the rate of growth too much.

This is all worth emphasizing, because there is a tendency to think of "social justice" with respect to wages in terms of a distributional conflict between workers and factory owners. Factory owners, according to this view, try to lowball workers, and the average wage rate is determined by the extent to which they succeed. There is an element of truth in this, but it personalizes the issue in an unhelpful way. The crucial variable is "the extent to which they succeed." Whether or not factory owners succeed in hiring someone at a low wage rate depends crucially upon what other options that person has. If the alternative to factory work is dirt farming, then that person is likely to settle for a low wage. If the alternative is another factory down the street, then that changes things. This is why the wages of factory workers in China have been rising by about 10% per year for the past decade. The entire Chinese economy has been growing at approximately this rate.

Finally, it is important to remember that the assignment of individuals to jobs in a market economy is *unplanned*. In order for our society to run smoothly, a certain number of people have to agree to become doctors, pilots, primary-school teachers, chefs, mechanics, garbage collectors, computer programmers, and so on. Yet if you took a poll of high school students and asked them what they wanted to be when they grew up, you'd find that people don't just spontaneously divide up into the relevant occupational groups. (And needless to say, an economy in which half of the people are rappers, actresses, or art-house filmmakers would not work very well.) So you need to have some mechanism that channels people into the occupations where they are needed and diverts them from the occupations that are overcrowded. This process is necessarily coercive, since it requires most people to give up on what they themselves would like to be doing (artist, actor, musician), in order to do something that "society" requires (waiter, data-entry clerk, administrative assistant, salesperson).

This coercion can be achieved in various ways. One can imagine a planned economy, where students all take an aptitude test upon graduation and are then assigned to a job by some giant computer that keeps track of who's doing what. Obviously, this is unattractive. The alternative solution, in a market economy, is simply to have a competitive labor market. When all goes smoothly, this will ensure that wages in overcrowded sectors will be bid down, while wages in undersupplied sectors will rise. As a result, people will shuffle around until all the jobs are filled, attracted by the high wages available in some sectors, repelled by the low wages and unemployment in others. The fact that people are choosing to do so should not obscure the fact that the labor market is still, at some level, serving a coercive role—pushing people to give up on their dreams and to accept a more pedestrian life than they might have hoped for. And the way this is achieved is through changes in the wages that are paid, along with the unemployment rates that prevail within the relevant sectors. (Think of how much effort society must expend on this front in order to discourage too many people from becoming actors.) It is important, then, when thinking about how "fair" or "unfair" a particular wage is, to keep in mind that we rely upon the labor market to impose a lot of hard decisions upon people. The mere fact that it is impossible to earn a living wage in a particular occupation does not mean that there is any unfairness in the fact that people are paid that wage. It may mean that "society" does not require any more people to enter that occupation: Too many people are doing it already.

$ $ $

One of the reasons that inequality in poor countries often seems so extreme has to do with the number of personal servants people have. Even fairly middle-class people will often have households that are teeming with hired hands. It goes without saying that everyone has a maid, nanny, and cook (social class is reflected in whether they have one, two, or three people to do these jobs). Many people have drivers, tutors of various sorts, and, of course, security guards. When I was much younger, I spent a couple of weeks working in Mexico City. Invited over to my manager's house one Sunday afternoon, I was appalled to discover that they had a guy whose job seemed to be to hang around waiting for me to finish my Corona so that he could run get me a new one. I appeared to be the only person who found it difficult to relax by the pool under these conditions.

I sometimes think about this when I'm assembling a particularly recalcitrant piece of Ikea furniture, or trying to rewire a light socket.

"Here I am, living in one of the richest countries in the world," I say to myself. "Why do I have to build my own furniture and do my own electrical work?" The answer, of course, is that it's precisely *because* I live in one of the richest countries in the world that I have to do my own electrical work. Because labor is so productive, most people have better things to do with their time than hook up other people's light fixtures. As a result, it is punitively expensive to lure them away from these other, more productive occupations. Getting an electrician to come wire your light fixture would typically cost more than the light fixture itself.

This is also why we tend to throw things away rather than get them repaired. It's not because of some general ailment called "consumerism"—it's because getting something repaired is incredibly expensive. One day my stove beeped loudly and the nifty digital display started blinking "Error 5." I looked it up in the manual, which told me to call for immediate servicing. Since it's a gas stove, I figured I wouldn't take chances. I called the company. Two days later, a guy in coveralls showed up at my door during breakfast time. He opened up the oven, yanked something out, tore open a bag, stuck something new in, mumbled something about a "broken sensor," then handed me a bill for $169. He was in my house less than 10 minutes. The sensor cost $70; the rest of the bill was labor and taxes. Imagine how much it would have cost if the stove itself had been broken (as opposed to just the system designed to tell me when the stove is broken).

It is a general feature of advanced economies that, as the country as a whole becomes richer, services become more expensive relative to manufactured goods. The basic reason is that productivity growth in the service sectors lags behind that of the manufacturing sector. In a sense, it's not that services get expensive, it's that everything else get incredibly cheap. What's amazing is not that it costs me $169 to get my stove repaired; it's that it costs me only $599 to buy a brand-new one. When you think about it, the amount of value produced by the guy who goes around repairing gas stoves has not increased all that significantly over the course of the last 50 or 60 years. He wastes a huge amount of time traveling from one house to another. And despite the bells and whistles, the basic technology has not changed all that much—pressurized gas in a pipe, something to light it and control the burn, and so on. The technology for checking it all to see if it is in working order also has not changed much. The factory that manufactures stoves, on the other hand, has been completely revolutionized over the past 50 years. It would not be surprising to discover that workers there were producing three or four times as many stoves per capita, thanks to improvements in manufacturing technology.

This improvement in manufacturing, combined with relative stagnation in the service sector, produces what the economist William Baumol called the "cost disease" in services.[8] When productivity increases in the manufacturing wing of the firm, the gains will typically be divided up—by hook or by crook—among all the firm's constituency groups. As a result, that productivity increase will tend to generate (among other things) wage increases. Yet suppose that there is considerable labor mobility between those who repair and those who manufacture stoves—that anyone qualified to do the former can also do the latter. If the wages of factory workers go up, some people who work in service will want to switch jobs. This will have the effect of putting downward pressure on the wages in manufacturing and upward pressure on the wages in repair. The firm will have to pay more to keep people working in repair even though there have been no productivity gains in this sector. This increases the "unit cost" of providing the service.

Thus the benefits to workers that come from increased productivity in one sector will tend to be shared by other workers, regardless of whether or not they themselves are working any more productively. In the short term, some set of workers may be able to capture the benefits of a particular set of productivity gains, particularly if they have some special skill or have undergone costly or time-consuming training that makes it harder for others to enter their corner of the market. But in the long run labor is quite mobile between occupations. This is why, if you look at productivity growth in various sectors of the economy over the course of a few decades and compare it to changes in wages, you see very little correlation (unlike, say, changes in output price, which track changes in productivity fairly closely).[9] Yet there is a strong correlation between average productivity growth (across the entire economy) and wage increases. This is why wages in underdeveloped countries are very low, even in highly automated factories where the level of productivity of the individual worker is comparable to that in wealthier parts of the world. What they are paid bears only a slight relationship to what they produce. It is the average level of productivity in the economy, or in the broader sector in which they are employed, that determines wages.

This is why personal services become more expensive as the country as a whole becomes wealthier. Everyone's wages get pushed up, even if there is no change in the way particular services are provided. While posing as a maid (Ehrenreich-style), the *Globe and Mail* journalist Jan Wong contemplated the absurdity of a client having asked her to do some ironing:

> The client has left written instructions on little yellow sticky papers stuck to three small mountains of ironing. 1. "Iron for sure this pile. Must do." 2. "Iron if time allows." 3. "Fold and iron IF TIME ALLOWS." I snort at the things she wants ironed: jeans, T-shirts, cotton turtlenecks . . . We're booked for four hours, at $171. After two hours, I'm only midway through the second pile of ironing. After three hours, I have seven items left. There are 51 items in all, including sheets and pillowcases, which means it costs the client $1.25 per item.[10]

The observation is perfectly sensible, yet Wong fails to draw the obvious implication: Even when working somewhat below the minimum wage, she is essentially being overpaid *relative to the value of the service that she is providing*. This is why maids don't make very much money and are subject to such constant pressure to work harder and faster. It's because—save perhaps for the invention of the vacuum cleaner—the basic level of productivity among housecleaners has not increased much since the nineteenth century. Housecleaning is time-consuming manual labor with no economies of scale. As a result, it is only the existence of nasty working conditions that makes it possible for people outside the upper classes to hire maids. (Wong was working for an agency and points out, astutely, that only middle-class clients hire maids through agencies.) The alternative to having maids who do grueling work at minimum wage working for agencies is not well-paid maids, but rather the absence of maids (in the same way that our economy currently features an absence of butlers).

If people were paid for the value of what they create, the cost of hiring a maid would have changed very little since the late nineteenth century. Yet if the wages paid to maids were stuck at nineteenth-century levels, no one would be willing to work as a maid. Wages have therefore risen, enough to keep a certain number of people willing to do the job. But as they have risen, the advantages of hiring someone to clean your house, as opposed to doing it yourself, have declined. And so various forms of domestic service have essentially been squeezed out of the economy. The problem is not that employers are mean; it's that the amount of value produced through that sort of labor is intrinsically very low. People used to pay their butlers to iron the newspaper in the morning, so that the ink would not rub off on their fingers. This was cost-effective at the time, because the overall productivity level of human labor was so appallingly low that a butler, released from this sort of service, couldn't actually produce that much more value in another occupation. In the present day, however, hiring a butler to do this means outbidding all of the other people who might be able to make use of this person's skills in a highly automated assembly plant or any of a multitude of other employments where significant value is produced. The scarcity price of labor means that if you want to divert someone from a useful occupation in order to have him sit around ironing your morning newspaper, then you have to compensate everyone else who might have made use of his time in some other way. As labor in general becomes more productive, the amount of compensation you have to offer for it increases, until at some point hiring servants becomes simply not worth the trouble, even for those who are quite wealthy.

There are many examples of occupations getting squeezed out of the economy by the "cost disease," but one data set I particularly like compares the cost of having a shirt washed and ironed to the prevalence of commercial dry cleaners in several different countries (Table 10.1).[11] (One can see here the effects of the immigration system in the United States, which floods the country with low-skilled labor. I use the word "system" here loosely, to include the wink-wink, nudge-nudge features of the American system that make it possible for employers to hire illegal immigrants.)

	Cost per shirt ($US)	Ratio of population to laundry workers
Denmark	$5.20	3,500
Sweden	$4.25	727
Spain	$3.90	905
West Germany	$3.70	667
United Kingdom	$2.20	750
United States	$1.50	391

Table 10.1 Squeezing out laundries

The alternative to having a particular service squeezed out is that it becomes an object of luxury consumption. Baumol initially developed his argument using the example of symphony orchestras—pointing out that it takes exactly the same number of musicians to play a Beethoven symphony now as it did a century ago.[12] By rights, they should be paid pennies, not dollars, per hour for live performances. Yet of course they aren't. Their wages have, by and large, kept up with those of factory workers. Some of this has been recouped through a shift to studio work and recorded music. But the more obvious result has been the transformation of live performances of classical music into a luxury good, and even then, one available only with massive public subsidy.

An exception to this rule occurs when it is the employee's time itself that is valued by the consumer. The problem with maids is that they are valued primarily for the *output* they produce. Some of Ehrenreich's clients seemed to have derived enjoyment from watching her scrub the floor, but most didn't. In fact, they weren't even home. All they wanted was to have the house clean when they got back from work. This is what imposes the upper bound on how much they are willing to pay. With other sorts of employment, on the other hand—anything that is advertised as "pampering"—the waste of someone else's time constitutes a significant element of that which is being consumed. This is why there are fewer maids than there once were but more massage therapists. The more expensive the other person's time is, the greater the sense of luxury produced through the act of wasting it.

$ $ $

Most of us are quite lucky that wages aren't determined by the intrinsic value of what we create; if they were, we'd be very poor. One of the ways of thinking about this is to take your job, consider your daily routine, and ask yourself whether you're producing 10 times more than someone doing the same job a century ago. Farmers, construction workers, miners, accountants, engineers, filing clerks, and factory workers can easily answer yes to this question. The rest of us cannot. Yet for those of us who answer no, it means that we are basically hitching a ride on the coattails of workers in sectors that have undergone more significant productivity gains. We are taking advantage of the fact that markets have something of an equalizing tendency with respect to wages.

In a sense, you get paid not so much for what you do, but rather for what you *could* do. If you weren't being paid at least that much, then you would stop doing what you're doing and start doing that other thing. This is why, despite the fact that we all do approximately the same job, law professors make about twice as much money as philosophy professors. The difference is that the law professors have better outside options. In fact, most of them could earn even more money than they do now if they quit the university and went to work as lawyers. Philosophy professors, on the other hand, can't really use their skills to do anything but teach philosophy. If the salaries of philosophy professors around the world were one day cut in half, across the board, I doubt that a single department of philosophy would close down. The same would not be true of law schools.

All this raises a second question: Why are philosophy professors paid as much as they are, given that they have such terrible outside options? The answer has to do with a second equalizing tendency within our economy, which is that large organizations tend to flatten out wage spreads between employees. This is a claim that surprises many people, but there is plenty of evidence to support it. The economist Robert Frank has proposed the following thought experiment, to see the equalizing tendency in academic departments. Generally speaking, "any three people in a given age group will collectively earn more than any other two."[13] Now, he asks the reader to consider which would hurt the organization more: having the two best employees quit, or having the three worst employees quit. The answer, typically, is that losing the two best would be far, far worse. But this just shows that these two are being paid less than what they contribute relative to the other three.

Even in companies that have highly individualized compensation, the difference between what the most productive employee earns in a particular occupational class and what the least productive employee earns is not nearly proportional to the differences in their contributions to the revenues of the firm. When compensation is adjusted directly for the level of individual contribution, as for sales staff who earn commissions, the differences are not as great as one might expect if each employee had simply tried to negotiate the best deal possible for himself with the employer, tied to a credible threat to leave and work for a rival firm. We tend not to realize this, because we ignore just how much better good employees are at their jobs than bad employees. Frank conducted a small survey of car dealerships in upstate New York and found that "most of these dealers reported that their best salespersons consistently make several times as many sales as do their least productive salespersons, and even during generally depressed years will make more sales than the average salesperson does in an average year."[14] Yet even with commissions their compensation does not even come close to reflecting these differences in output.

It's not difficult to see why there might be this flattening of wages within firms. Ultimately, people need to work together, and wage inequalities are one of the most important sources of internal conflict and dissension. As I've already mentioned, I consider myself overpaid (in the grand scheme of things). As a result, I make it a point never to complain about my salary. There is only one thing in the world that is capable of making me feel underpaid: looking up how much my colleagues are making. And by "colleagues," I mean "people working in my department, at my university." I may casually glance at what philosophy professors at other universities are earning, but I don't really get excited about it. Why? Because it's no reflection on me. It's not the same as when the guy across the hall, who reports to the same dean and has his compensation determined in exactly the same way, earns more than me. (This is why public-sector disclosure legislation, such as the act that is responsible for my salary appearing on the Web, tends to have the perverse effect of putting upward pressure on public-sector salaries. The public cares only a little bit about these salaries, but the people who are earning them care a *lot*. Telling people how much the person down the hall from them is earning is one of the best-known ways of generating demands for wage increases—which is precisely why businesses tend to keep this information secret.)

The upshot is that equality functions as an important constraint on wages within firms. (There is one glaring exception to this rule: the wage gap between executives and other employees, which has been steadily rising. This is, however, largely an American phenomenon, one that has more to do with a breakdown in governance between chief executives and boards of directors of large, publicly traded firms. It is, in other words, a consequence of market failure, not of the ordinary operations of the labor market.) One of the major challenges facing firms after a merger or acquisition is trying to deal with differences in salary levels and, in particular, trying to achieve greater equality without simply raising everyone to the highest level.

Philosophy professors have seen their salaries rise quite considerably in the last couple decades. This is because we are, in effect, hitching two free rides. First of all, we benefit from the fact that average wages have been increasing across the board as a result of increased productivity in completely unrelated sectors. So even though universities have not dramatically increased their productivity (there are limits to how many more students can be squeezed into classrooms), we still get the benefits of rising wages. Second, we benefit from the fact that wages for highly skilled employees have been rising even faster. This gives faculty members in areas like engineering, finance, and law much better outside options, and so pushes up their salaries. In order to avoid bitter recriminations and infighting, the university then raises the wages of all faculty members.

Obviously, I benefit from these two equalizing tendencies. Unfortunately, it is not clear that society as a whole benefits as much. The first tendency is relatively benign. As the wages of philosophy professors rise, demand for their services declines, and studying philosophy becomes more and more of a luxury good. Some people may lament the cultural consequences of this, but at least it has the advantage of channeling labor toward its more productive employments (in the same way that scarcity pricing channels all resources toward their most productive employment). The second tendency is less benign. The equalizing pressure on wages within the university means that some departments have difficulty retaining faculty, because they can't pay salaries that are high enough to compete with the outside options. Usually, the only way they are able to lure people in is through the superior status that being a university professor confers (which is, in many respects, a form of adverse selection). Meanwhile, other departments (like philosophy) find themselves turning away job applicants literally by the hundreds. The wage rate, which should be sending a signal to the effect that "the world does not need more philosophers," is sending the opposite message. As a result, society must rely upon unemployment, rather than low wages, to deter entry into the field. Because of this, something of a "lottery economy" develops, where some people win big and most wind up with nothing. The structure of this is similar to the shea-butter nut rush that the Body Shop created in Ghana by paying above-market rates for the product.

This may all seem rather esoteric, but the principles generalize to any other sector of the labor market. Consider, for example, the campaign for pay equity (codified in the International Covenant on Economic, Social and Cultural Rights, adopted by the United Nations in 1966). Women typically earn less than men. There are a variety of reasons for this, one of them being sex-based discrimination. In order to eliminate the latter, it is generally accepted that men and women doing the same job (with the same level of seniority, the same level of training, and so on) should be paid the same. "Equal pay for equal work" is fairly uncontroversial. (Although that doesn't stop some people from arguing against it, on the ridiculous grounds that men more often have families to support whereas women have husbands who work. My wife hears this sometimes from her co-workers. The suggestion that wages should somehow be a function of household budget is, of course, crazy as soon as you think about it. Should people with kids be paid more? And the thought that *all* men are entitled to earn more just because *some* of them have dependent spouses is self-evidently absurd.)

Yet people have not been satisfied with just that uncontroversial principle, because it does nothing to address the problem of "pink ghettos"—sectors of low-paid work in which *all* employees are women. Here there are often no men to serve as a comparison class, making it difficult to say that the low pay is a consequence of discrimination.

As a result, in the past few decades, the basic antidiscrimination intuition has been extended to the somewhat more dubious claim that men and women should receive "equal pay for work of equal value," where "value" is typically taken to be determined by four factors: skill, effort, responsibility, and working conditions.[15] (This is known as "comparable worth" in the United States, "pay equity" in Canada.) The four-factor evaluation scheme is then used to assess jobs across completely different sectors of the labor market. Consider Table 10.2, a typical illustration of how such a system of evaluation can be used (from a report by the Canadian Human Rights Commission):[16]

Job	Skill score	Effort score	Responsibility score	Working conditions score	Total score	Wage
Receptionist	120	30	150	20	320	$28,000
Warehouse worker	90	60	130	40	320	$33,000

Table 10.2 Comparing apples and oranges

The suggestion is made that, in cases such as this, the receptionist's work is not being "equitably recognized and compensated." The use of the word "recognized" is important here—it suggests that the reason receptionists are paid less than warehouse workers has something to do with a larger failure, on the part of either society or the employer, to achieve an unbiased assessment of the difficulty of the work that they do. In other words, because we are all sexist, we think that lifting boxes is harder than talking on the telephone, and so we pay warehouse workers more than receptionists. (Elsewhere, it is suggested that work done mostly by women has not, historically, been as "well-appreciated" as work done mostly by men, "and thus, has not been fairly paid."[17] The word "thus" in this sentence is crucial—it suggests that there is some causal relationship between how well workers are paid and how well "appreciated" their contributions are. This is the "social recognition" fallacy.)

Let us suppose that the assessment in Table 10.2 is correct. If warehouse workers are making more than receptionists for jobs that involve exactly the same level of difficulty, then why don't the receptionists apply to work in the warehouses? The answer may be that they would have difficulty getting hired at the warehouse, because of gender discrimination. But if this is the explanation, then the correct way to combat the pay differential is to ensure that women have equal access to such occupations—get rid of the discrimination in hiring. The easiest way to get rid of ghettos is to make it easy for people to leave.

But of course, it is doubtful that many receptionists would be interested in working in warehouses. One reason is that people have different sorts of abilities and tastes, and tend to seek out work that will be the least onerous, given these preferences. Warehouse workers and receptionists are not being drawn from the same labor pool; vacancies in one area will not be filled by applicants from the other. As a result, there could be a dozen applicants for every job opening as a receptionist, and only two or three for jobs in the warehouse. Warehouse workers wind up getting paid more simply because they are in a less competitive labor market.

The point is not to suggest that this is what actually happens. The point is that one cannot infer the presence of discrimination from the mere fact that work of the same difficulty is being paid at different rates. In order to make such an inference, there would also have to be a very high level of short-term labor mobility between the two sectors.

The competitiveness of the labor market could easily be incorporated into the job evaluation scheme, simply by having another category with a score that went up as the number of qualified applicants per job opening went down. It could be called "scarcity." Workers whose skills were in greater demand or subject to a shortfall in supply could then legitimately be paid more. The failure to treat this sort of factor as relevant to compensation reflects a very conscious choice on the part of the architects of these schemes. In the background is clearly a moral theory about the source of entitlement to wages, one that unfortunately bears no relationship to the way wages are determined in a capitalist economy. The implicit claim is that wages should be based upon the difficulty of a job and the skill required to do it, regardless of whether "society" requires fewer or more people with these skills. If this principle were universalized, we would be left without any mechanism for channeling labor into sectors where it is most needed.

Part of the "pink ghetto" problem usually comes from the fact that too many women are seeking the same type of work (it's called a "ghetto" because it's overcrowded), which has the effect of bidding down wages. As Rhona Mahony has observed, if the entire graduating class from university one year decided to go into the ice-cream business, then the wages of workers in that sector would plummet. But the same thing happens if half the cohort decides to become waitresses, primary-school teachers, daycare workers, and nurses.[18]

Of course, the constrained set of career options that women have historically faced is the legacy of discrimination in other sectors. Women have traditionally done certain types of work because they were denied other options. The solution, though, is not to raise the wages in the female sector—that sends precisely the wrong signal. Women should be discouraged from seeking work in overcrowded fields, not rewarded with higher pay. Large employers, such as the government, do have the discretion to equalize wages to some degree (the same way the universities can over-pay philosophy professors), but the incentive effects are often perverse.

Take the case of nursing, a classic pink ghetto. Doctors used to be almost all male, because of very active discrimination against women both in medical-school admissions and in the professional culture of medicine. Doctors are also paid a lot more than nurses. But this pay differential is not there because society failed to place enough value on work in the "caring" professions. It's because an entire generation of women who could have been doctors were instead forced to work as nurses. The removal of barriers to entry has generated a massive influx of women into medical schools (so that the U.K. and Canada are now graduating more female than male doctors, while in the United States the two groups are about tied). Part of the reason women have been keen to become doctors is no doubt that they want to make more money than they could as nurses. Unsurprisingly, hospitals are now beginning to suffer from a shortage of trained nurses (and are facing retention problems). So the wages of nurses are going up, just as the earnings of doctors are going down (in part because female doctors work, on average, less than male doctors).[19]

In other words, the universe is unfolding more or less as it should. Once the active discrimination against women in medical schools is eliminated, the pay inequity works itself out, without requiring any further intervention. The temptation to step in and fiddle around with wages is one that should be resisted. Artificially raising the salaries of nurses 20 years ago would have been inimical to the broader goal of achieving gender equality, insofar as it would have diminished the incentive that so many young women have to become doctors.

So while pay equity may help certain specific women, it does not advance the general cause of gender equality. Indeed, in many cases the language of equality is simply being hijacked to serve other ends. The fact that there is no genuine commitment to equality underlying that language can be seen in the fact that "equity" is always achieved by increasing women's wages. Yet if women are being underpaid, it is *necessarily* true that men are being overpaid. It would not be unreasonable for an employer hit with a pay-equity lawsuit to insist that every dollar of increased salary that goes to a female employee be "paid for" by a decrease in a male employee's salary. Yet no court would even impose such a settlement, and no union would ever accept one.

$ $ $

One of the major consequences of the success of Ehrenreich's book was renewed attention in the United States to the issue of the minimum wage. Concern about the minimum wage was also something of an inevitable consequence of the Clinton "welfare" reforms, which put a five-year lifetime cap on eligibility for social assistance. Much of this culminated in the subsequent adoption of the Fair Minimum Wage Act of 2007 in the United States, which is slated to raise the federal minimum wage from $5.15 to $7.25 an hour.

As we have already seen, there is an active debate among economists about the impact of the minimum wage. The Economics 101 argument, which says that such laws do more harm than good because of the unemployment they create, has been shown to be too simplistic given the complexities of real-world labor markets. At the same time, it is absurd to maintain that minimum-wage laws do not have some perverse consequences. For example, very few primary breadwinners work at the minimum wage—the sorts of jobs that are paid minimum wage are typically done to earn supplemental income within the household. In particular, 30% of minimum-wage earners in the United States are teenagers.[20] But the fact that so much of the benefit from minimum-wage legislation flows to teenagers can itself have perverse consequences. For example, some evidence has been produced to show that it may increase high school dropout rates.[21] The money itself increases the attractiveness of working, rather than staying in school, but it may also have more subtle effects, such as leading teenagers to overestimate the extent to which the economy will reward unskilled labor.

All of this is not to say that the minimum wage is a bad idea; it just means that we should disabuse ourselves of the notion that it is a useful tool for fighting poverty. Even David Card and Alan Krueger, whose empirical research has done the most to undermine the received opposition to minimum wages, have observed that the minimum wage is an extremely "blunt instrument" when it comes to correcting poverty.[22] Aside from its perverse consequences, its benefits are not particularly well targeted. If the goal is to combat poverty, a more useful measure would be to ensure that no single-income, minimum-wage household has to pay income tax (a principle that is frequently violated in many jurisdictions). Personally, I support having a minimum wage, and I think it should be set at a reasonably high level. My support for it, however, is based upon an entirely non-economic consideration—I think that wage rates below a certain level are incompatible with human dignity. The fact that people may be willing to sell their services at this price is not a decisive consideration. People may be willing to sell themselves into slavery as well, but the law will not uphold such contracts, on the grounds that they are incompatible with human dignity. (Why it is permissible, then, to purchase products from workers in other countries who are paid much less than the domestic minimum wage is a much longer and more complicated story.)

Ehrenreich's diagnosis of the basic problem confronting the working poor is actually somewhat more nuanced than simply a focus upon wages. In her view, the issue is that "wages are too low and rents too high" (something that "you don't need a degree in economics to see").[23] She takes this to be a simple consequence of the rich outbidding the poor in order to "buy up their tenements or trailer parks, and replace them with condos, McMansions, golf courses, or whatever they like."[24] Unfortunately, this makes things seem a bit too straightforward. Housing is not intrinsically scarce, since we can always build more of it or increase the density of what we have. Both land and building materials are cheap across most of the United States. If the market is failing to deliver an adequate supply of low-income housing, it is actually an interesting question to ask why.

Many people point the finger of blame at housing codes.[25] In fact, there is an interesting similarity between housing codes and minimum-wage laws. One of the reasons traditional, high-density workers' housing is so hard to find is that municipal bylaws have ratcheted up standards over time, making institutions like the rooming house or the cold-water flat illegal in many jurisdictions. In Toronto, for instance, the property standards bylaws specify how much habitable space must be available per occupant (nine square meters), how large each bedroom must be, and so on. It regulates the temperature of the hot water, and specifies that "every dwelling unit shall have at least one water closet, one wash basin, one kitchen sink and one bathtub or shower" and that "every room in which meals are prepared in a dwelling unit shall have a sink that is installed in a counter having a backsplash and a drain board made of material impervious to water."[26]

Part of the motivation for adopting such codes was obviously to reduce the squalor of the conditions in which poor people often find themselves living. Yet it should also be recognized that these rules increase the cost of rental housing (in particular, by outlawing the sharing of kitchens and bathrooms between units), which in turn leads to a reduction in supply. It is not clear that there was much sensitivity to the impact upon the poor when these codes were adopted. Much of the Toronto code, for instance, is clearly intended to deal with complaints from middle-class homeowners (length of grass must not exceed 20 centimeters, firewood may not be stacked to a height of more than 1.5 meters in the yard, driveways must be "kept free from dirt, surface dust and refuse . . . maintained in good repair and free from cracks, holes and ruts," etc.).[27]

Again, this is not an argument against having minimal standards for rental housing (just as the specter of unemployment is not a knockdown argument against minimum wages). Living conditions are also closely related to issues of human dignity, and a wealthy society should want to ensure that no one is forced to live below a certain level. What needs to be recognized, however, is that all these well-intentioned policies are win-lose from the standpoint of the poor, because of the perverse effects caused by interference with the price mechanism. As a result, while these policies do confer some benefits upon some people, they also impose very tangible harms upon others. If *other* ways of delivering benefits become available, ways that are not associated with the same harms, we should seize the opportunity to adopt them.

To the non-American reader, for instance, the thing that leaps off the page of Ehrenreich's book—and that of pretty much every other ethnographic account of poverty in America—is health care. It is the lack of reliable access to medical care that makes the life of poverty in America not just uncomfortable, but positively scary. No amount of fiddling with the minimum wage is going to make a difference on that front. While the introduction of a universal health care system in the United States would not directly affect the problem of low wages or high rents, it could generate a lot more in the way of benefits for the working poor—without the perverse effects that come from interfering with prices in the labor or housing market.

In general, it is far too easy to jump to the conclusion that so-and-so or so-and-so is being underpaid. It's not enough simply to look at what people do and make some sort of intuitive judgment of how much that job is "worth." Wages, in a market economy, are prices, and the price of one thing always depends upon the price of everything else. Furthermore, prices are fundamentally intended to track relative scarcity, which is why wages are powerfully affected by how many people are willing or able to do a particular job. Because the amount that people are paid is affected by all sorts of factors that are completely extraneous to the actual work that they do or the amount of effort that it requires, relying upon intuitive moral judgments about the fairness or unfairness of particular wage rates is bound to lead to simplistic political judgments and, in the extreme, to unworkable labor-market policies.

CHAPTER 11

SHARING THE WEALTH

Why capitalism produces so few capitalists

There was a time when people used to complain about "the idle rich." This is something that, for better or for worse, has been changing. Rather than being the layabout grandchildren of long-deceased industrial tycoons, the rich today are more likely to be hyperactive overachievers who got to where they are through 80-hour workweeks and eye-popping salaries. Part of this is due to runaway executive compensation. Disney CEO Michael Eisner went from earning $10 million in 1984—considered a large amount at the time—to $203 million in 1994, a sum equal to 68% of the company's annual profits.[1] No wonder being a shareholder is not as exciting as it once was. While inherited wealth may have been the big scandal of nineteenth-century capitalism, it has since been edged out by the problem of runaway income.[2]

Still, the fact that the wealthy can sit around and do nothing, living comfortably off their investments, still rankles many people. No matter how you feel about Eisner's pay package, the fact remains that he had to get out of bed every morning and do *something* to earn it; but the same cannot be said of those, like the Walton, Cox, or Mars heirs, who became billionaires simply by inheriting money that their parents or grandparents had worked for. In most industrial democracies, the richest 10% of households own somewhere between 50% and 70% of the wealth, while the bottom half own close to nothing.[3] Since a significant fraction of the national income flows to those who hold this wealth, its disposition remains a matter of public concern. Many people who have made peace with the market as a mechanism for coordinating production and consumption still find its consequences for the distribution of wealth unpalatable. If redistributing income can have perverse effects, insofar as it affects people's work incentives, surely something can be done to make the distribution of these large stocks of wealth more equitable.

The problem with capitalism, according to this view, is simply that it produces too few capitalists.[4] If we want to maintain our standard of living, then we can't consume everything we produce. We also need investment, to replace all the factories, machinery, and computers that we use in our day-to-day economic activities. And we therefore need people to "put in," in the form of labor, somewhat more than they "take out," in the form of individual consumption. The easiest way to do this is to give individuals an incentive to save, in the form of a return on their savings. In this way, those who find it easiest at any given time to put in more than they take out will do so, allowing society to reproduce its stock of capital goods in the least intrusive way. The alternative is to have some form of mandatory collective savings orchestrated by the state. This typically has the disadvantage of imposing a uniform savings rate upon everyone despite the fact that some people might have legitimate reasons for wanting to consume their entire income at some particular period of their lives. For example, a household with young children will want to ratchet up its consumption, while one with grown children may want to scale back.

Once you accept the principle of individual savings, however, and grant that this should be accomplished by giving individuals some sort of incentive to save, then you've basically conceded the principle that it's okay for people with accumulated wealth to be paid despite the fact that they haven't actively "done" anything to earn it. Karl Marx famously made fun of the idea that capitalists could be entitled to their profits by virtue of their heroic "abstinence" from consumption (if you want to see abstinence from consumption, he suggested, take a walk through a Manchester factory slum). Yet it is undeniable that those who save money in order to lend it to others at interest are in fact performing a valuable social service. And if this is so, then it is not difficult to show that forgone consumption should be a legitimate basis for reward.[5]

Yet it is possible to accept the basic principle at work here—that capitalists can be paid merely for being capitalists—and still lament the fact that so few people seem to have gotten a piece of the action. If we're going to have a system that simply pumps out money to reward passive investors, then why not have a system that disperses this money as broadly as possible, so that everyone gets a stake in the success of the system? This idea, often referred to as "people's capitalism" or the "ownership society," tries to make capitalism more equitable by distributing its advantages out more broadly. More formally, blueprints of this sort are referred to as "asset redistribution" plans (as opposed to "income redistribution"). Unfortunately, plans of this sort have encountered their own difficulties. It's very easy to give people money, but a lot more difficult to persuade them not to spend it. The capacity for abstinence, it turns out, is not quite as well distributed in the population as one might hope. Still, there is a persistent unwillingness on the part of many to believe that poverty might be caused by anything other than a lack of money. The result is a dramatic overestimation of the power of straightforward redistribution to achieve significant gains in social welfare.

$ $ $

In the nineteenth century, economists used to fret about what was called "the improvidence of the poor." At the time, they were primarily concerned with the problem of poor people having children that they couldn't support. These days the discussion is a lot more circumspect. It is couched in terms of "hyperbolic discounting," "dynamic preference instability," and "pathologies of intertemporal choice." But the problem that is being identified is very much the same. Poor people don't just suffer from a lack of money; they also have a tendency to make extraordinarily bad choices with the money that they do have. While there are many cases of poor single mothers scraping and saving, sacrificing themselves to give their kids a good start in life, this is not the dominant phenotype. Even very sympathetic observers, time and again, have pointed to the lack of "money-management skills" as a major problem in poor households.

It is a commonplace observation that poor people often, perversely, wind up paying more for basic necessities than those who are somewhat better off. In jurisdictions where landlords are permitted to demand "security deposits" or "first and last month's rent," the poor are often excluded from renting apartments, and so wind up paying a much higher daily rate to live in motels. When banks require large minimum deposits, the poor wind up having to use check-cashing outlets that charge extremely high fees (plausible in cases where the check might bounce, but more difficult to justify when it is a welfare, unemployment, or pension check). The poor also pay much higher rates for credit, through pawn shops, payday loans, rent-to-own sales, and the like.

Ethnographic accounts of poverty provide a wealth of more concrete examples. In his book *The Working Poor,* David Shipler works through the household budget of a couple who paid $200 a month for laundry, because their washing machine was broken, and another $200 or so a month for restaurant meals, "because the gas company wouldn't turn on their gas until they paid $400 in overdue bills."[6]

In each case, the problem is caused by the need to come up with a lump sum of money, at the "front end" as it were, in order to avoid higher periodic payments. Table 11.1 shows a highly schematic representation of the kind of trap that poor people wind up in. The first payment stream is what middle-class consumers wind up paying, whether it be for rent, food, laundry, banking services, or consumer credit. The second payment stream represents what the poor wind up paying, whether it be to live in a motel, eat fast food rather than cook, go to the laundromat, or use a check-cashing service.

	Series of payments							
	1	2	3	4	5	6	7	Total
Payment stream 1 (middle class)	$100	$5	$5	$5	$5	$5	$5	$130
Payment stream 2 (poor)	$20	$20	$20	$20	$20	$20	$20	$140

Table 11.1 The poverty trap: initial and subsequent payments

There is a straightforward explanation for how a person could get locked into the second payment stream. If you look at the total amount spent, it is clear that while the poor person can "afford" her upfront payment, there is a problem with the way the payment scheme is organized over time. In order to switch from payment stream 2 to payment stream 1, a person would need to save up $100. It takes at most five periods to do so, but because the good that is being consumed is essential (housing, food, etc.), it's impossible to survive without it for that long. Thus the person has no choice but to continue paying the high price, which effectively prohibits her from setting aside the required amount of money. This is why people often describe the greatest frustration of poverty in terms of the impossibility of "getting ahead."

This is the charitable explanation for why there is often such a mismatch between the total income of poor households and the quality of life that their members are able to attain. And there are many cases where this explanation is clearly correct. In developing countries in particular, the "can't get ahead" scenario is quite common, which is why microcredit—the practice of giving small loans to the very poor—can generate such significant improvements in welfare. Yet in wealthy industrial countries the charitable explanation is often a lot less plausible. The fact that acceptance of it remains de rigueur on the left is an unfortunately indication of dogmatism (nourished, it should be noted, by the milk of human kindness, but nevertheless still dogmatism). This easily shades over into the fallacy of thinking that poverty is its own explanation—that the only thing wrong with poor people is that they have no money. Would that this were true, since then we would know how to fix their problems. In reality, poverty tends to be a symptom, rather than a cause, of a much deeper set of problems. Most of the poverty in wealthy societies (or at least those with reasonable social welfare systems) is not like old-fashioned Dickensian poverty (what used to be called "pauperism"). It could perhaps better be described as "recalcitrant poverty," on the grounds that it's poverty that we don't exactly know how to get rid of.

To see this, one need only look at the sort of poverty traps that many poor people get into. Much of what goes on in these households is difficult to explain in strictly financial terms. Partly this is because one can find the same pattern of expenditure—a stream of high periodic payments that could be reduced by a single lump-sum payment—but in areas that are clearly discretionary. The family budget that Shipler dissected, which included $200 a month for laundry because the washing machine was broken, also included $161 for tickets to an Ozzy Osbourne concert, $50 a month for movie rentals, $100 a month to buy Kraft "Lunchables" for their preschooler, and so on.[7] The budget was also marked by a constant stream of small, impulsive purchases. As Willie, the father, explained, "I know if we were smart people, we could be well off. Sometimes I bring home $700 a week. I know I could be well off. But, you know, neither of us can just sit home and say, OK, this is what we've got for dinner, and that's it. If we had $10 in our pocket and we were sick and tired of sitting in the house, we'd go out and spend $10 on ice cream and supper."[8]

This sort of impulsiveness is something that companies serving the "poverty industry" understand very well. The same firms that run "payday loan" services are often in the "rent-to-own" business as well. While payday loans (typically very short-term loans at annualized rates of interest between 300% and 1,000%) may be used to cover emergency expenses, such as avoiding having one's power disconnected, the same generally cannot be said for renting a television or a living-room sofa. (Rent-to-own stores evade the laws governing consumer credit by claiming that they are offering rental agreements with an option to purchase, rather than a purchase with financing. As a result, they are able to charge an implicit interest rate several times higher than that of even the most expensive credit cards—typically without having to disclose this to the consumer.)

In many cases, the structure of the business model is quite clear. These firms are profitable because they cater not so much to those who are poor, but rather to those who are *extremely impatient*. (They are often quite up-front about this. One of the major players in the Canadian market, Rentcash Inc., launched two services: Instaloans for payday loans and Instarent for rent-to-own. The prefix "insta" tells you everything you need to know about the clientele that they are targeting.) One study in Canada showed that 25% of users of check-cashing services used them to get access to the money more quickly (to avoid the hold that banks often impose on payment), while only 7% did so because they had no bank account.[9] Of course, there is no reason to think that being poor makes you more short-sighted or impatient than the average person. But there is good reason to think that being unusually impatient will make you poor. Especially when there is an entire industry that has sprung up to take advantage of people with this precise disposition.

Many of the mortgage products that contributed to the U.S. subprime fiasco were also obviously structured in such a way as to take advantage of people with a very short planning horizon. This is particularly true of "negative amortization" loans, where the initial monthly payments did not even cover the interest charges, and so the size of the principal grew from month to month. In a market where house prices are rising rapidly and the buyer intends to sell, such a loan could make sense. But for the most part these products were used just to exploit short-sighted or unsophisticated borrowers.

$ $ $

Economists have a very nice tool that they use to represent people's impatience. It's referred to as a *discount function*. The discount function is introduced to account for the fact that people have a general preference for present over future satisfaction. Given a choice between having something nice happen today or having it happen in a week, all things being equal, most people prefer to have it happen today. Some of this reflects uncertainty about the future (you may die tomorrow, and so not get a chance to enjoy things in a week), but some of it constitutes a *pure time preference*. We are simply impatient. We want happiness now, rather than later.

It's fairly easy to measure the level of impatience people exhibit. If I have a preference for present satisfaction over future satisfaction, the only way to persuade me to defer some particular satisfaction is to promise me a greater amount in the future. This is why it is thought necessary to pay people interest on their savings. If I decide to consume $100 now rather than save it, at a time when interest rates are at 5%, this means that I prefer $100 now to $105 in a year's time (because that's what my $100 will turn into, if I let it sit in the bank for a year). But as the interest rate goes up, it must presumably reach a point at which it makes me willing to save. Suppose that when it reaches 10% I become willing to save the $100. This means that $100 right now is worth the same to me as $110 in a year. Thus we say that the *present discounted value* of "$110 in a year" is $100. And since the value a year from now of "$110 a year from now" will also be $100, it follows that the present value of "$110 in two years" will be around $91.

Thus the discount factor is like the opposite of the interest rate. In this example, an interest rate of 10% corresponds to a discount factor of just under 91% (arrived at through the following calculation: $1/1.1$). The way to figure out the present value of some quantity of satisfaction is therefore to multiply it by the discount factor once for every time period that one must wait before experiencing it. So when people look at something like the payoff streams shown in Table 11.1, the way they make their decision is not by comparing the total cost. They tend to assign somewhat greater importance to up-front cost. For a person with a discount rate of 80% per period, the two payoff streams look like Table 11.2.

	Series of payments							Discounted total
	1	2	3	4	5	6	7	
Payment stream 1	$100	$4	$3.20	$2.56	$2.05	$1.64	$1.31	$114.76
Payment stream 2	$20	$16	$12.80	$10.24	$8.19	$6.55	$5.24	$79.02

Table 11.2 The poverty trap made worse: initial and subsequent payments

One can see here why energy-saving appliances are a hard sell. The first payoff stream "feels" like more money at the point of decision because the cost is up-front; the benefits are realized only in the future. So a person who appears to be "stuck" in the high-cost payment stream may not actually be stuck—he may simply lack the incentive to switch, given the way that he discounts the future. Naturally, a person who discounts the future more sharply is more likely to end up in these sorts of "poverty traps."

If that seems bad, don't worry—it gets worse. When economists started introducing discount rates into their models, they didn't actually go and study people in order to determine how much the average person discounts future satisfaction. They just looked at interest rates, and assumed that these could serve as a model for the way that individuals discount the future. But when psychologists came along and started looking at the choices people actually make, a very different sort of pattern began to emerge.

Some of the most important early studies were actually done on animals. The psychologist George Ainslie, for instance, started out studying pigeons.[10] He would put a pigeon in a cage with two buttons. One button would release a small amount of food right away, and the other would release a larger amount of food after some delay. By varying the length of the delay, he could find the exact point at which the pigeon would switch from the "larger, later" reward to the "smaller, sooner" one. Collecting enough data points of this sort allowed him to figure out the rate at which pigeons discount future satisfaction.

What he discovered, however, was rather surprising. The interest-rate model in economics had led investigators to expect that aversion to delay would be uniform across all time periods: delay would "count" for the same amount regardless of when it was scheduled to occur. Instead, Ainslie found that there is a warp in our attitude toward the future. Delay tends to loom much larger in the very near term, whereas future delays are assigned disproportionately lower significance. With pigeons, a food reward would lose something like *half* of its allure through the first second of delay, but subsequent seconds had a much less dramatic impact. A better approximation of the pigeon's discount rate could be achieved by taking the quantity of food and simply dividing it by the number of seconds of delay prior to its consumption, resulting in a better representation of its present value.

Ainslie called this a *hyperbolic* discount rate, because the effects of delay are highly exaggerated in the near term. And when he turned to studying people, he found that the way we discount the future has very much the same structure. We are more patient than pigeons— we discount over the course of years, not seconds—but we share the same tendency to exaggerate the near term. So if you take something like payment stream 2 from Table 11.2 (suppose it's lease payments, over a seven-year term), the way that it really looks to people at the beginning is more like the second stream in Table 11.3. Instead of slow, steady decay, what you get is rapid initial decay followed by significant leveling off.

	Series of payments							Discounted total
	1	2	3	4	5	6	7	
Interest rate model	$20	$16	$12.80	$10.24	$8.19	$6.55	$5.24	$79.02
Hyperbolic discounting	$20	$10	$6.66	$5	$4	$3.33	$2.85	$51.85

Table 11.3 The poverty trap made even worse: initial payment and subsequent payments

What makes this sort of discount function so unfortunate is not just that it generates short-sighted behavior, but that it also generates inconsistencies of choice over time. Ainslie illustrates this with a very simple example. He asks audiences what they would do given a choice between a check for $100 that can be cashed right away and a check for $200 that can be cashed in three years. Many people will choose the $100. But many of these same people, when given a choice between a $100 check that can be cashed in six years and a $200 check that can be cashed in nine years, will take the $200.[11] It's not difficult to imagine what they are thinking. In the first case people think, "Three years is a long time—I might as well take the $100." In the second case they think, "Since I'm already waiting six years, an extra three years is no big deal—I might as well go for the $200." But these same people, in six years, will want to reverse this decision. The three years that don't seem like a big deal when they are far away become a much bigger deal as they approach the present.

Hyperbolic discounting thus generates not only short-sightedness, but also the phenomenon that philosophers have traditionally referred to as "weakness of the will." This phenomenon plays a very important role in addiction and other patterns of self-defeating behavior. When the time to act is far away, we resolve to choose the greater good, but as the moment of decision approaches we give in to temptation and choose the lesser, more immediate good. So we resolve to floss more, or save more, or eat less, or interrupt other people less, or go to bed earlier, or stop smoking, but when the time comes to make good on this commitment, we can't bring ourselves to do it. For the hyperbolic discounter, the initial delay generates a massive reduction in the present value of a particular event. But the fact that value decays so quickly in the near term means that it also tends to spike up as the event comes closer to happening. This is what leads people to choose the "smaller, sooner" reward over the "larger, later" one—even though they had initially resolved not to do so, and will subsequently regret their choice.

Consider the example shown in Figure 11.1. It shows a situation in which a person of limited means has to choose between going to a movie on Saturday evening and having money for dinner on Sunday. Eating dinner on Sunday is worth more than seeing the movie. The two graphs show the expected utility for these two outcomes on each day of the week preceding, starting on Monday. On the left, one can see a person with a standard discount function (80% per day), while the right shows someone with a hyperbolic discount rate (utility divided by "number of days plus one"). Both individuals can see clearly that having money for dinner on Sunday represents the greater good. They also both start out, on Monday, with a preference for the greater good. The central difference is that, for the hyperbolic discounter, that preference gets reversed on Friday, remains inverted throughout the day on Saturday, and then switches back again on Sunday. So this person, left to his own devices, will resolve to save his money for dinner on Sunday but then change his mind and go to the movie when the opportunity presents itself.

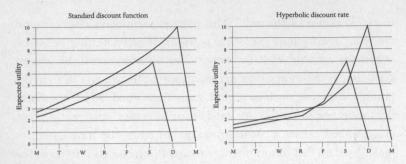

Figure 11.1 Dynamic preference inconsistency

It should be clear from all this that hyperbolic discounting is a very bad thing. Unfortunately, everyone seems to be naturally disposed to discount the future in this way. As a result, most of us spend a lot of energy trying to ensure that our attitude toward the future looks more like the left-hand side of Figure 11.1 than like the right-hand side. Often we do this through straightforward self-control, but we also rely quite heavily upon other people and the environment. (I'm convinced that this is why married people—despite all the trials and tribulations associated with that institution—are on average happier than everyone else:[12] all the nagging and mutual insult, while painful in the short term, serves the larger purpose of preventing bad habits from getting too much out of control. People who live alone for too long, on the other hand, often become unmarriageable, simply because their bad habits become more and more extreme as time goes by.)

It may come as no surprise to learn that people's discount functions become less hyperbolic (on average) with age. People with higher levels of educational attainment also tend to discount the future less hyperbolically. In both cases, the causal relation probably runs both ways. People who discount their future satisfaction more sharply are more likely to drop out of school and/or die young. It would also come as no surprise to learn that what are euphemistically referred to as "low-SES individuals" (SES stands for "socioeconomic status") discount the future hyperbolically. Even if being poor doesn't make you discount the future more sharply, discounting the future too sharply is certainly a recipe for becoming poor. Again, if one thinks of Galston's "three rules" for avoiding poverty in American society—finish high school, marry before having a child, and wait until you're at least 20 before having that child (and maybe add a fourth rule, don't become a drug addict)—it's easy to see the connection between excessive discounting and poverty.

$ $ $

By now it should be clear how all this relates to the "improvidence of the poor." Unfortunately, talking about the self-defeating choices poor people so often make generates a lot of discomfort, because it is usually the first step of an argument that seeks to blame the poor for their own misfortune (followed by a "you made your bed, now lie in it" admonition). As a result, many people on the left choose to deny the phenomenon and insist that any appearance of improvidence is entirely a product of the circumstances that people find themselves in, rather than of the choices they have made. There is an element of wishful thinking in this. Wouldn't it be nice if all the social problems that one finds among the poor were merely a *product* of their poverty? Then these problems would be easy to fix, just by redistributing income. But what if, as a matter of fact, poverty is a *consequence* of the underlying social problem? This puts significant constraints on how much can realistically be achieved through redistribution.

A better approach would be to grant the obvious fact that a lot of poverty (in wealthy countries with a robust labor market and a generous welfare state) is extremely recalcitrant, and often exacerbated by self-defeating patterns of behavior on the part of the poor, but then to deny the right-wing policy implications that are often thought to follow from this. The problem with these policies is that, under the banner of "personal responsibility," conservatives ignore the distinction between moral hazard problems and the effects of hyperbolic discounting. While forcing people to live with the consequences of their own choices may be effective in the former case, it is unlikely to have much effect in the latter. The problem with people who discount the future too sharply is that they disregard certain incentives (those that occur too far off in the future). To propose those very same incentives as a solution to the problem amounts to little more than piling on.

Consider, for instance, Thomas Robert Malthus's view on the problem of indigent children:

> When the wages of labour are hardly sufficient to maintain two children, a man marries and has five or six. He of course finds himself miserably distressed. He accuses the insufficiency of the price of labour to maintain a family. He accuses the parish for their tardy and sparing fulfillment of their obligation to assist him. He accuses the avarice of the rich, who suffer him to want what they can so well spare. He accuses the partial and unjust institutions of society, which have awarded him an inadequate share of the produce of the earth. He accuses perhaps the dispensations of Providence, which have assigned to him a place in society so beset with unavoidable distress and dependence. In searching for objects of accusation, he never adverts to the quarter from which all his misfortunes originate. The last person that he would think of accusing is himself, on whom, in fact, the whole of the blame lies.[13]

Malthus proceeds to draw the tough-love conclusion: "If he cannot support his children, they must starve; and if he marry in the face of a fair probability that he shall not be able to support his children, he is guilty of all the evils which he thus brings upon himself, his wife, and his offspring."[14] The thought here is pretty straightforward: The most effective deterrent to having children you can't support is to have to sit there and watch them die. Now, if Malthus had thought that this was a moral hazard problem—that people were having too many children *because* they could count upon the "parish" or the government to support them—then cutting off all assistance might help to resolve the overpopulation problem. But if the problem is that people are listening "to the voice of passion," and thus disregarding the consequences of their choices, promising to internalize the costs of these choices is not going to change the behavior—it's merely going to kill a lot of children. Malthus may have wanted to do it anyhow, just to prove a point, but that doesn't provide a very powerful public policy argument.

The left-wing response to the problem of improvidence exhibits greater generosity of spirit, but is unfortunately no more promising. Insofar as anyone is willing to admit that the poor make bad choices, they chalk it up to effects of bad information. As a result, "more education" is proposed as the universal panacea. If teenagers are having babies, or dropping out of school, or committing crimes, or smoking, it must be because they have (in some sense) no choice, or because they don't fully understand the consequences of the choices that they do have. The reflex is to call for more education. People need more *information,* so they can make the right choices.

The problem with this proposed solution is obvious: You can't educate people who aren't willing to sit and learn anything. You can give people information, but you can't make them care about it. The whole problem with extreme hyperbolic discounting is that it makes people unwilling to tolerate short-term deprivations in order to achieve long-term benefits. Acquiring an education is an example of *precisely* the sort of deprivation that these people are unwilling to accept. The solution, in other words, presupposes that the problem has already been fixed.

The tendency to overprescribe education as a solution to social problems stems from a very general failure to look at these problems from a motivational perspective. People who make terrible life choices are often perfectly aware of the consequences of these decisions. The problem is that they can't help themselves. They lack the incentive to stop, not in general, but rather at the crucial point in time at which decisions have to be made. Making alcoholics ineligible for liver transplants or telling cigarette smokers they'll have to pay for their own chemotherapy isn't going to deter anyone, because the threatened punishment is too far off in the future. If these people were capable of being motivated by such distant concerns, then the threat of cirrhosis or cancer alone would be enough to deter them. What they need are incentives *right here and now.* Alcohol and cigarette taxes, for example, are surprisingly effective at reducing drinking and smoking.[15]

One can see this thinking beginning to influence the design of social programs. The Oportunidades program in Mexico is the pioneering example and is rapidly being imitated around the world (such as by the Bolsa Familia program in Brazil). The basic idea involves making welfare payments conditional upon good parenting. For example, mothers cannot pick up their monthly support payments unless they can show that their children have been attending school regularly, that they have appropriate vaccinations, and that they been to the doctor for scheduled checkups. What makes programs such as this so successful is that they do not change people's incentives: They merely rearrange the temporal sequence in which these incentives are experienced. Naturally, parents don't want their children to be caught in a vicious circle of poverty, and they understand that education and good health dramatically improve their chances of escaping from it. Yet when the costs of prevention are up-front and the potential benefits are decades removed, people face a significant motivational challenge bringing themselves to do the right thing. The Oportunidades program simply makes it in their interest, here and now, to do the right thing. This has proven to be more valuable than a thousand recitations of the fable of the ant and the grasshopper. (In the same way, everyone wants to save for their retirement, but doing this through voluntary contributions is very difficult. So we negotiate benefits through our employer, essentially forcing ourselves to make the contributions that we know we should be making.)

The right-wing formula—defending freedom of choice at the front end, combined with massive punishments at the back end—thus amounts in practice to little more than kicking people after they're down. The left-wing formula of education, social work, and other "talking cures" feels less coercive, but in practice tends simply to make people more aware of how badly they are screwing up. What people with highly exaggerated discount functions need is a *restructuring of incentives*, in order to facilitate more effective strategies of self-control.

$ $ $

Most of us know from everyday experience that not everyone is equally good at handling cash. We talk about people with money "burning a hole in their pockets." Even those who are fairly sophisticated at managing their finances usually take specific measures aimed at reducing the liquidity of their assets—by purchasing real estate, locked-in retirement savings plans, dedicated education savings funds, back-loaded mutual funds, and so on. Furthermore, the creation of these illiquid assets is strongly encouraged by the tax system. Yet despite this, the majority of the population fails to take advantage of these opportunities and—perhaps unsurprisingly—fails to accumulate any wealth or savings.

Consider the distribution of financial wealth (excluding owner-occupied housing) in the United States. In 1995, 93% was held by the wealthiest 20%, 6.9% by the next quintile, and 1.4% by the middle, while the bottom two quintiles held −1.3%.[16] It is easy to show that this distribution reflects not just inequality in the distribution of income, but also a systematic failure to save on the part of large segments of the population (including many who are quite rich, not just by global standards, but even by relative American standards). So while it's all well and good to want to see less inequality in the distribution of wealth, it is worth stopping first to ask why the distribution is so unequal to begin with.

Yet many people on the left have resolutely shied away from asking this question. Consider, for example, the proposal made by Bruce Ackerman and Anne Alstott in *The Stakeholder Society*, a proposal designed to break up large concentrations of wealth and guarantee every American a fair start in life.[17] Ackerman and Alstott suggest that inheritance taxes be increased in order to finance a cash transfer to each new generation of American citizens—$80,000 per person, to be received between the ages of 18 and 25. The idea is to create equality of opportunity by "leveling the playing field" at the beginning of adulthood. This is presented as a serious legislative proposal, complete with calculations of how much it would cost ($225 billion per year), how the financing could be arranged, and so on.

The hope is obviously that people will do something sensible with the $80,000, such as acquire a university eduction or buy into a mutual fund. If a person were to invest the capital wisely, the sum of $80,000 could generate an income stream that would be more generous than the welfare payments available to single individuals in most jurisdictions. Unfortunately, $80,000 also covers the sticker price of a fully loaded Cadillac Escalade. What's to stop people from buying the SUV, rather than the mutual fund? There are empirical studies that examine how people handle large lump-sum cash transfers—such as lottery winnings or bequests—and the results are pretty devastating. A 2001 study in the United States suggested that about 70% of people who receive large lump-sum payments spend it all in the first two years.[18]

To take a practical example, large "coming of age" payments are common in North America on Native reserves with significant oil and gas revenues. Consider, for example, the case of the Samson Cree reserve in Hobbema, Alberta, which sits on top of a massive oil field. During the 1980s, the federal government in Canada collected over $783 million in royalties for the Samson Cree. At the time, families were collecting nearly $3,000 in royalties each month and teenagers were given $100,000 on their eighteenth birthday. And at the same time, Hobbema became the suicide capital of the country. In this community of 6,000, there were over 300 suicides a year, and a violent death was occurring once a week.[19]

These types of social problems tend to have very complex causes, especially in Native communities. However, many tribal elders identified the "coming of age" royalty checks as a major contributing factor. According to one, "A lot of these kids, they will not listen. They will rebel, simply because of the fact that they have this money coming. It's more of a detriment than anything. Kids will drop out of school.

They see it as a career—turning 18. I've seen kids get $150,000, spend it in two months, then commit suicide."[20] Even after drilling was complete and royalty checks began to dwindle (down to between $30,000 and $40,000), Mel Buffalo, a member of the Samson Cree Nation said, "I've seen people spend that in three or four days on booze, casinos and cars."[21]

Of course, Ackerman and Alstott recognize that their plan may give rise to some serious problems involving improvident use of the funds. Yet they treat the issue primarily as an educational challenge, one that can be overcome through public education initiatives, combined with the wise counsel of teachers and parents:

> *At present, most teenagers have little reason to prepare themselves*
> *for the responsibilities of managing eighty thousand dollars.*
> *This will change over time as parents, teachers, and friends spend*
> *endless hours telling them of the perils of blowing their stakes.*
> *We believe that, after hearing years of such talk, most young*
> *Americans will surprise the skeptics and make responsible use of*
> *their new-found freedom.*[22]

What reason is there for such optimism? The suggestion that "endless hours" of lecturing from parents and teachers represents a solution to the problem of irresponsible conduct among teenagers falls somewhere between the comical and the culpably naive. Furthermore, as the Hobbema elder observed, the fact that young people are expecting a large cash transfer makes them *less* likely to listen to others, and more likely to drop out of school. Education cannot correct the problem of improvident spending, because the expectation of the cash transfer undermines the incentive to acquire an education.

Looking at how American adults currently manage their own money certainly offers no grounds for encouragement. Americans are carrying over $650 billion in credit-card debt alone, at punitively high interest rates. Adults are exposed to countless advertisements from debt consolidation and refinancing companies, telling them the perils of such debts, yet they persist in abusing the "new-found freedom" of consumer credit. Moreover, credit-card debt is simply the most extreme manifestation of a more general savings crisis in the United States. Although there are a variety of explanations for the decline in savings, the economist David Laibson has argued that financial innovation may share a large part of the blame, because it increases liquidity and therefore makes it harder for individuals to exercise self-control. Improvements in banking service, in particular, have made it much more difficult to create illiquid assets. It used to be that you had to give your bank several days' notice when you wanted to withdraw money from your savings account. Now the difference between savings and checking accounts has become purely nominal. Furthermore, the introduction of banking machines has meant that everyone has access to their money at all hours (and so withdrawing a fixed amount at the beginning of the week can no longer be used as a self-control mechanism). Reverse mortgages allow people to drain the asset value of their homes. And, of course, various forms of consumer credit have rendered the practice of "saving up" for a purchase almost obsolete.

The general lesson is clear. The existing level of flexibility in the financial system is already causing serious problems for many Americans. In this context, large lump-sum transfers are unlikely to do much good. If most people were capable of accumulating any large sums of money, they would already be doing so. Trying to increase the financial wealth of the population by spreading money around is like pouring water into a sieve. While it would be nice to turn every worker into a capitalist, so that everyone could enjoy a "free" income supplement, the problem is that capital can too easily be spent.

$ $ $

The American economist James Tobin once wrote that "while concerned laymen who observe people with shabby housing or too little to eat instinctively want to provide them with decent housing and adequate food, economists instinctively want to provide them with more cash income . . . This answer rarely satisfies the intelligent egalitarian layman. He knows, partly because he has learned it from economists, that there are pragmatic limits on the redistributive use of taxation and cash transfers."[23]

This is undoubtedly one of the reasons that the "intelligent egalitarian layman" is often tempted to fiddle with prices, rather than simply providing people with cash transfers. The advantage of subsidizing electricity, from this perspective, is that poor people have no choice but to spend their portion of the subsidy on electricity. Then you don't have to worry as much about them getting their heat cut off in the middle of winter. Letting the market set electricity prices, then providing the poor with an income supplement to defray the expense, is a riskier strategy. Some people will inevitably fail to spend it on electricity, and so will wind up getting their heat cut off.

One way to get around this problem is to give people vouchers, rather than cash (then try to prevent the emergence of secondary markets for these vouchers). This is another way of giving the poor an income supplement that can *only* be spent on electricity, one that has the advantage of leaving the price of electricity intact. People have also recommended housing vouchers and education vouchers, and, of course, in the United States, people receive food vouchers. The difficulty with these sorts of schemes is that they are overtly paternalistic, and are therefore thought to stigmatize their intended beneficiaries. Indeed, one of the major reasons that people on the left support price subsidies is that it allows them to implement a paternalistic policy without having to explicitly acknowledge the paternalistic concern. From this perspective, the loss of efficiency associated with the price distortion is simply the price that must be paid in order to avoid having to admit that you don't want to give people cash because you don't trust them to spend it properly.

A proper understanding of hyperbolic discounting, however, serves to dissolve much of this old-fashioned antagonism between liberty and paternalism. Many social policies that force people to act in their own best interests can be understood not as the high-handed intervention of the "nanny state," but rather as a self-binding strategy that individuals themselves may be perfectly happy to support. In the state of Alaska, for instance, rather than having surplus oil and gas royalties disbursed directly to individuals, residents voted to create the Alaska Permanent Fund, which invests the money on their behalf and pays an annual dividend. Subsequent proposals to dissolve the fund and transfer the principal to residents, for them to invest (or spend) as they see fit, have all been rejected. Residents of Alaska have exhibited a strong preference to keep the principal locked away, not just from politicians, but also from themselves. They prefer to receive the income stream rather than to hold the asset. Those who seek to dissolve the fund argue that this is paternalistic. Yet if individuals are regarded as hyperbolic discounters, it may be regarded as a rational self-binding strategy, carried out with the assistance of the state.

Many of the more nannyish features of the welfare state can be understood in the same way—including various types of forced savings and mandatory insurance. Instead of trying to fiddle with these programs in order to make them seem less paternalistic, a more promising strategy would be to challenge the old assumptions that fail to distinguish between institutions that tell people how to live their lives and those that help people carry through on the commitments needed to live their lives more successfully.

CHAPTER 12

LEVELING DOWN

The wrong way to promote equality

Kurt Vonnegut's story "Harrison Bergeron" is set in a future society where people have finally achieved the ideal of perfect equality: "They weren't only equal before God and the law. They were equal every which way. Nobody was smarter than anybody else. Nobody was better looking than anybody else. Nobody was stronger or quicker than anybody else."[1] The task of ensuring this happy outcome belonged to the Handicapper General, whose office had equipped all smart people with a special earpiece that disrupted their concentration at regular intervals, preventing them from developing very sophisticated thoughts. Those who were beautiful were obliged to wear masks. The healthy and athletic were saddled with weights to slow them down.

The story presents, in somewhat crude form, what philosophers refer to as the "leveling down" objection to egalitarianism. One way of achieving greater equality is to improve the condition of those who are at the bottom. But it is just as easy—and in many cases easier—to achieve equality by worsening the condition of those who are at the top. When this is done without improving anyone else's condition, it is referred to as *leveling down*. It amounts to cutting down the tall poppies while leaving the rest of the field intact.

Most people agree with Vonnegut that leveling down is unattractive. And while the tendency to level down is not exactly a fallacy, it does lead many people to advocate policies that, if they thought about the consequences more carefully, they would be much more hesitant to endorse. We are inclined to think that in order for an outcome to be classified as *better*, from the moral point of view, there must be someone *for whom* it is better.[2] Naive formulations of the principle of equality violate this principle: They classify more egalitarian distributions as better even if these outcomes are achieved in a way that doesn't make any actual person better off. Unfortunately, people who care about equality are not always as careful as they should be to avoid the charge of leveling down. In particular, they are often not as sensitive as they should be toward what economists call the "equality-efficiency trade-off."

The potential for an efficiency gain is present whenever one person's condition can be improved in a way that doesn't worsen anyone else's. Unfortunately, there is no guarantee that the benefits of efficiency gains will be equally distributed. Thus a temptation may arise to block these efficiency gains in the name of equality. For example, many people are opposed to private schools, or private health care, *merely* because it allows some people to get a better education, or better medical treatment, than others. But unless it can be shown—non-tendentiously—that the benefit to the wealthy person generates some tangible *harm* to the poor, then this egalitarian impulse represents a commitment to leveling down. When defending state monopolies in the area of education or health care, it is important to be able to show that there is some sort of "value-added" associated with the monopoly.

It's very easy to level down without realizing it. Consider the example from chapter 2 of an inegalitarian society growing at an annual rate of 5% and a more egalitarian one growing at a rate of only 0.5%. In the short term, the efficiency losses in the egalitarian society may be compensated for by the benefits flowing to the lowest-paid workers. But after 16 years, the choice of the more egalitarian path becomes an exercise in pure leveling down, since by that time *everyone* in the inegalitarian society—including the lowest-paid workers—will have become richer than their counterparts in the more egalitarian society. When this happens, people might reasonably begin to wonder what the point of equality is, since it seems to be making everyone, including the very poorest, worse off. Of course, money isn't everything, and there may be *other* reasons for preferring the egalitarian arrangement; it's just important to realize that helping the poor, financially, can't be one of them.

$ $ $

Unfortunately, when people talk about the "equality-efficiency trade-off," they sometimes speak as though there were some established result in modern economics that demonstrated the inevitability of such trade-offs. In fact, what modern mathematical economics has proven is the exact opposite: There is no necessary trade-off between equality and efficiency. In an ideal world—more or less the same ideal world in which perfectly competitive markets generate perfectly efficient outcomes—there would be no tension whatsoever between efficiency and equality. We would be able to have capitalist efficiency and socialist equality both at the same time. (Indeed, the initial flush of enthusiasm for "market socialism" was motivated by precisely this discovery.)[3]

The relevant result is known as the Second Fundamental Theorem of Welfare Economics. It shows that the market is basically transparent with respect to equality; it is biased neither toward it nor against it. If you take any outcome that you happen to like, for whatever reason, it is possible to rig up a market economy that will deliver precisely that outcome as a competitive equilibrium. This means that if you happen to like perfect equality, it is possible to configure initial allocations in a way that will induce individuals to trade their way to perfect equality.

The inequality we see in the world around us is not, then, the fault of the market as such. The market, like many institutions, is governed by the "garbage in, garbage out" principle. If you take a totally unequal distribution of resources and productive assets as input, the market will give you a totally unequal distribution of income and consumption as output—the only difference is that it will give you a more efficient, totally unequal distribution. In other words, the difference between rich and poor will be just as great, it's just that everyone will be happier (to varying degrees).

Of course, the real world never even comes close to satisfying the conditions under which this would be true. The theorem is still important, however, because it shows that being committed to both efficiency and equality is not like wanting to have your cake and eat it too. There is no conceptual incoherence involved in wanting both—and as a result, there is no reason *in principle* that egalitarian policies must level down. In other words, the "Harrison Bergeron" scenario is one possible consequence of a simple-minded commitment to equality, but there is no reason that a sophisticated egalitarian cannot avoid such an outcome.

The proof of the Second Fundamental Theorem is a bit complicated, but there is a very simple graphical way of representing the compatibility of a concern for both equality and efficiency. Figure 12.1 shows the distribution of some quantity of goods between two people, Bill and Ted. The status quo, shown as the black dot, assigns more to Bill than to Ted (and is in this respect unequal). Any change in the status quo necessarily falls into one of four categories. Movement up and to the right represents an efficiency gain—both Bill and Ted are better off, and neither is worse off. Movement down and left makes them both worse off. Movement up and to the left, on the other hand, makes Bill worse off and Ted better off. This outcome cannot be judged from the standpoint of efficiency but can be judged superior from the standpoint of equality.[4] Movement down and to the right has the opposite consequence—it exacerbates inequality, while leaving efficiency unchanged. (The "sweet spot," in terms of stable social arrangements, is to be as far out as one can be on the efficiency axis, and as close as one can be to the middle on the equality axis. The advantage of this allocation is that it eliminates all but the most self-serving complaints—no one has any desire to switch places with anyone else, and no one can propose any change that would not leave someone else worse off.)[5]

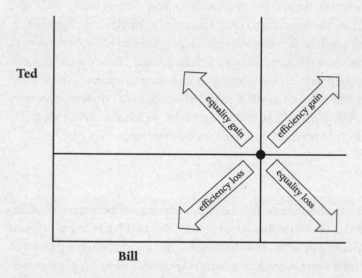

Figure 12.1 The equality and efficiency axes

In this way, one can think of every outcome as the result of two choices: a decision "how much" is to be allocated, and a decision about "who gets what." In principle, these two choices are unrelated to each other; the decision made in one dimension does not constrain the range of options available in the other. Thus the trade-offs that we encounter when dealing with actual public policy questions are typically the result of pragmatic or empirical difficulties. In particular, the type of institutional arrangements needed to promote equality tend to have perverse incentive effects, which diminish efficiency. We have already seen several examples of this, when it comes to fiddling with prices as a way of trying to promote distributive justice. Lower the price of electricity and you will benefit the poor somewhat more than the rich; but at the same time, you will give everyone an incentive to waste electricity (or, more precisely, you will diminish the incentive *not* to waste it). Increase the wages for unskilled work and you will generate a benefit for the poor; but you will also diminish the incentive people have to acquire skills. Impose a gigantic inheritance tax and you will break up large estates; but you will also undermine the incentive to save. The list of examples could quite easily be multiplied. In fact, coming up with proposals to enhance equality at the expense of efficiency is as easy as falling down. The real art of progressive public policy involves coming up with ways to improve equality that *don't* require a major sacrifice on the efficiency front. Modern economics has taught us that it is possible. The job of the left should be to look for these sorts of opportunities, and to seize them when they arise.

$ $ $

As a point of reference, it is helpful to distinguish between two different kinds of redistributive social policy. I like to think of them as "good redistribution" and "bad redistribution." Bad redistribution is the sort of program where government simply takes money away from one person and gives it to someone else. People on the right complain about this all the time, even though that doesn't stop right-wing political parties from doing it once they are in power.

Take, for example, the recent Universal Child Care Benefit adopted by the Conservative government in Canada in 2006 (similar to the "family allowance" schemes that one can find in Norway). The program is pretty simple: The government sends out a $100 check every month to parents for every child under the age of six. The policy was introduced as part of a broader initiative, which primarily involved dismantling the previous government's more hands-on approach to the development of a national daycare program.

Of course, you don't have to be Malthus to wonder why government should be involved in the daycare business at all. It's one thing to provide daycare subsidies so that poor single mothers can get into the workforce. But it's something else entirely to argue that the state should provide subsidized daycare to everyone, or that it should be in the business of owning and operating daycare centers. Where is the market failure? How is it a club good? Why shouldn't middle-class or wealthy parents pay the full cost? One can see why government would want to *regulate* daycares. But why would it want to own, operate, or subsidize them?

Insofar as there is a defensible role for government in this sector, it probably has to do with problems arising at the level of ownership structure. Many people are uncomfortable with standard profit-oriented corporations owning and operating daycare centers, because of the moral hazard problems involved in child care. (How often is my child's diaper being changed? What quality of food is being served? How carefully are toys being washed?) Regulation is a blunt instrument; concern about "mutilating percentages" will always be in the background. As a result, there is a strong incentive to operate daycare centers as consumer cooperatives. These, however, suffer from chronic problems. Because parents know that they will only be members for a fixed (and relatively short) period of time, they tend to exercise poor governance (compared to a condominium, for instance, where people remain in the co-op for longer, and cannot leave without finding someone willing to take their place). Because of this, daycares are often best run on a non-profit model. The problem with nonprofits, however, is that there is no real market incentive to create them. This can result in undersupply of daycare spaces, even when prices are quite high. Thus one argument for government involvement in this sector is simply that a certain amount of organizational work and subsidy is required in order to get the relevant "third sector" institutions into place.

The "family values" crowd, on the other hand, objects to such involvement, on the not-entirely-unreasonable grounds that it arbitrarily privileges one particular lifestyle choice at the expense of others. Women (and men, but for the sake of honesty and convenience, we'll say women) often do a straightforward cost-benefit calculation when deciding whether to stay at home with the kids or return to work: How much will I earn vs. how much it will cost for daycare, a second car, and so on? If they choose to put a child in daycare and return to work, typically this will be because it increases their net income. So why should they receive a government subsidy on top of this increase in income? If anything, they're the lucky ones, because they have access to reasonably good employment opportunities (enough to justify the cost of daycare). Why should women who choose to stay home and raise their own children be penalized for doing so?

This was more or less the reasoning of the Conservative government. If you're going to subsidize child care, they said, you should subsidize *all* child care, regardless of whether it is obtained from paid workers at a daycare or through the "unpaid" labor of mothers in the home. So they withdrew the government from active involvement in the daycare sector, and instead started simply sending out checks. The result, however, became a classic case of bad redistribution.

As economists never tire of pointing out, collecting taxes almost always imposes inefficiencies, by distorting incentives and increasing transaction costs. One of the arguments sometimes made for free public transit is that a significant percentage of each fare is absorbed by the cost of collecting the fare—minting tokens, counting coins, paying attendants, and so on.[6] Standard consumption or income taxes should be thought of in the same way. A nontrivial percentage of each dollar collected in taxes is used to pay the costs of collecting that tax. It is important to be aware of the indirect costs as well, such as the transactions that do not occur because they would be taxed.[7] When people try to put an exact number on this, it tends to be very much influenced by their ideological proclivities, but let's say, for the sake of argument, that on average it "costs" the government 15¢ to collect a dollar's worth of tax revenue.[8] This is called the "deadweight loss" of taxation. Because of the deadweight loss, the total cost of any public project will be larger than the dollars-and-cents cost. When the government spends $1, the "social cost" of this is actually more like $1.15. Thus a public project would have to generate at least $1.15 of benefits for every dollar that the government spends in order to be worthwhile undertaking.[9]

In certain cases, this standard can quite easily be met. With public or "club" goods, for instance, where there is an underlying market failure, the state is often the only institution able to provide a particular good. When the government builds roads, provides vaccinations, or operates a judicial system, there is very little doubt that the benefits outweigh the total cost. This is because the state is not just handing money over to people; it is providing them with a good that they would otherwise be unable to obtain (or unable to obtain at a price that would make it worth buying).

With pure redistribution, on the other hand, the government is not providing a good; it is just handing over money. If the government imposed a tax upon Bill in order to give the money to Ted, it would only be in a position to give Ted 85¢ for every $1 in losses imposed upon Bill (speaking roughly). From the perspective of financial cost, it looks like a losing proposition. The only way it could be justified is if Bill were richer than Ted, so that the welfare cost to Bill of losing $1 was less than the welfare gain to Ted of receiving a mere 85¢. This is called a "progressive" redistribution. The important point is that a redistribution, in order to be worthwhile, must be not only progressive, but significantly so, in order to outweigh the losses imposed by the tax system itself. (Using the tax system to do pure redistribution is sort of like using a leaky bucket to bring water from one person to another: You lose a certain amount in transit. As a result, the transfer will be worthwhile only if the recipient is *really* thirsty compared to the donor; otherwise it's a waste of water.)

With a system that involves simply sending money to all parents, there is no particular reason to think that the redistribution will be progressive. Wealthy suburbanites get the same check as poor single parents living in the projects. Its primary effect is to take money away from people who don't have children (or who had children a while ago) and give it to those who do. This itself seems a bit unfair. After all, most people who have children do so as an expression of their self-interest, not as a benefit to society (the world is, after all, not underpopulated). It is unclear why people shouldn't be expected to save their own money, or perhaps work a bit harder, in order to raise their own children. (I also get $4,000 a year as a "child care benefit" from my employer, on top of my government check. I admit to being somewhat mystified as to why my co-workers should be giving me money merely on the grounds that I have young children.)

In order to avoid the bad optics of sending government checks to rich people, the Canadian government went one step further, deciding to "claw back" the universal benefit by making it count as taxable income. The end result is madness. In my own case, I get $200 a month from the government, about $90 of which I must then *pay back* to the government at the end of the year, so that they can turn around and give it to someone else. This is kind of like bringing me water in a leaky bucket, giving me just a sip, then carrying it back to the person it came from. At some point, it starts to look more like an irrigation system than a water delivery mechanism.

$ $ $

If this is bad redistribution, then what does good redistribution look like? The general problem with just moving money around is that there is no value added by the state. But because there is always a cost associated with making a transfer, the state faces an uphill battle when trying to improve social welfare in this way. It's not impossible, but it's hard. And it's easy to overlook the true social cost of such activities, because many of these costs do not show up on the balance sheet. So cash redistribution often becomes bad redistribution, where the loss on the efficiency front is too great relative to the gain on the equality front.

There is, however, an easier way to improve equality. If you impose a tax upon people with the sole purpose of redistributing the money, then whatever improvements you get at the level of equality are achieved at the expense of decreased efficiency. But if you *already* have to tax people in order to achieve a certain sort of efficiency gain, then why not just fiddle with the system to make it more egalitarian? In particular, in cases where the government is obliged to tax the population in order to resolve a collective action problem, one can simply tweak things on either the taxation or the spending side to make the program as a whole more egalitarian in its consequences. The bulk of the dead-weight loss generated by the taxation scheme is then "paid for" by the efficiency gain associated with the program as a whole. Making it more progressive generates perhaps a small increment, but nothing compared to the initial imposition of the tax. The result will be much closer to the ideal, in which there is no trade-off required between equality and efficiency. I call this approach "opportunistic egalitarianism," because it involves refraining from pursuing too much redistribution until such time as the opportunity presents itself to do so without taking a huge hit on the efficiency front.

One of the first major opportunities to have presented itself, historically, involved Keynes's recommended solution to the problem of the business cycle. As we saw in chapter 9, recessions occur when there is a sudden change in liquidity preference, leading to a shortage of money in circulation. One way to address this is to increase the money supply (as they did in the babysitting co-op) or to lower interest rates. Keynes, however, thought that there were limits on the effectiveness of either strategy. As a result, if people weren't willing to spend their own money, the next-best solution was for the government to spend it for them. Keynes recommended that the state engage in "countercyclical spending"—running a surplus in times of economic expansion, then deficit-spending during recessions. In Keynes's view, it didn't really matter what the state spent the money on during a recession; the important thing was simply that it be spent on *something*. To illustrate the point, he suggested that the government could stuff bottles full of banknotes, bury them in abandoned coal mines, then leave it to the private sector to dig them up again: "It would, indeed, be more sensible to build houses and the like; but if there are political and practical difficulties in the way of this, the above would be better than nothing."[10]

The basic structure of the argument is quite clear. A recession is caused by a certain form of collectively self-defeating behavior. The state is in a position to break people out of the vicious cycle by spending their money for them (on something, it doesn't matter what). Whatever deadweight losses may be caused by the forcing are more than outweighed by the beneficial effects of the fiscal stimulus generated. That's why spending the money on something completely stupid would still be better than nothing. But as long as the state has to spend people's money, why not spend it on something useful? Or, more specifically, why not spend it in a way that promotes greater equality? For example, one could undertake public works projects, like building bridges, libraries, highways, or subways—projects that will either benefit everyone equally or generate a slightly greater benefit for the poor. (This is, in fact, how some of the best and most beautiful public infrastructure in North America came about.)

Since Keynes's time, serious doubts have been raised about the need for an expansion of state spending during times of recession. Many feel that Keynes underestimated the power of monetary policy and overestimated the effectiveness of fiscal measures (not to mention the willingness of governments to eliminate the deficits once the recession was over). The result has been a waning of enthusiasm for classic Keynesian measures, and with it diminished opportunities to use countercyclical spending as a way of promoting greater equality. The traditional left has tried to fight this tide, clinging to the traditional Keynesian remedies. The opportunistic egalitarian, on the other hand, is willing to move on, looking for new opportunities to improve equality without economic sacrifice.

$ $ $

There are some cases in which good redistribution actually looks a lot like bad redistribution: The state takes money away from some people and hands it over to others, so it seems like just a cash transfer with no value added—but what the government is actually doing is running an insurance system. This is obviously true in the case of public pensions, health care, workers' compensation, and unemployment insurance. In a sense, all insurance involves a simple redistribution of funds. Private insurers also take money away from some people (in the form of premiums) and give it to others (in the form of indemnity payments). But there is obviously value added here; that's why people voluntarily buy insurance. What looks like pure redistribution is actually a risk-pooling arrangement (of the sort outlined in chapter 6), which generates benefits for everyone involved.

In some cases, adverse selection problems make it impossible for private insurers to offer a particular form of insurance at a reasonable price, because they have no way of separating the bad risks from the good ones. Governments are able to eliminate these sorts of problems by imposing mandatory insurance upon the entire population (essentially forcing everyone into a single insurance pool). This is the primary rationale for "single payer" health care systems as well as for state pension plans. The premium, in this case, is imposed in the form of a tax (sometimes imposed separately and sometimes drawn from general government revenues). There are no doubt deadweight losses associated with such taxes, but these are also no doubt outweighed by the benefits that flow from the insurance scheme.

Once a system of this sort is in place, one of the ways the state can promote greater equality is to impose non-actuarial premiums. In a purely private insurance scheme, the ideal procedure for setting premium levels is to calculate the magnitude of the loss that a policyholder may suffer, multiply it by the probability that such a loss will occur, and then charge the person precisely that sum. For example, to set a

ECONOMICS WITHOUT ILLUSIONS

fire insurance policy, you start by looking at how much a house and its contents are worth, then look at how likely the house is to burn down in the coming year—tack on about 30% for overhead, and there you have the annual cost of a policy. (This is why expensive homes with antique wiring cost a lot to insure.)

This calculation generates what's known as the *actuarial premium*. In reality, however, it can be very hard to do this calculation properly, both because relevant information is unknown and because prospective policyholders have an incentive to dissemble—to not tell the full truth. Thus insurance premiums tend to be something of an approximation. In some jurisdictions there are legal restrictions on actuarial pricing as well, such as regulations that prevent car insurance companies from charging men more than women (despite the fact that men are statistically far more likely to have accidents).[11] Many people also have moral objections to actuarial pricing, which is one of the reasons why so-called flat-premium friendly societies (in which all members pay the same amount) that were the dominant insurance model throughout the nineteenth century persisted well into the twentieth.[12]

Thus even in the private sector, where people voluntarily sign up for insurance, there is a fair bit of free play when it comes to determining premium levels. What most "social insurance" systems do is simply take advantage of this free play in order to devise a premium scheme that will be progressive with respect to income. It is already necessary, in order to avoid adverse selection problems, to force everyone into a single risk pool. Once that's been done, it's easy to charge them a premium that is based not upon the anticipated loss that they bring to the pool (the actuarial model), but upon their income. This is how health insurance is delivered under a "single payer" system—it is paid for out of general tax revenue, and thus through a progressive income tax. Instead of thinking of the health insurance system as a redistributive program that takes money away from the healthy and gives it to the sick, it is better to think of it as an insurance product, provided to the entire population, paid for through a radically non-actuarial premium.

Thus social insurance presents one of the most significant opportunities for improving equality without creating huge losses on the efficiency front. Even a government that didn't care at all about equality would still have to have a massive tax-collection system in order to finance all the public and club goods that a modern state provides. Furthermore, most of the exemptions, deductions, and special loopholes in the tax code would still be there, since these don't have anything to do with promoting equality. People would also have the same incentive to evade taxes that they have now, and so the standard sort of enforcement apparatus would need to be in place. Yet once this entire system is up and running, it doesn't add *that* much to the complexity of the tax system to have three or four tax brackets rather than just one (so that wealthier individuals are forced to pay a higher percentage of their income in taxes). As the economists Joel Slemrod and Jon Bakija have observed, one of the "great red herrings" in the debate over the 1986 tax act in the United States was the idea that reducing the number of tax brackets constituted an important simplification: "Once taxable income is computed, calculating tax liability from the tax tables is a trivial operation that is not perceptibly simplified by having fewer brackets."[13]

The only significant advantage to eliminating progressivity in the income-tax system is that it might permit the wholesale replacement of the income-tax system with a consumption tax (recall that consumption is equal to income minus savings). Experts are divided, however, over the merits of such a proposal, since the taxation rate would be so high that it would create fairly significant incentives for tax evasion. Most tend to favor a system that features a small number of very broad-based taxes at relatively low rates.

Thus the principle of social insurance—that the state provides insurance to all citizens at a premium level that is progressive with respect to income—greatly enhances equality, while imposing very little in the way of a trade-off with efficiency (because the alternative to state provision is not private provision at actuarial prices, but rather market failure in the private insurance sector). Again, this sort of equality is achieved not by pursuing a comprehensive egalitarian project, but simply by making the most of an opportunity that happens to present itself.

$ $ $

I have been discussing social insurance as merely an "opportunity" that happens to come along and that permits the state to achieve greater equality without significant compromise on the efficiency front. This should not be taken to imply that it is inconsequential. Welfare states typically "redistribute" 10% to 15% of GDP through the mechanisms of old-age pensions and health insurance alone.[14] At the same time, it should be recognized that this opportunity is one that might conceivably fade away. In particular, if some radical innovation in medical forecasting were to take the guesswork out of determining who will suffer from what disease or how long a person can expect to live, then the efficiency gains arising from the relevant insurance markets would dissipate. People would know how much they need to save, and so would derive little benefit from pooling their savings with others.

In the same way that more effective monetary policy diminished the need for Keynesian countercyclical spending, more effective medical technology might diminish the need for social insurance. This would in turn deprive the state of one of the major tools that it has used in recent years to promote greater equality among citizens. (There would still be the distributive justice question of what to do with those who expect to develop very costly, debilitating illnesses. It's just that we would have to confront this as a problem of pure distribution—we would no longer be able to piggyback our redistributive policies onto a mutually advantageous risk-pooling arrangement.)

It is worthwhile, therefore, to keep an eye on the horizon for other opportunities that may present themselves to achieve "good redistribution." Two immediately spring to mind. The first is green taxation.

So far I've been speaking as though taxes always distort incentives in undesirable ways. (I've argued that these distortions are not as bad as people on the right usually make them out to be, but I have granted the basic point.) This is not actually true of all taxes. Apart from lump-sum taxes, which are non-distortionary, there are also Pigovian taxes (named after the economist Arthur Cecil Pigou). These are taxes that are imposed upon goods that are associated with significant negative externalities (a bit like so-called sin taxes on tobacco and alcohol). In this case, the incentive effects of the tax are themselves desirable from an efficiency perspective. Take, for example, the gasoline tax. The general problem with gasoline is that the market price is too low—the purchaser does not fully compensate those who are inconvenienced by her consumption. In particular, those who suffer as a result of the atmospheric pollution generated are not compensated. As a result, the price of gasoline is much lower than it would be in an ideal market economy (in which we all lived in bubbles and were able to charge other people for introducing foul emissions into our airspace).

The result, among other things, is that too much gasoline will be consumed. When the state imposes a tax upon gasoline, the incentive effect of the tax is to discourage gasoline consumption, and therefore to bring total consumption down closer to what it should be (closer to the point where the social cost is warranted by the private benefit). Thus the tax itself can be efficiency-promoting. (I say "can" because of the Second Best Theorem, which shows that, in an economy with multiple price distortions, fixing one price will not necessarily lead to a more efficient outcome; the argument must be made on a case-by-case basis.) Most important, the beneficial effects of the tax can be achieved *regardless* of what the government does with the revenue raised (even if it were to stuff it in bottles and bury them in abandoned mines). Indeed, many people think the government should impose a range of Pigovian taxes, then just turn around and give the money back to people. One sophisticated strategy is to push for the introduction of "green taxes" on a revenue-neutral basis, by matching them with cuts in the income tax. The general slogan: "Tax bads, not goods!"

Of course, it is easy to think of better things to do with the revenue generated. In particular, it can be used to promote greater equality.

Thus a shift toward environmental taxes could offer an important opportunity to achieve the greater good of equality without significant compromise on the efficiency front. It is worth recalling Peter Lindert's observation that more sophisticated welfare states tend to have more efficient tax regimes—value-added taxes, low corporate taxes, and so on. It is perhaps no accident that the higher rates of green taxation are also being introduced in these same states.[15]

From this perspective, global warming creates a huge opportunity for the egalitarian welfare state. The imposition of a tax on carbon emissions—the "carbon tax"—is fully justifiable on efficiency grounds alone. Such a tax would "pay for itself," through its own incentive effects (namely, reducing carbon-dioxide emissions). This would in turn leave the state free to spend the revenue more or less as it saw fit, for such objectives as poverty relief and social assistance.

$ $ $

One of the major preoccupations of the New Left over the course of the twentieth century was the problem of consumerism. This concern arose because of the widespread perception that increased material well-being did not seem to be translating very well into increased happiness, or "quality of life." Thorstein Veblen, who was the first to give a name to the problem, argued that increased material prosperity had given consumption an increasingly competitive character. Goods were valued not so much for their intrinsic properties, but because of the status that they conferred. The problem with status is that we can't make more of it: It's a socially constructed hierarchy. Whenever one person moves up, it effectively bumps someone else down. Thus trying to pursue status competition through increased consumption winds up being collectively self-defeating. When *everyone* ratchets up their consumption, the result is that relative positions remain unchanged.

For example, it used to be very common for doctors to go out and buy a BMW within a few years of opening their practice. (At the hospital where my wife works, there is a single parking garage, so everyone knows what everyone else is driving. Because of this, status considerations play an important role in the decisions people make about what car to buy.) Over time, however, BMWs—especially the 3-series—came to be seen as merely "entry-level" luxury cars. Preferences began shifting toward more expensive vehicles, like the X3 or X5. The result is that the doctors wind up paying much more for their cars—but the pecking order hasn't really changed. The chief of surgery may have a 6- or 7-series BMW instead of a 5-series, doctors will have an SUV instead of a 3-series, and medical residents will now be driving a 3-series instead of a Volkswagen. But no one is getting any *more* status out of the new arrangement—people are simply preserving their relative positions at a higher level of expenditure.

John Stuart Mill argued, a century and a half ago, that this pattern made luxury items a logical target for taxation. "The consequence of cheapening articles of vanity," he wrote, "is not that less is expended on such things, but that the buyers substitute for the cheapened article some other which is more costly, or a more elaborate quality of the same thing; and as the inferior quality answered the purpose of vanity equally well when it was equally expensive, a tax on the article is really paid by nobody: it is a creation of public revenue by which nobody loses."[16]

Take, for example, golf club memberships. The price of membership at an exclusive club has very little to do with how much it actually costs to run the place. The purpose of the price is to maintain exclusivity, by making the club unaffordable to most people. (This is particularly true of clubs with large up-front "debenture" or entrance fees.) Often clubs wind up spending this money on fairly frivolous things that are of no particular value to the members. People are willing to pay the fee because of the exclusivity that it confers; they don't really care about what it is used for. This means that if the state seizes some portion of it, in the form of a tax on golf club and country club memberships, the individuals who wind up paying this tax remain largely unaffected. They still get what they want, which is the exclusivity; it's just that now their money can be used for more socially beneficial purposes.

As the quote from Mill suggests, this is an idea that has been kicking around for some time.[17] A tax on status goods is unfortunately a bit difficult to implement, simply because of the fickleness of status hierarchies and the perfidy of luxury-goods retailers. It does, however, suggest that a progressive income tax does not have nearly as deleterious an impact upon the incentives of the wealthy as is often supposed. Once a certain threshold of expenditure is reached, pretty much everything that a person consumes is in some way or other a status good. A tax that affects *everyone* in an upper income bracket equally makes no one any less able to afford a home in a "nice" neighborhood or to send their child to a "prestigious" college. Because everyone will have less to spend on these positional goods, the prices will simply be lower.[18] Thus the efficiency-equality trade-off in the domain of taxation is probably much less significant than an Economics 101 perspective would lead one to expect.

As for targeting status goods directly, a more sophisticated approach involves nudging those who are participating in the status competition to generate the social benefits all on their own. This is the idea underlying what the economist Roger Congleton calls "efficient status seeking."[19] People engaged in status competition tend to create negative externalities for one another (through their "one-upmanship"). But the status competition as a whole can also generate negative or positive externalities for society more generally. "Bad" status competitions are those that generate negative social effects. The "potlatch" tradition in Native communities on the west coast of Canada would be a good example of this. Although it began as a ritualized form of competitive gift-giving among clans, it eventually became standard to destroy the goods rather than give them to others. So the competition changed from being one that benefited the less fortunate to one that simply resulted in the large-scale destruction of goods. Compare this to the charity auction. Here the dominant motive is still status-seeking. The difference, however, is that the proceeds go to some worthwhile purpose, and so the competition as a whole has beneficial effects for society. It constitutes, therefore, what Congleton calls an "efficient status game."

This sort of efficient status competition has been a fixture of upper-class culture for some time. Endowments for university chairs, grants to the performing arts, additions to hospitals, and straightforward charitable donations are some of the most popular conduits. Furthermore, the sums involved are not insubstantial (the Bill and Melinda Gates Foundation, with an endowment of over $37 billion, is a colossus in the field of global health). But as society becomes more affluent, there is no reason that the same model of efficient status competition cannot move downward. Consider, for example the (RED) brand, launched with some fanfare by the U2 singer Bono and Bobby Shriver in 2006. Their basic approach is to partner with companies like Apple, Motorola, and Nike, which agree to produce and sell special (RED)-branded versions of their popular consumer good (iPods, cell phones, Converse sneakers, etc.). These firms then *voluntarily* take a portion of the purchase price of (RED) products they sell and donate it to the Global Fund, which uses it to combat AIDS in Africa. What's happening here is substantially similar to what would occur if the fight against AIDS were funded through a luxury tax that targeted the brand premium on these items. The difference is that here it is all being done voluntarily, precisely because the firms see it as a way of cultivating a brand premium.

The (RED) brand naturally makes purists quite uneasy, because it seems to be persuading people to do the right thing for the wrong reason. This is basically correct. Rather than trying to combat status competition or defeat the "brand bullies," what (RED) is doing instead is redirecting the forces of competitive consumption in such a way that it at least generates beneficial side effects. And why not? Members of the upper class have been doing the right thing for the wrong reasons for centuries. It's obvious that, despite 40 years of scathing social criticism, members of the middle classes are not about to stop caring about brands. Furthermore, they're not about to stop engaging in status competition (keeping in mind that "cool" is the central status hierarchy in contemporary urban society). In a sense, the guys at (RED) are throwing in the towel when it comes to the traditional left-wing critique of consumerism. What they have, however, is a good backup plan: "Okay, okay," they say. "So you insist on wasting your money buying the latest 'must-have' phone, or sneakers. The least you can do is waste the money by sending it to Africa."

This may not seem like a very big deal, but the fact is that as our societies become wealthier and wealthier, more and more of our consumption becomes directed toward goods that are valued for their relative qualities. Thus more and more of the economy gets channeled into one or another form of competitive consumption. Anything that serves to redirect this competition in such a way as to produce socially beneficial side effects seems to me a highly worthwhile initiative.

$ $ $

People on the left sometimes claim that they don't care about efficiency, that they're interested only in equality. For the most part, this cannot be taken seriously. To promote equality without any regard for efficiency considerations is to exhibit a crazed indifference to human well-being. After all, it can't be a matter of indifference whether people are equally miserable or equally happy. Yet people on the left do consistently find themselves in a position where they are essentially defending leveling down.

As we have seen, many of the policy preferences of the "traditional" social-democratic left come with a cost on the efficiency front. The use of price subsidies, the habit of fiddling with wages, and the preference for pure redistribution all generate substantial deadweight losses. This doesn't mean that there cannot be compensating benefits, but it does mean that such policies should be approached with caution. Opportunistic egalitarianism, by seeking out ways to promote equality without leveling down, is a far more promising strategy. It does require, however, somewhat greater forbearance. Most of the mistakes that people on the left make involve failures of self-restraint—an unwillingness to tolerate moral flaws in society, even when we have no idea how to fix them and no reason to think that the cure will not be worse than the disease.

EPILOGUE

Everyone loves a happy ending. Not only that, but after years of feel-good Disney adaptations and test-marketed blockbusters, we've begun to feel entitled to happy endings. This is true not only of fiction, but of nonfiction as well. In works of social criticism, the nonfiction equivalent of a happy ending is a short chapter showing how all the problems identified throughout the work can be resolved through a series of simple and effective policy measures.

This book lacks a happy ending. While I have been trying to encourage people who hate capitalism to take economics more seriously, this is not because the study of economics offers any simple solutions to the problems of poverty, inequality, or social exclusion. Quite the opposite. The study of economics often just complicates things, by showing how many of the simple solutions so often proposed by people of good will have no reasonable chance of success. In this book, I have focused upon fairly abstract conceptual errors that people make in the way that they reason about economic questions. But one can see quite easily how this percolates down to the level of everyday politics and political ideology.

For example, the left constantly tries to avoid owning up to the consequences of the policies they advocate by claiming that tax burdens can be imposed on corporations rather than individuals. This is a classic example of an easy solution that turns out, on closer analysis, to be entirely nonsensical. Many traditional left-wing parties, for instance, oppose carbon taxes on the grounds that oil companies and polluters should be the ones to pay the penalties, not consumers. But how could that possibly work? When the price of oil goes up, oil companies don't become less profitable—they simply charge people more for gas. If the taxes they pay go up, their response will be exactly the same. It makes absolutely no difference whether the tax is imposed upon consumers or upon corporations: It will be the consumer who pays.

To see this, consider the way a value-added tax works. People on the left sometimes complain, erroneously, that taxes on corporations have declined in the past 25 years. This is not entirely true, since a VAT is, technically speaking, a tax on corporations. After all, have you ever written the government a check to pay the VAT (the way that you pay your income taxes)? If you're incorporated, you do this routinely. But if you're a consumer, then you've never actually paid VAT. Of course, you've paid the VAT indirectly, since companies charge it to you every time you purchase a good or a service. But this just shows that it's impossible to make corporations pay taxes—they pass it along to consumers (or workers, suppliers, or shareholders). In the case of Canada's VAT— the GST—you actually get an itemized receipt at the cash register, showing how much of what you just paid will be used by the company to pay the VAT owing on your purchase. The important point is that you do not pay the tax, and you do not owe it; the corporation is charging you for the tax liability that *it* incurs as a result of your purchase. They could also put an item on the receipt showing how much of what you just paid will be used to pay the "tax on profits" that they owe as a result of your purchase. The only reason they don't is that it's harder to work out a firm number in this case.

None of this should be taken to suggest that there should be no taxes on corporations. It just means that the question is complicated. The ability to incorporate confers genuine advantages upon individuals. In particular, a corporation provides a plethora of opportunities for individuals to minimize their income-tax burden (such as the ability to carry forward income from year to year, to "expense" personal consumption, etc.). I know a lot of people who have moved from self-employment to incorporation; in each case the sole motive for doing so was to reduce their personal tax burden. There should be some costs associated with these benefits. What matters is simply that corporations not be treated as a magic hat out of which the government can pull arbitrarily large tax revenues. Taxes on corporations increase the transaction costs associated with organizing economic transactions outside the market (such as building things in-house rather than outsourcing). This is, in general, undesirable, which is why the most progressive, redistributive welfare states in Europe typically have some of the *lowest* rates of corporate taxation.[1]

Or take the case of international trade. For all the bluster and protest about globalization, the basic problem comes down to something that is quite simple. International trade is controversial because it allows individuals to engage in transactions that would be illegal (and immoral) if conducted domestically. People in China may find it normal to work for 10 hours a day six days a week, but in the United States it is illegal to hire workers for that long. Thus a company that closes down a plant in the United States and moves it to China is effectively doing an end-run around American labor regulations. It will also be doing an end-run around minimum-wage laws, workplace safety regulations, and probably a whole host of environmental regulations. So from a certain moral point of view, it seems obvious that these transactions should be prohibited.

Yet it is also easy to see that the consequences of such a prohibition would be extremely damaging to people in China—precisely those whose welfare ostensibly provides the motivation for the prohibition. The problem is that these trades, despite their apparent unfairness, are nevertheless *mutually advantageous*. Chinese workers take these jobs because they are better than the alternative, in a very poor country.

Workers in Europe took jobs at comparable wages under similar conditions back in the nineteenth century. The only reason they don't have to anymore is that *everyone* is richer. People will someday look back at *us* and marvel that we were willing to work under the conditions that we do at the abysmal level of pay that we currently accept; that doesn't make it immoral for us to work the way that we now do.

Furthermore, it is essential to remember that when China exports goods to the United States, it uses the currency that is earned to import American goods to China. This is an important part of China's development strategy, because it relieves China of the need to do everything that an advanced industrial economy must do, all at the same time. It allows the Chinese to import most of the equipment that is in their factories from Japan or Europe, rather than build it themselves. Or, to take a more interesting example, it allows them to import legal services from the rest of the world (China being a country that, until recently, had almost no lawyers). For a very long time, India followed a policy of economic autarky (self-sufficiency), convinced that trade with the West was a source of exploitation and dependency. The result, however, was economic stagnation, because Indians had to waste countless amounts of time and energy building things that they were not particularly good at building, things they could easily have bought elsewhere.

The important point is that trade between rich countries and poor countries, like all trade, is not a win-lose, but rather a win-win transaction. The consumer in the rich country is not literally gaining at the expense of the worker in the poor country, and the accumulated wealth of the rich country is not achieved through a transfer from the poor. In other words, there is no actual exploitation here—no one is made worse off. International trade is simply a system of mutually beneficial cooperation between people who live under highly unequal conditions. This is not to say that globalization is great, or that it has no problems. It just means that globalization is a very tricky issue, from the moral point of view. On the one hand, there is enormous unfairness in the terms of trade; but on the other hand, the trade is beneficial to both parties, and it is unclear how the terms could be modified without eliminating a lot of the benefits. Thus we need to weigh the pros and cons very carefully before deciding to outlaw certain transactions. Banning child labor should be fairly uncontroversial, but the question of what sort of adult labor or environmental standards to impose strikes me as being very difficult to resolve. Requiring anything like first-world standards is just an indirect way of creating trade barriers, which harm the poor. But at the same time, you don't want to say that anything goes—that as long as everyone is benefiting, everything is okay. That would make child labor okay, too. Somewhere the line must be drawn: We just can't really use our intuitions about what would be appropriate or fair in a domestic context to do so.

The sort of complications that one can get into—along with the moral ambiguities that they generate—have led many people to want to dispense with the market entirely. One of the most extravagant bits of wishful thinking on the part of the progressive left over the course of the twentieth century was the thought that we might be able to get around these problems just by getting together and hammering out some sort of cooperative solution, without any recourse to the market. Some believed that democratic decision-making could actually replace the price system as a means of coordinating production and consumption, both domestically and internationally. Economic decisions, according to this view, would be made by "the community of associated producers."

Again, this is the sort of proposal that falls apart the moment it is subjected to even basic economic analysis. The central problem is that economic decision-making requires a feedback loop, which democracy has a difficult time providing. Take a very concrete example. Suppose that we decide to coordinate economic output by having all the workers at all the factories hold their own meetings to decide how much they are going to produce in the upcoming year. All these "proposals" could then go to a planning board, which would examine them for consistency. Of course, each proposal for a given level of output will be based upon certain assumptions about inputs. In order to make a certain number of batteries, for instance, workers at a given factory are going to need a certain quantity of various metals, use of heavy equipment, and so on. These inputs are in turn the outputs of other work groups, such as the miners, who are responsible for digging up the metals. But these miners use equipment that runs on batteries! The battery makers, when they submit their plan, are going to be making certain assumptions about how much metal the mines are going to produce. The miners, in order to calculate how much they can produce, are going to be making certain assumptions about how many batteries they will have access to. In order to avoid a complete fiasco, it is essential that these assumptions be mutually consistent. This is extremely difficult to do without the market. (In the former Soviet Union, for instance, giant piles of manure used to accumulate by the side of railroads due to lack of coordination between those who manufactured fertilizer and those responsible for producing the bags to put it in[2]—this *despite* the giant planning bureaucracy.) No serious person believes that it is possible to make the sort of fine-grained alignment of proposals needed here through democratic mechanisms.

Even a system in which worker cooperatives used the market to coordinate their production would have very serious problems. The basic flaw in worker cooperatives—which has been observed since the early nineteenth century—is that they have an incentive to restrict both hiring and production. This is relatively innocuous in an economy dominated by capitalist firms, but it would become an extremely serious problem if the model were to become more widespread. It pretty much precludes the organization of an entire economy on a cooperative basis.[3] Because a genuine co-op is essentially a profit-sharing arrangement, workers often find themselves in a situation where bringing in new members would increase net revenue and yet nevertheless lower average profitability. Thus workers typically face a choice between letting productive capacity sit idle, voluntarily lowering their own wages in order to expand employment, or bringing in new workers on contractual terms (that is, not as full members). The temptations of the last option are so great that successful cooperatives have a tendency, over time, to become very much like capitalist firms, with the initial members becoming more and more like shareholders. One can see this explicitly in many law firms, where the partners (the full members of the co-op) make out like bandits, while an army of associates (the contract workers) does all the heavy lifting. It was precisely because of this tendency that many nineteenth-century socialists, such as Beatrice Webb, were so critical of the worker cooperative movement.[4] And yet if you prohibit the practice of hiring on contract, many cooperatives will respond simply by not hiring at all, which in turn generates unemployment.

None of this should really come as big news to anyone on the left, since all these issues have been extensively discussed by economists, including socialist economists (whose left-wing credentials should be beyond reproach), for well over a hundred years. And yet it has had almost no impact on what one might call the "working political ideology" of the left. The same bad ideas continue to attract widespread popular allegiance (while politicians who abandon them continue to be accused of selling out to big business). This is the scandal of economic illiteracy on the left. It's one thing to hope for a better world, but it's essential that we not ignore the enormous investment of intellectual effort over the past two centuries on the part of people trying to figure out how we might actually improve things.

When I was younger, I thought that questions of social justice were easy. It seemed to me that there were two sorts of people in the world—those who were basically selfish, and those who were more generous and caring. Insofar as there was injustice or suffering in the world, it was because those who were selfish had managed to see their interests prevail. Thus the solution to these problems was to persuade people to care more or, failing that, to ensure that people who did care more were given access to political power. Furthermore, because of all the "invisible hand" rhetoric, it seemed obvious to me at the time that capitalism was a system designed by the selfish to advance the interests of the selfish, and that right-wing political parties existed in order to give ideological cover to this operation. Anticapitalism therefore struck me as being a straightforward moral imperative. Government was good; the market was bad.

Now that I'm older, I think there are so many things wrong with this view that I wouldn't even know where to begin enumerating them. Many different factors contributed to this dawning realization. Part of it, no doubt, had to do with spending a fair bit of time, over the course of many years, in Asia, and seeing what an incredible force for development even a poorly structured market economy can be (not to mention what a fiasco the state can be, particularly in places where corruption is an issue). Part of it came from meeting more people outside my immediate circle of left-wing acquaintances, and discovering that "the system" is made up of people pretty much like everyone else, acting on the basis of the usual mix of selfish and altruistic motives that one encounters in any walk of life. But a lot of it came from reading economics, and from trying to work through systematically the alternatives to the existing order of things. What one discovers through this exercise is that for any ridiculous, destructive, or unjust state of affairs, there is usually an understandable reason why that state of affairs persists. Our problem is often not that we lack the will to fix our problems, but that we don't know how to fix them.

William Easterly, in a recent book on aid and development, illustrates this in a dramatic way.[5] He begins by citing the usual blandishments about poverty in Africa, which we have all heard a thousand times. How is it possible in a world as affluent as our own that so many children are still dying of malaria, when "medicine that would prevent half of all malaria deaths costs only twelve cents a dose"? Such miserliness! Obviously we all need to dig deeper into our pockets. But then Easterly reverses the question in a startling way. How is it possible, he asks, in a world where Western countries spent over $2.3 *trillion* on foreign aid in the past five years, that aid organizations are still failing to prevent half of all malaria deaths by providing children with pills that cost only

12¢? The moment you think about it, you realize that it *can't* be from a simple lack of funds. Africa is littered with incredibly expensive, high-tech development projects—factories, irrigation systems, electrification programs, even Internet initiatives. So why not 12¢ antimalarial pills?

What do we learn from all this? The primary thing we learn is that development is complicated. It is not a simple morality tale, with good guys (the poor) and bad guys (the rich). Nobody actually knows how to "develop" a country, or even why things that work in one place don't work in another. The same is true with a lot of economic problems. Nobody really knows how to fix the problem of homelessness, or health care waiting lists, or aboriginal poverty. In each case, the status quo is a product of a number of different forces and considerations, which pull in different directions. Canadians are routinely embarrassed by photos showing terrible living conditions on Native reserves, yet the government also transfers rather eye-popping sums of money to these same communities every year. Part of the problem, pretty much everyone acknowledges, is that people living on reserves do not own their own houses. As a result, they act like tenants rather than like owners—much of the decaying housing one sees is a product of the residents themselves failing to do routine maintenance. But the obvious way to fix this—give them individual title to their land—has serious problems as well. Ownership is useless without the right to sell, but the right to sell is of little value unless it includes the right to sell to people outside the community. Thus individual title would quickly undermine the cultural integrity of the reserve. What's the solution? There is no obvious one. Addressing what *appears* to be a straightforward problem of poverty turns out to demand considerable ingenuity.

It's because the world is complex that I chose to write this book as a handbook of economic fallacies. Strictly speaking, a *fallacy* is simply an argument that takes you from true premises to a false conclusion. What makes it a fallacy, though, as opposed to simply a mistake, is that a fallacy *sounds* right when you first hear it. In fact, it often requires considerable subtlety to see why a fallacious inference is, in fact, invalid.

Fallacies are especially thick on the ground in the field of economics because people fail to appreciate complexity. We ignore the fact that everything depends upon everything else. We forget that people are likely to change their behavior when their environment changes. We overlook the fact that certain things have to add up, if not right away then at least in the long term (consumption and production, imports and exports, etc.). We propose simple arguments to deal with complex situations. The right would have us believe that markets provide the best of all possible worlds, or the best of all pragmatically attainable worlds. Competition is presented as a universal panacea and market "solutions" are recommended even when the hope of organizing anything like a competitive market is self-evidently absurd. Government "inefficiency" is condemned not through appeal to empirical evidence, but on the basis of imaginary first principles ("Government is doing it, therefore it must be inefficient"). Ordinary people are cut loose from mutually beneficial risk-pooling arrangements, or given enough rope to hang themselves, all in the name of individual liberty and personal responsibility. Yet the left would have us believe that any apparent "injustice" in the economy can be resolved by giving orders or changing laws in order to directly modify the terms on which transactions are conducted. Landlords are charging too much? Force them to charge less. Industry is polluting? Make them stop. Employers not paying enough? Get them to pay more. People are poor? Give them more money. Or, better yet, let the government take over, so that we can do the right thing directly, without all the annoyances of having to work through the greedy, profit-oriented private sector.

Is there a quick and easy solution? No. This is why there is no happy ending to the book. For all the hatred and suspicion of capitalism in the world, finding something better has proven to be devilishly difficult. The best we've come up with so far is a set of improvements, along with a set of intellectual tools for thinking about what *other* improvements might be possible. Therein lies the value of modern economic science.

POSTSCRIPT TO THE U.S. EDITION

The great financial crisis of 2008 has provoked an extraordinary round of soul-searching among economists. The reasons for this are not difficult to find. Not only did most members of the profession fail to predict the impending catastrophe, but many aided and abetted it by aggressively rationalizing the very practices and institutional arrangements that gave rise to the collapse of the U.S. investment-banking system.

In the background was the assumption, widely shared among economists, that contractual arrangements entered into by private parties were efficient until proven otherwise. Thus buckets of ink (or terabytes of keystrokes) were wasted, essentially intellectualizing the work of financiers and bankers (much the way academics in the humanities intellectualize the work of artists and writers). The implosion on Wall Street was therefore a source of considerable embarrassment. Imagine an art historian, invited to offer his impressions of a long-lost work by Marcel Duchamp. After waxing poetic for several minutes about its "transgressive" and "post-auratic" qualities, he is informed that a mistake has been made, that the work in question is actually just a urinal. This is basically the situation that many academic economists found themselves in last fall.

The repercussions have been swiftly felt. While the public debate has been dominated by finger-pointing at a bewildering range of suspects, the debate in the economics profession has become quite narrowly focused on two rival theories.

The dominant view of markets had been that they were rational and efficient. Yet in the fall of 2008 it became clear that financial markets had failed to perform efficiently. One obvious explanation was that people were behaving irrationally. For proponents of behavioral economics, the crisis created a huge "I told you so" moment. Many were quick to hop on this bandwagon, arguing that economists were blindsided as a result of their failure to acknowledge the role that "animal spirits" play in investment decisions.

The other possibility is that no one acted all that irrationally, but that rationality and efficiency just don't go together quite as neatly as had been assumed. Perhaps it's the same old story (recounted in chapter 1) of collective action problems and market failure. Yet why then did so many economists miss all the warning signs? The problem is not that they assumed people were rational. The problem stemmed from what the Harvard law professor Robert C. Clark once described as "facile optimism about the optimality of existing institutions."

The first theory is the easier sell. It certainly seems to be the one that everyone wants to believe. It appeals to the outrage of the public and the desire to condemn the eggheads who got us into this mess. It also, however, feeds into the lamentable tendency to treat all of economics as hogwash, or as a castle in the sky invented by ivory-tower intellectuals. This is terribly unhelpful.

While the second view is a bit stodgy, it has a lot more to recommend it. I mention this because, while many of the economic ideas in this book may strike some people as being "outside the box," I am actually a partisan of the conventional, old-fashioned rationality-based approach. This isn't to say that I think people are rational all the time. It means that we have no choice but to act as if most people are mostly rational most of the time. This view is becoming sufficiently unpopular that I feel I should say a few words in defense of it.

It is here that my day job as a philosopher becomes relevant, since

there is a well-established argument—incredibly famous in philosophical circles, mostly unheard-of by the rest of the world—in support of
the rationality-based approach. It was developed by the American philosopher Donald Davidson, and it hinges upon what he called "the principle of charity."

The basic idea is pretty simple. We can observe people's actions,
but we cannot observe their motives. We don't really know what people
are thinking or what they are trying to achieve. Thus any story we con-
coct about a person's behavior is going to be just one of many different stories that are consistent with what we see. So how do we choose
one story? Essentially, we pick the one that makes the person come out
sounding best. We favor the interpretation that minimizes the ascription of error. If we didn't, we would never be able to understand one
another, even with respect to simple things.

Allow me to illustrate this with an example. One of the downsides
of working in philosophy is that it attracts a lot of people with mental-
health problems. It's not all that uncommon for students to submit
notebooks of crazed ramblings in lieu of essays, or for professors to
barricade themselves in their offices. Many years ago I had a colleague
who was facing some challenges of this sort. At the time, he was writing
a book about the great German philosopher and logician Gottlob Frege.
He was very frustrated by the university administration's failure to give
him adequate credit for his work-in-progress. At one point, in a fit of
anger, he exclaimed, "Don't these people realize they're dealing with
the greatest philosopher of the twentieth century?" My friend who was
speaking to him tried gently to correct this, saying, "Wasn't Frege more
of a nineteenth-century philosopher?" To which my colleague replied,
"Frege? I'm not talking about Frege; I'm talking about *me*."

So what exactly happened here? My colleague started out saying
something that was obviously false. This created an interpretive challenge for my friend. Clearly a mistake had been made. The way he constructed his interpretation was by ascribing the *smallest* error possible to
the speaker—having confused the date of Frege's major work. It turns

out this wasn't right; the speaker had made a much larger mistake—having confused himself with the greatest philosopher of the twentieth century.

The point of the story is not that there is anything wrong with interpreting people charitably. On the contrary, it shows why we must do so. Imagine leading with the second interpretation. If you're willing to start with the assumption that people make mistakes of that magnitude, then there are almost no constraints on the crazy things that you can take them to be saying. You would never be able to settle upon a good interpretation, because there would be no way to tell a good one from a bad one. This is not to say that people can't be irrational (my former colleague being a case in point). It's that any explanation that appeals to irrationality shoulders a massive burden of proof (*eo ipso*, as we say in the business).

The same thing applies to understanding people's actions. We assume that these are by and large rational because if we didn't there are no limits on what we could take people to be doing or how we might expect them to behave. If the story you're telling about someone's actions makes them come out sounding completely irrational, it suggests a problem with the story, not the person. This doesn't exclude the possibility that you're right; it just means that you take on a huge burden of proof.

From this perspective, it seems apparent that behavioral economists have been far too cavalier in their ascription of irrationality to economic agents. Consider the case of a bank run, which many proponents of the "animal spirits" view present as an example of mass-hysterical behavior. What is striking about the actions of depositors in the case of a bank run is that their actions are perfectly rational. Two things make the whole thing *seem* irrational. First, because what each person does depends upon what that person thinks that everyone else is going to do, the interaction is subject to very dramatic tipping-point effects. Second, once the run gets started, it is collectively self-defeating or inefficient.

But neither of these two features adds up to genuine irrationality. Indeed, if bank runs were irrational, it's not obvious what one could do to fix them. And yet the introduction of deposit insurance during the New Deal era all but eliminated bank runs in the conventional banking sector. It did so by changing the incentives faced by depositors.

Now take the financial crisis. It's all well and good to blame animal spirits, until one stops to think about what an attractive regulatory response to the crisis would be. Indeed, if the problem is that banks periodically go crazy, how could the situation ever be corrected? We design roads based on the assumption that drivers are trying *not* to run into one another. Similarly, we design the system of financial regulations based on the assumption that firms want to stay solvent. It's not clear how we could approach either design question in the absence of these assumptions.

Thus the rationality postulate is not just an intellectual fantasy or a strange fixation of economists. It's a prerequisite for any useful understanding or critique of our institutions. It is certainly not something that should be abandoned lightly.

ACKNOWLEDGMENTS

I would like to thank the following people for helping me, in one way or another, with this book: Vida Panitch, Sareh Pouryousefi, Andrew Potter, Alisa Kim, Sergio Tenenbaum, Wayne Norman, Rodolphe Dudebout, Justin To, Jacqueline To, Adrian Scotchmer, and Simon Heath. Special thanks to Abraham Singer for the "Atkins diet" analogy and Arthur Ripstein for the "trip to Hawaii" analogy.

I had the opportunity to test-drive some of these arguments in columns that I wrote for the Montreal *Gazette* and *Policy Options* magazine, as well as in an article in *THIS Magazine*. I would like to thank the editors, Brian Kappler, L. Ian MacDonald, and Julie Chrysler, respectively. I would also like to acknowledge a debt of gratitude to HarperCollins Canada for supporting my work, and to Jim Gifford for whipping it all into shape. Finally, I would like to thank the Social Sciences and Humanities Research Council of Canada for financial support of this project.

NOTES

INTRODUCTION

1. See Michael Prowse, "The Old Ideas Can't Constrain Us Forever," *Financial Times*, January 6, 2001.
2. John Kenneth Galbraith, *American Capitalism*, rev. ed. (Cambridge, MA: Riverside, 1956), p. 85.
3. Marc Hauser, *Moral Minds* (New York: HarperCollins, 2006), pp. 92–93.
4. Bryan Caplan, *The Myth of the Rational Voter* (Princeton, NJ: Princeton University Press, 2006), p. 197.
5. Steven E. Landsburg, *The Armchair Economist* (New York: Free Press, 1993), pp. 225–26. See also John Kay, "Thinking Outside the Blue Box on Recycling," *Financial Times*, February 25, 2004. My favorite line is the following: "Most virgin paper comes from Canada and Scandinavia, where there is little other economic activity."
6. Henry Hazlitt, *Economics in One Lesson*, 3rd ed. (New York: Three Rivers, 1979).
7. W. Kip Viscusi, "Cigarette Taxation and the Social Consequences of Smoking," in James Poterba, ed., *Tax Policy and the Economy*, vol. 9 (Cambridge, MA: MIT Press, 1995), pp. 51–101 at 75.
8. Cornelius Walford, "Early Bills of Mortality," *Transactions of the Royal Historical Society* 7 (1878): 212–48 at 230.
9. Or the son of an economist, to be precise. See David Friedman, *Hidden Order* (New York: HarperCollins, 1996), pp. 10–11.
10. Andrew Duany, Elizabeth Plater-Zyberk, and Jeff Speck, *Suburban Nation* (New York: North Point, 2000), p. 90.
11. Joseph Heath and Andrew Potter, *The Rebel Sell* (Toronto: HarperCollins, 2001), p. 112.

CHAPTER 1: CAPITALISM IS NATURAL

1. "The Churchill You Didn't Know," *The Guardian*, November 28, 2002.
2. V. I. Lenin, *State and Revolution* (New York: Independent, 1971), pp. 83–84.

3. See Timothy Miller, *The 60s Communes* (Syracuse, NY: Syracuse University Press, 1999), pp. xviii–xx.

4. Friedrich A. Hayek, *Law, Legislation, and Liberty: Rules and Order* (Chicago: University of Chicago Press, 1978), pp. 36–40.

5. Incidentally, this style of reasoning cast a long shadow on the debate over "rights" throughout the twentieth century. It was precisely to avoid this sort of reasoning, for example, that the "notwithstanding" clause was inserted into the Canadian Charter of Rights, essentially allowing the legislature to immunize particular acts of legislation from judicial review. It was inserted at the insistence of the then-socialist government of Saskatchewan, which wanted it in order to ensure that courts could not block social legislation. This is mildly ironic, given that judicial activism has since become almost exclusively a conservative bugbear.

6. Herbert Spencer, *The Principles of Biology* (New York: D. Appleton and Company, 1902), vol. 1, p. 530.

7. Spencer, *Principles of Biology*, vol. 2, p. 528. By way of elaboration, Spencer noted that "families and races" in which the struggle for survival "does not stimulate to improvements in production—that is, to greater mental activity—are on the high road to extinction; and must ultimately be supplanted by those whom the pressure does so stimulate. This truth we have recently seen exemplified in Ireland." The reference is to the potato famine, which killed approximately one million people in Ireland and created about the same number of refugees (including my own great-grandparents). The ability to maintain such equanimity in the face of catastrophic human suffering became one of the hallmarks of the Victorian moral sensibility.

8. John Locke, *Second Treatise of Government*, ed. C. B. MacPherson (Indianapolis, IN: Hackett, 1980), p. 9, also p. 32.

9. It is typically assumed that an elaborate train is a sign of superior health in the male. See Marion Petrie, "Improved Growth and Survival of Offspring of Peacocks with More Elaborate Trains," *Nature* 371 (October 13, 1994): 598–99.

10. David Hume, *A Treatise of Human Nature*, 2nd ed., ed. P. N. Nidditch (Oxford: Clarendon, 1978), p. 526.

11. This observation is drawn from Thomas Schelling, *The Strategy of Conflict* (Cambridge, MA: Harvard University Press, 1960), pp. 123–37.

12. For discussion, see Drew Fudenberg and Jean Tirole, *Game Theory* (Cambridge, MA: MIT Press, 1991), pp. 367–95.

13. For a more rigorous version of this argument, see Walter J. Schultz, *The Moral Conditions of Economic Efficiency* (Cambridge: Cambridge University Press, 2001), especially chap. 4. See also Avinash K. Dixit, *Lawlessness and Economics* (Princeton, NJ: Princeton University Press, 2004), pp. 1–20.

14. William J. Baumol, *Welfare Economics and the Theory of the State* (Cambridge, MA: Harvard University Press, 1952), p. 92.

15. Steven Holmes and Cass R. Sunstein, *The Cost of Rights: Why Liberty Depends on Taxes* (New York: W. W. Norton, 1999), p. 65.

16. Holmes and Sunstein, *The Cost of Rights*, p. 64.

17. Gary Gorton, "Banking Panics and Business Cycles," *Oxford Economic Papers* 40 (1988): 751–81.
18. This is why it was so surprising to see a bona fide bank run on the IndyMac Bank in California in August 2008. In this case, the primary motivation was that about $1 billion of the $19 billion in deposits held by the bank was uninsured.
19. Gilbert Geis, *White-Collar Criminal* (New York: Atherton, 1968), p. 10.
20. David A. Moss, *When All Else Fails: Government as the Ultimate Risk Manager* (Cambridge, MA: Harvard University Press, 1992), p. 125.
21. Prior to that, the U.S. government passed bankruptcy laws and then repealed them once economic crises were over (1800, 1841, 1867).
22. On limited liability, see Frank H. Easterbrook and Daniel R. Fischel, *The Economic Structure of Corporate Law* (Cambridge, MA: Harvard University Press, 1991), pp. 41–44. Limited liability in *tort* is a separate issue from limited liability for debts—and is rightly more controversial. See Reinier Kraakman, Paul Davies, Henry Hansmann, Gérard Hertig, Klaus J. Hopt, Hideki Kanda, and Edward B. Rock, *The Anatomy of Corporate Law* (New York: Oxford University Press, 2005), pp. 76–77.

CHAPTER 2: INCENTIVES MATTER

1. Steven Landsburg, *The Armchair Economist* (New York: Free Press, 1993), p. 3.
2. Philippa Foot, "The Problem of Abortion and the Doctrine of the Double Effect," in *Virtues and Vices and Other Essays in Moral Philosophy* (Oxford: Basil Blackwell, 1978). A famous variant can be found in Judith Jarvis Thomson, "The Trolley Problem," *Yale Law Journal* 94 (1985): 1395–1415. See Frances Kamm, *Intricate Ethics* (Oxford: Oxford University Press, 2006) as well.
3. For a discussion of this history, see Joseph Heath, *Following the Rules: Practical Reasoning and Deontic Constraint* (New York: Oxford University Press, 2008), pp. 71–85.
4. Steven D. Levitt and Stephen Dubner, *Freakonomics* (New York: HarperCollins, 2005), p. ix. Dubner takes this to be one of Levitt's endearing characteristics.
5. Niccolò Machiavelli, *The Prince*, trans. Harvey C. Mansfield Jr. (Chicago: University of Chicago Press, 1985), p. 66.
6. Landsburg, *The Armchair Economist*, p. 9.
7. Joseph Henrich, Robert Boyd, Samuel Bowles, Colin Camerer, Ernst Fehr, Herbert Gintis, and Richard McElreath, "In Search of Homo Economicus: Behavioral Experiments in 15 Small-Scale Societies," *American Economic Review* 91 (2001): 73–78.
8. The reference is to Richard Thaler's column "Anomalies" published in the *Journal of Economic Perspectives* from 1987 to 1990, collected in Richard H. Thaler, *The Winner's Curse* (Princeton, NJ: Princeton University Press, 1994). "Anomalies" turns out to be something of an understatement.
9. David Sally, "Conversation and Cooperation in Social Dilemmas: A Metaanalysis of Experiments from 1952 to 1992," *Rationality and Society* 7 (1995): 58–92.
10. Varda Liberman, Steven M. Samuels, and Lee Ross, "The Name of the Game: Predictive Power of Reputations versus Situational Labels in Determining Prisoner's Dilemma Game Moves," *Personality and Social Psychology Bulletin* 30 (2004): 1175–85.

11. See the discussion in Chip Heath, "On the Social Psychology of Agency Relationships: Lay Theories of Motivation Overemphasize Extrinsic Incentives," *Organizational Behavior and Human Decision Processes* 78 (1999): 25–62.

12. Heath, "On the Social Psychology of Agency Relationships," pp. 39–44.

13. Richard G. Lipsey, Douglas D. Purvis, and Peter O. Steiner, *Economics*, 6th ed. (New York: Harper & Row, 1988), p. 371.

14. David Card and Alan B. Krueger, *Myth and Measurement: The New Economics of the Minimum Wage* (Princeton, NJ: Princeton University Press, 1997).

15. Assar Lindbeck, *The Political Economy of the New Left* (New York: New York University Press, 1977), p. 39.

16. Joel Slemrod, "The Consequences of Taxation," *Social Philosophy and Policy* 23 (2006): 73–87.

17. Henry Ford, *My Life and Work* (Garden City, NY: Doubleday, 1922), p. 147.

18. George Akerlof, "Labor Contracts as Partial Gift Exchange," *Quarterly Journal of Economics* 97 (1982): 543–69.

19. Daniel M. Hausman, "Problems with Supply-Side Egalitarianism," in Samuel Bowles and Herbert Gintis, *Recasting Egalitarianism*, ed. Erik Olin Wright (London: Verso, 1998), p. 75.

20. Gøsta Esping-Anderson, *The Three Worlds of Welfare Capitalism* (Princeton, NJ: Princeton University Press, 1990), p. 156.

21. János Kornai, *The Socialist System* (Princeton, NJ: Princeton University Press, 1992), p. 317.

22. Peter Lindert, *Growing Public*, vol. 1 (Cambridge: Cambridge University Press, 2004), p. 18. See also Joel Slemrod and Jon Bakija, *Taxing Ourselves* (Cambridge, MA: MIT Press, 1996), pp. 100–101.

23. Lindert, *Growing Public*, p. 227.

24. See Slemrod and Bakija, *Taxing Ourselves*, pp. 196–99.

25. Lindert, *Growing Public*, pp. 235–45.

26. Eric Lipton, "'Breathtaking' Waste and Fraud in Hurricane Aid," *New York Times*, June 27, 2006.

27. For a good discussion of this, see William Greider, *The Soul of Capitalism* (New York: Simon & Schuster, 2003), pp. 263–99.

28. Henry Mintzberg, "Managing Government, Governing Management," *Harvard Business Review* 74 (1996): 75–83 at 83.

29. Lindert, *Growing Public*, pp. 254–55.

30. The most important exception is Robert H. Frank, *Choosing the Right Pond* (New York: Oxford University Press, 1986).

31. Gerald J. S. Wilde, *Target Risk* (Toronto: PDE Publications, 1994).

32. See Colin F. Camerer, Linda Babcock, George Loewenstein, and Richard H. Thaler, "Labor Supply of New York City Cab Drivers," in Daniel Kahneman and Amos Tversky, eds., *Choices, Values and Frames* (Cambridge: Cambridge University Press, 2000).

33. Camerer et al., "Labor Supply of New York City Cab Drivers," p. 364.

CHAPTER 3: THE FRICTIONLESS PLANE FALLACY

1. Interview with the author. Original publication, Joseph Heath, "What Economists Don't Want You to Know," *THIS Magazine*, March/April 2001.
2. See Joseph Heath, *The Efficient Society* (Toronto: Penguin, 2001).
3. See Marc Blaug, *Economic Theory in Retrospect*, 4th ed. (Cambridge: Cambridge University Press, 1985), p. 594.
4. John Kay, *The Truth About Markets* (London: Penguin, 2003), pp. 112–13.
5. See Michael Trebilcock, *The Limits of Freedom of Contract* (Cambridge, MA: Harvard University Press, 1994).
6. Robert Nozick, *Anarchy, State and Utopia* (New York: Basic Books, 1974), p. 163.
7. Kenneth J. Arrow and Gerard Debreu, "The Existence of an Equilibrium for a Competitive Economy," *Econometrica* 22 (1954). 265–90.
8. Note that I am using the term "externality" in the very broad sense that was popularized by David Gauthier, *Morals by Agreement* (Oxford: Clarendon, 1986). Economists define an externality more narrowly, as an uncompensated effect created by a transaction for an otherwise uninvolved third party. The more general definition makes it possible for one person to generate an externality for one other person (e.g., for a free rider in a prisoner's dilemma to create a negative externality for the other person), while the economic definition requires at least three people to be involved.
9. Michael McCloskey, "Intuitive Physics," *Scientific American* 249 (1982): 122–30.
10. Milton Friedman, *Capitalism and Freedom*, 2nd ed. (Chicago: University of Chicago Press, 1982), p. 120.
11. Richard E. Just, Darrell L. Hueth, and Andrew Schmitz, *The Welfare Economics of Public Policy* (Northampton, MA: Edward Elgar, 2004), pp. 27–28.

CHAPTER 4: TAXES ARE TOO HIGH

1. All hospitals in Canada are in the public sector, broadly defined.
2. Data drawn from Peter Lindert, *Growing Public*, vol. 1 (Cambridge: Cambridge University Press, 2004), pp. 12–13.
3. Paul Samuelson, "The Pure Theory of Public Expenditure," *Review of Economics and Statistics* 36 (1954): 387–89.
4. James M. Buchanan, "An Economic Theory of Clubs," *Economica* 32 (1965): 1–14 at 1.
5. For the relevant theory, under which one could get perfect efficiency, see Charles Tiebout, "Pure Theory of Local Public Expenditure," *Journal of Political Economy* 64 (1956): 416–24.
6. Tiebout, "Pure Theory of Local Public Expenditure."

CHAPTER 5: UNCOMPETITIVE IN EVERYTHING

1. See Paul Krugman, *Peddling Prosperity* (New York: W. W. Norton, 1994), pp. 285–91.
2. Rick Haglund, "GM Chief Blasts Gloomy Analysts," *Mlive.com*, May 4, 2007.
3. Thomas L. Friedman, *The Lexus and the Olive Tree* (New York: Anchor, 2000), p. 232.
4. Thomas L. Friedman, *The World Is Flat* (New York: Farrar, Straus & Giroux, 2005), p. 377.
5. Paul Krugman, "Toyota, Moving Northward," *New York Times*, July 25, 2005.

6. Paul Krugman, "Ricardo's Difficult Idea," http://web.mit.edu/krugman/www/ricardo.htm (accessed August 2008).

7. John Ralston Saul, "Canada Today, Mexico Tomorrow . . . ," in Laurier Lapierre, ed., *If You Love This Country* (Toronto: McClelland & Stewart, 1988), p. 189.

8. The one exception being the U.S. dollar, which people sometimes do want to hold for its own sake. This means that the U.S. is in a position to run larger trade deficits than most other countries, although in so doing it does run the risk that a "day of reckoning" will come. One commentator has compared the situation of the U.S. to that of a person being able to write checks that recipients don't cash, but rather use to mediate further exchanges with one another. This is great for the person writing the checks, but it is always possible that some day the recipients will start cashing them.

9. Charles Wheelan, *Naked Economics* (New York: W. W. Norton, 2002), p. 108.

10. The mathematical expression of this idea is known as the Heckscher-Ohlin model of comparative advantage. For useful discussion, see Edward E. Leamer, "The Heckscher-Ohlin Model in Theory and Practice," *Princeton Studies in International Finance* 77 (1995).

11. This version of the tale is from Tim "The Undercover Economist" Harford. See *The Undercover Economist* (Oxford: Oxford University Press, 2006), p. 211. For the original, see David Friedman, *Hidden Order* (New York: HarperCollins, 1996), pp. 69–72.

12. Krugman, "Ricardo's Difficult Idea."

13. John Kay, *The Business of Economics* (Oxford: Oxford University Press, 1996), p. 79.

14. See the discussion in Paul Krugman, *Pop Internationalism* (Cambridge, MA: MIT Press, 1996), pp. 96–98.

15. All quotes from Francis Cullen, William Maakestad, and Gray Cavender, "Profits vs. Safety," in Douglas Birsch and John H. Fielder, *The Ford Pinto Case* (Albany: State University of New York, 1994), pp. 267–68.

CHAPTER 6: PERSONAL RESPONSIBILITY

1. Inaugural address, January 20, 2001, http://www.whitehouse.gov/news/inaugural-address.html (accessed August 2008.)

2. François Ewald, *L'Etat providence* (Paris: Grasset, 1986), pp. 185–86.

3. Ian Hacking, *Introduction to Probability and Inductive Logic* (Cambridge: Cambridge University Press, 2001), p. 191.

4. Assuming stochastic independence of returns. More concretely, failure has to be caused by bad luck, not an absolute scarcity of game (which will affect all hunters equally).

5. Karl Polanyi, *The Great Transformation* (Boston: Beacon Press, 1957), p. 49.

6. For example, see Hillard Kaplan, Kim Hill, and A. Magdalena Hurtado, "Risk, Foraging and Food Sharing Among the Aché," in Elizabeth Cashdan, ed., *Risk and Uncertainty in Tribal and Peasant Economies* (Boulder, CO: Westview Press, 1990).

7. Gary D. Thompson and Paul N. Wilson, "Common Property as a Response to Environmental Variability," *Contemporary Economic Policy* 12 (1994): 10–21.

8. This is the (somewhat self-congratulatory) story that we used to tell each other back in Saskatchewan. For a more nuanced analysis, see Seymour Martin Lipset, *Agrarian Socialism* (New York: Doubleday, 1968), pp. 153–58.

NOTES TO PAGES 129-155

9. Robert Ellickson, "Property in Land," *Yale Law Review* 102 (1993): 1315–1400.

10. Peter Singer, "Famine, Affluence and Morality," *Philosophy and Public Affairs* 1 (1972): 229–43.

11. David Schmidtz, "Islands in a Sea of Obligation: Limits on the Duty to Rescue," *Law and Philosophy* 19 (2000): 683–705 at 686.

12. Thomas Robert Malthus, *An Essay on the Principle of Population*, vol. 2, Patricia James, ed. (Cambridge: Cambridge University Press, 1989), p. 161.

13. Schmidtz, "Islands in a Sea of Obligation," p. 688.

14. Jacob S. Hacker refers to this, in the United States, as the "personal responsibility crusade." See *The Great Risk Shift* (New York: Oxford University Press, 2006), p. 51.

15. James Q. Wilson, "Why We Don't Marry," *City Journal* (Winter 2002). Galston offers the following important clarification (personal communication): "It's 79 percent if you break all three, not just one. The statistic comes from research by Nicholas Zill and was recently updated. The numbers are a bit lower now, but the basic 10 to 1 ratio between those who break and those who follow all three rules remains the same."

16. Robert Moffitt, "Incentive Effects of the U.S. Welfare System: A Review," *Journal of Economic Literature* 30 (1992): 1–61 at 27.

17. Moffitt, "Incentive Effects of the U.S. Welfare System," p. 27.

18. There are some products sold under the title of "divorce" or "marriage" insurance in various countries, but so far none of them are true insurance products (often they are loans, or complicated annuity schemes).

19. Moffitt, "Incentive Effects of the U.S. Welfare System," p. 31.

20. David Gratzer, *Code Blue* (Toronto: ECW Press, 1999).

21. Organization for Economic Co-operation and Development, *OECD Health Data 2006*, http://www.oecd.org/health/healthdata (accessed August 2008).

22. See, e.g., Gratzer, *Code Blue*, pp. 192–94.

23. David Dranove, *Code Red* (Princeton, NJ: Princeton University Press, 2008), pp. 131–32.

24. François Ewald, *L'Etat providence* (Paris: Grasset, 1986).

CHAPTER 7: THE JUST PRICE FALLACY

1. "Drivers 'Panic Buy' as Supplies Remain Tight Through to Next Week," *Globe and Mail*, February 27, 2007.

2. H. Michell, "The Edict of Diocletian: A Study of Price Fixing in the Roman Empire," *Canadian Journal of Economics and Political Science* 13 (1947): 1–12.

3. John C. Rolfe and Frank B. Tarbell, "A New Fragment of the Preamble to Diocletian's Edict, 'De Pretiis Rerum Venalium,'" *American Journal of Archaeology* 5 (1889): 428–39 at 433.

4. "Chavez Threat to Seize Food Shops," *BBC News*, February 15, 2007, http://news.bbc.co.uk/2/hi/business/6364515.stm (accessed August 2008).

5. Marc Hauser, *Moral Minds* (New York: HarperCollins, 2006), pp. 92–93.

6. Abba P. Lerner, "Marginal Cost Pricing in the 1930's," *American Economic Review* 67 (1977): 235–43 at 236.

7. Statistics from United States Government Energy Information Administration, http://www.eia.doe.gov/ (accessed April 2008).

8. "The Elusive Negawatt," *The Economist*, May 10, 2008.

9. All statistics from Statistics Canada's 2005 Survey of Household Spending.

10. As James Q. Wilson once observed, the problem with moral issues is that they tend to "obscure practical issues, even when the moral question is a relatively small one and the practical matter is very great." See Wilson, "Corruption Is Not Always Scandalous," in J. A. Gardinar and D. J. Olsen, eds., *Theft of the City* (Bloomington: Indiana University Press, 1968), p. 29.

11. Andrew Potter, "Not the Brightest Bulbs in the Pack," *Maclean's*, April 9, 2007.

12. Abba Ptachya Lerner, *The Economics of Control* (New York: Macmillan, 1946), p. 48.

13. John W. Baldwin, *The Medieval Theories of the Just Price* (Philadelphia: American Philosophical Society, 1959).

14. Aristotle, *Nicomachean Ethics*, trans. Roger Crisp (Cambridge: Cambridge University Press, 2000), p. 88.

15. Augustine, *On the Trinity*, ed. Gareth B. Matthews (Cambridge: Cambridge University Press, 2002), p. 110.

16. Marjorie Grice-Hutchinson, *The School of Salamanca* (Oxford: Clarendon, 1952), p. 48.

17. In a fairly typical misrepresentation of the issue, Henry Hazlitt heaps scorn upon the search for "just" prices, arguing instead that economists employ a notion of "functional" prices—"those that encourage the largest volume of production"; *Economics in One Lesson*, 3rd ed. (New York: Three Rivers, 1979), p. 152. But of course, "volume" as such is irrelevant; it is satisfaction of human need that counts. Thus the appeal of scarcity pricing is entirely moral, not functional. It simply responds to a different set of moral concerns than those that animated the old "just price" view.

18. Oskar Lange, "On the Economic Theory of Socialism, Part 2," *Review of Economic Studies* 4 (1937): 123–42 at 123.

19. As the philosopher Ronald Dworkin put it, in *Sovereign Virtue* (Cambridge, MA: Harvard University Press, 2000), markets fix "the value of any transferable resources one person has as the value others forgo by his having it" (p. 149).

20. Lerner, "Marginal Cost Pricing in the 1930's," p. 236.

21. One of the clearest formulations of this idea can be found in Henry Simons, *Economic Policy for a Free Society* (Chicago: University of Chicago Press, 1948). Simons wrote, "It is urgently necessary for us to quit confusing measures for regulating relative prices and wages with devices for diminishing inequality. One difference between competent economists and charlatans is that, on this point, the former sometimes discipline their sentimentality with a little reflection on the mechanics of an exchange economy" (p. 83).

22. See Edward L. Glaeser and Erzo F. P. Luttmer, "The Misallocation of Housing Under Rent Control," *American Economic Review* 93 (1997): 1027–46. Also Rolfe Goetze, "Rent Control: Affordable Housing for the Privileged, Not the Poor: A Study of the Impact of Rent Control in Cambridge" (Cambridge, MA: GeoData Analysis, 1994). Goetze writes, "This study, based on extensive empirical data, makes clear that the special protection promised by rent control—for families, for less affluent households, and for the elderly—has failed. Instead, rent control has caused the gradual displacement of a large disadvantaged renter population by a younger, higher income, better educated,

singles population. In short, rent control has spurred gentrification . . . Rent control is paradoxical in that it produces the opposite of the promised results; it is an initially well-intentioned but ultimately destructive housing policy that actually reduces supply, hurts the poor and displaces the needy" (p. 24).

23. Ronald Dworkin, "Liberalism," in *A Matter of Principle* (Cambridge, MA: Harvard University Press, 1985).

24. Joseph E. Stiglitz and Andrew Charlton, *Fair Trade for All* (Oxford: Oxford University Press, 2005).

25. For a thorough history, see Gavin Fridell, *Fair Trade Coffee* (Toronto: University of Toronto Press, 2007), pp. 53–63.

26. Charis Gresser and Sophia Tickell, *Mugged: Poverty in Your Coffee Cup* (London: Oxfam International, 2002), p. 19.

27. Gresser and Tickell, *Mugged*, p. 40.

28. Gresser and Tickell, *Mugged*, p. 46. Fridell, in his book *Fair Trade Coffee*, manages to write just under 300 pages without mentioning the possibility of overproduction generated by these price distortions. He is too busy employing a "historical materialist approach to development" in order "to identify the macro-structures of power and their historical, social and political-economic roots" (p. 11).

29. John Stackhouse, *Out of Poverty* (Toronto: Vintage, 2000), p. 108.

30. Stackhouse, *Out of Poverty*, p. 113.

CHAPTER 8: THE "PSYCHOPATHIC" PURSUIT OF PROFIT

1. Anup Malani and Eric Posner, "For-Profit Charities," *Virginia Law Review* 93 (2007): 2017–67.

2. Regarding charity, the George Mason University economist Tyler Cowan writes, "My preferred approach is pure cash transfers to rural Mexicans, vis-à-vis Western Union. You don't get the tax break but administrative expenses are *very* low. Think of Western Union as a for-profit charity" (www.marginalrevolution.com).

3. Maude Barlow and Tony Clarke, *Blue Gold* (Toronto: Stoddart, 2002), write, "The Earth's fresh water belongs to the Earth and all species, and therefore must not be treated as a private commodity to be bought, sold, and traded for profit" (p. xvii). Yet despite this principle, and the fact that they get very upset about the possible privatization of public water supplies, neither sees any reason to nationalize the bottled-water industry (see p. 242).

4. Joel Bakan, *The Corporation* (Toronto: Viking, 2004), p. 28.

5. Bakan, *The Corporation*, p. 69.

6. Bakan, *The Corporation*, pp. 112–13. For more of the same, see Barlow and Clarke, *Blue Gold*, p. 87.

7. For example, see the report of the Commission on the Future of Health Care in Canada, *Building on Values* (Ottawa, 2002).

8. Adolph Berle and Gardiner Means, *The Modern Corporation and Private Property*, rev. ed. (New York: Harcourt, Brace, 1968).

9. Bakan, *The Corporation*, p. 99. Similarly, a group of Harvard Business School professors, discussing ways to restore trust in American business, denounced the

"profit-maximizing abuses unmasked in the recent wave of corporate scandals"; see Rakesh Khurana, Nitin Nohria, and Daniel Penrice, "Management as a Profession," in J. W. Lorsch, L. Berlowitz, and A. Zelleke, eds., *Restoring Trust in American Business* (Cambridge, MA: MIT Press, 2005).

10. Margaret Blair, *Ownership and Control* (Washington, DC: Brookings, 1995), pp. 100–106, 217.

11. As the Delaware Supreme Court ruled in the influential *Guth v. Loft* 5 A.2d 503 (Del. Ch. 1939) decision, "The rule that requires of corporate officers and directors an undivided and unselfish loyalty to the corporation demands that there should be no conflict between duty and self-interest."

12. Lucian Bebchuk and Jesse Fried, *Pay Without Performance* (Cambridge, MA: Harvard University Press, 2004).

13. This is a "bread and butter" Economics 101 claim (see N. Gregory Mankiw, *Principles of Economics* [Fort Worth, TX: Dryden, 1998], p. 295), although the result is unknown to many people.

14. John Kenneth Galbraith, *American Capitalism*, rev. ed. (Cambridge, MA: Riverside, 1956), pp. 112–13.

15. The term was coined by GE chairman and CEO Jeff Immelt.

16. Jerry Useem, "America's Most Admired Companies," *Fortune,* March 7, 2005.

17. Bakan, *The Corporation,* p. 39.

18. Henry Hansmann, *The Ownership of Enterprise* (Cambridge, MA: Harvard University Press, 2000), pp. 12–16.

19. Hansmann, *Ownership of Enterprise,* p. 13.

20. Statistics Canada, *The Daily,* December 7, 2004.

21. Hansmann, *Ownership of Enterprise,* pp. 39–44.

22. The exception to this is minority shareholders, which is why corporate law contains so many provisions aimed at protecting them from majority shareholders. See Reinier Kraakman, Paul Davies, Henry Hansmann, Gérard Hertig, Klaus J. Hopt, Hideki Kanda, and Edward B. Rock, *The Anatomy of Corporate Law* (New York: Oxford University Press, 2005), pp. 54–60.

23. Harvey Feigenbaum, "Public Enterprises in Comparative Perspective," *Comparative Politics* 15 (1982): 101–22 at 109.

24. Joseph Stiglitz, *Whither Socialism?* (Cambridge, MA: MIT Press, 1994), p. 250.

25. Anthony E. Boardman and Aidan R. Vining, "Ownership and Performance in Competitive Environments: A Comparison of the Performance of Private, Mixed, and State-Owned Enterprises," *Journal of Law and Economics* 32 (1989): 1–33.

26. For a fascinating and very careful analysis of one such case, see John Palmer, John Quinn, and Ray Resendes, "A Case Study of Public Enterprise: Gray Coach Lines Ltd.," in Robert Prichard, ed., *Crown Corporations in Canada* (Toronto: Butterworth, 1983). The authors analyze two intercity bus companies in Canada from 1969 to 1997, one private, the other public. They attempt to determine why the public firm had the highest fares yet had an average rate of return on net worth of only 6.3%, compared to 20.6% for the private firm. They conclude that, although the public firm ran some unprofitable routes

that otherwise would not have had service, the primary reason for its weak returns was overcapitalization, due to weak political oversight.

27. Anthony Ferner, *Governments, Managers and Industrial Relations* (Oxford: Basil Blackwell, 1988).

28. Garth Stevenson, "Canadian National Railways and Via Rail," in Allan Tupper and G. Bruce Doern, *Privatization, Public Policy and Public Corporations in Canada* (Montreal: Institute for Research on Public Policy, 1988).

29. John Langford and Kenneth Huffman, "Air Canada," in Tupper and Doern, *Privatization, Public Policy and Public Corporations in Canada*, p. 99.

30. Stiglitz, *Whither Socialism*, p. 173.

31. Simon Nora, *Rapport sur les enterprises publiques* (Paris: La documentation française, 1967).

32. Charles Lindblom, *Politics and Markets* (New York: Basic Books, 1977), p. 146.

33. Or, more generally, having a single "maximand" makes it relatively easy to control corporate conduct. See Frank Easterbrook and Daniel R. Fischel, *The Economic Structure of Corporate Law* (Cambridge, MA: Harvard University Press, 1991), pp. 37–38.

34. Charles E. Lindblom, *Politics and Markets: The World's Political Economic Systems* (New York: Basic Books, 1977), p. 146.

CHAPTER 9: CAPITALISM IS DOOMED

1. As Paul Krugman put it in "Why Aren't We All Keynesians Yet?" *Fortune*, August 17, 1998.

2. Paul Krugman, introduction to John Maynard Keynes, *The General Theory of Employment, Interest and Money* (London: Palgrave Macmillan, 2007).

3. John Stuart Mill, *Principles of Political Economy* (Amherst, NY: Prometheus, 2004), pp. 322–23.

4. See Uriel H. Crocker, "The 'Overproduction' Fallacy," *Quarterly Journal of Economics* 6 (1892): 352–63, and Thorstein Veblen, "The Overproduction Fallacy," *Quarterly Journal of Economics* 6 (1892): 484–92. For a glaring instance of this fallacy, see William Greider, *The Soul of Capitalism* (New York: Simon & Schuster, 2003), p. 85. See also William Greider, *One World, Ready or Not* (New York: Simon & Schuster, 1997), pp. 48–49.

5. Mill, *Principles of Political Economy*, p. 522.

6. For a survey of pre-Keynesian views, see Warren M. Persons, "Theories of Business Fluctuations," *Quarterly Journal of Economics* 41 (1926): 94–128.

7. Thomas Homer-Dixon, *The Upside of Down* (Toronto: Knopf, 2006), pp. 194–95.

8. Thomas Robert Malthus, *Principles of Political Economy*, 2nd ed. (London: William Pickering, 1836), pp. 322–26.

9. This is how John Maynard Keynes put it, in *The General Theory of Employment, Interest and Money* (London: Macmillan, 1949), p. 32.

10. Bernard A. Corry, "Malthus and Keynes: A Reconsideration," *Economic Journal* 69 (1959): 717–24, at 722.

11. Paul Krugman, *Peddling Prosperity* (New York: W. W. Norton, 1994), p. 32.

12. http://www.reagan.utexas.edu/archives/speeches/1987/080387a.htm (accessed August 2008). Reagan approved because he was touting the merits of "people's capitalism" via ESOPs (employee stock ownership plans).

13. Henry Hazlitt, *Economics in One Lesson*, 3rd ed. (New York: Three Rivers, 1979), pp. 152–58.

14. Richard Florida, "Individual Identity vs. the Financial Crisis," *Globe and Mail*, October 4, 2008.

15. Russell Jacoby, "Infantile Liberalism," *The Nation*, May 21, 2007.

16. Mill, *Principles of Political Economy*, p. 522.

17. Homer-Dixon, *The Upside of Down*, p. 195.

18. Greider, *The Soul of Capitalism*, p. 130.

19. Dwight R. Lee, "Creating Jobs vs. Creating Wealth," *The Freeman* 50 (2000).

20. See Clifford Hugh Douglas, *Social Credit* (London: Palmer, 1924).

21. See Daniel Bell, *The Cultural Contradictions of Capitalism* (New York: Basic Books, 1976), and Jürgen Habermas, *Legitimation Crisis*, trans. Thomas McCarthy (Boston: Beacon Press, 1975).

22. This discussion is strongly indebted to David A. Moss, *When All Else Fails: Government as the Ultimate Risk Manager* (Cambridge, MA: Harvard University Press, 2002), p. 327.

23. Joel Kovel, *The Enemy of Nature* (London: Zed Books, 2007), p. 155. Weirdly, Kovel has nothing to say about the environmental impact of communism. In the 24-page section of the book intended to establish the internal connection between "capital" and environmental destruction, 12 pages are dedicated to a "case study" of the Union Carbide disaster in Bhopal. The Chernobyl nuclear disaster, on the other hand, which happened barely a year later, is not mentioned once in the book. Yet it seems highly relevant, insofar as it suggests that nature may have more than just one enemy.

24. Elizabeth May, speaking on *The Agenda* ("The Long Goodbye to GDP"), first broadcast June 7, 2007, by TVOntario.

25. "The Elusive Negawatt," *The Economist*, May 10–16, 2008.

CHAPTER 10: EQUAL PAY

1. See, for example, Jan Wong, "Maid for a Month," *Globe and Mail*, April 1, 8, 15, and 22, 2006. See also Morgan Spurlock, *30 Days*, Episode 1, first broadcast June 15, 2005, on FX.

2. James C. Riley, *Rising Life Expectancy* (Cambridge: Cambridge University Press, 2001).

3. Friedrich Nietzsche, *On the Genealogy of Morals*, trans. Douglas Smith (Oxford: Oxford University Press, 1996), p. 46.

4. Charles Tilly, *Durable Inequality* (Berkeley: University of California Press, 1999), p. 1. Part of this was due to delayed development—the differences among adults were less significant.

5. There is one very important exception to this, which is *land*. Land reform is often a crucial component of antipoverty programs in underdeveloped nations. In some cases, the tendency to overestimate the value of redistributing wealth comes from thinking of wealth as overly analogous to land. The difference is that wealth can be easily consumed, in a way that land cannot.

6. Andrea Brandolini and Timothy M. Smeeding, "Patterns of Economic Inequality in Western Democracies: Some Facts on Levels and Trends," *Political Science and Politics* 1 (2006): 21–26 at 25.

7. "Lovingly Touched by Mao," *The Economist*, January 31, 2002.

8. William J. Baumol and William G. Bowen, *Performing Arts: The Economic Dilemma* (New York: The Twentieth Century Fund, 1966).

9. Statistics Canada, *Productivity Growth in Canada* (Ottawa: Ministry of Industry, 2001), p. 31.

10. Jan Wong, "Modern Times," *Globe and Mail*, April 8, 2006.

11. Drawn from Gøsta Esping-Anderson, *Social Foundations of Postindustrial Economies* (Oxford: Oxford University Press, 1999), p. 113. The ratio is actually working-age population to laundry workers. Most but not all of the data is from 1996.

12. Baumol and Bowen, *Performing Arts*.

13. Robert Frank, *Choosing the Right Pond* (New York: Oxford University Press, 1985), p. 70.

14. Frank, *Choosing the Right Pond*, p. 64.

15. Mark R. Killingsworth, "Comparable Worth and Pay Equity: Recent Developments in the United States," *Canadian Public Policy* 28 suppl. (2002): S171–S186 at S176.

16. Canadian Human Rights Commission, *Time for Action: Special Report to Parliament on Pay Equity* (Ottawa: Minister of Public Works and Government Services, 2001), p. 18.

17. Canadian Human Rights Commission, *Time for Action*, p. 3.

18. Rhona Mahony, *Kidding Ourselves* (New York: Basic Books, 1995), pp. 15–17.

19. Abdul Rashid, "Earnings of Physicians," *Statistics Canada Perspectives* (Winter 1999), pp. 27–38. The fact that women doctors work less was popularized by a somewhat inflammatory article by Brian McKinstry, "Are There Too Many Female Medical Graduates: Yes," *British Medical Journal* 336 (2008): 748.

20. See also "A Blunt Instrument," *The Economist*, October 26, 2006.

21. David Neumark and William Wascher, "Minimum Wages and Skill Acquisition: Another Look at Schooling Effects," *Economics of Education Review* 22 (2003): 1–10; also Duncan D. Chaplin, Mark D. Turner, and Andreas D. Pape, "Minimum Wages and School Enrollment of Teenagers: A Look at the 1990's," *Economics of Education Review* 22 (2003): 11–21.

22. David Card and Alan B. Krueger, *Myth and Measurement: The New Economics of the Minimum Wage* (Princeton, NJ: Princeton University Press, 1995), p. 285.

23. Barbara Ehrenreich, *Nickel and Dimed* (New York: Holt, 2001), p. 199.

24. Ehrenreich, *Nickel and Dimed*, p. 199.

25. For example, Juliet Schor, *The Overworked American* (New York: Basic Books, 1992), p. 135.

26. Toronto Municipal Code Property Standards, sec. 629–38D, sec. 629–34A. http://www.toronto.ca/legdocs/municode/1184_629.pdf (accessed August 2008).

27. Toronto Municipal Code Property Standards, sec. 629–11B, sec. 629–10E, sec. 629–23F.

CHAPTER 11: SHARING THE WEALTH

1. "Eisner Pay Is 68% of Profit," *New York Times*, April 16, 1994.

2. On runaway income, see Robert H. Frank and Philip J. Cook, *The Winner-Take-All Society* (New York: Free Press, 1995), pp. 62–84.

3. James B. Davies, Susanna Sandstrom, Anthony Shorrocks, and Edward N. Wolff, "The World Distribution of Household Wealth," in Center for Global, International and Regional Studies, *Mapping Global Inequalities Conference Papers* (November 28, 2007).

The exceptions are Germany, Australia, Spain, Italy, and Finland, where the top 10% own between 40% and 50% of the wealth.

4. See Jeff Gates, *The Ownership Solution* (Reading, MA: Addison Wesley, 1998), p. 22.
5. Marx expressed concern "that the world continues to live solely through the self-chastisement of this modern penitent of Vishnu, the capitalist . . . The simple dictates of humanity therefore plainly enjoin the release of the capitalist from his martyrdom and his temptation" (*Capital*, vol. 1, trans. Ben Fowkes [London: Penguin, 1990], p. 745).
6. David K. Shipler, *The Working Poor* (New York: Knopf, 2004), p. 36.
7. Shipler, *Working Poor*, p. 36.
8. Shipler, *Working Poor*, p. 37.
9. Andrew Kitching and Sheena Starky, *Payday Loan Companies in Canada: Determining the Public Interest* (Ottawa: Library of Parliament, 2006), p. 3.
10. George Ainslie, "Impulse Control in Pigeons," *Journal of the Experimental Analysis of Behavior* 21 (1974): 485–89.
11. George Ainslie, *Breakdown of Will* (Cambridge: Cambridge University Press, 2001), p. 33.
12. Luigino Bruni and Pier Luigi Porta, *Economics and Happiness: Framing the Analysis* (Oxford: Oxford University Press, 2005), pp. 38–40.
13. Thomas Robert Malthus, *An Essay on the Principle of Population*, vol. 2, ed. Patricia James (Cambridge: Cambridge University Press, 1989), p. 106.
14. Malthus, *An Essay on the Principle of Population*, vol. 2, p. 105.
15. Studies from around the world put the price elasticity of cigarettes when deterrence is initiated at about –0.5 (e.g., S. Gallus, Anna Schiaffino, Carlo La Vecchia, Joy Townsend, and Esteve Fernandez, "Price and Cigarette Consumption in Europe," *Tobacco Control* 15 [2006]: 114–19). This means that a 10% increase in price results in a 5% decrease in consumption. As one might expect, elasticity declines as price increases. See Badi B. Baltagi and Rajeev K. Goel, "State Tax Changes and Quasi-experimental Price Elasticities of U.S. Cigarette Demand: An Update," *Journal of Economics and Finance* 28 (2004): 422–29; Siu Fai Leung and Charles Phelps, "My Kingdom for a Drink . . . ? A Review of Estimates of the Price Sensitivity of Demand for Alcoholic Beverages," in Michael Hilton and Gregory Bloss, eds., *Economics and the Prevention of Alcohol-Related Problems*, NIAAA Research Monograph no. 25 (Rockville, MD: National Institute on Alcohol Abuse and Alcoholism, 1993).
16. Edward N. Wolff, "Recent Trends in the Size Distribution of Household Wealth," *Journal of Economic Perspectives* 12 (1998): 131–50 at 135.
17. Bruce Ackerman and Anne Alstott, *The Stakeholder Society* (New Haven: Yale University Press, 1999).
18. Stephanie Hainsfurther, "Financial Planners Help Beneficiaries Weather Unexpected Windfalls," *New Mexico Business Weekly*, December 6, 2002. The study was conducted by the National Endowment for Financial Education.
19. Gordon Laird, "This Land Is Whose Land?" *THIS Magazine*, March/April 2000, pp. 16–24; see esp. p. 18.
20. Lisa Gregoire, "Suicide Still the Fastest Way Out of Oil-Rich, Dirt-Poor Reserve," *Montreal Gazette*, June 11, 2001.

21. Dawn Walton and Murray Campbell, "Violence, Suicides and Social Ills: Welcome to Our Native Reserves," *Globe and Mail*, November 24, 2005. One can see a similar drama being played out with the compensation checks that are being distributed across Canada in Native communities, as part of the settlement over residential school abuse; see Katherine O'Neill, "Residential School Money Hits the North," *Globe and Mail*, January 7, 2008.
22. Ackerman and Alstott, *The Stakeholder Society*, p. 63.
23. James Tobin, "On Limiting the Domain of Inequality," *Journal of Law and Economics* 13 (1970): 263–77 at 264–65.

CHAPTER 12: LEVELING DOWN

1. Kurt Vonnegut Jr., *Welcome to the Monkey House* (New York: Dial, 1998), p. 7.
2. The philosopher Larry Temkin refers to this constraint as "the Slogan" (before going on to argue against it); Larry Temkin, *Inequality* (New York: Oxford University Press, 1993), pp. 248–55.
3. Joseph Stiglitz, *Whither Socialism?* (Cambridge, MA: MIT Press, 1994).
4. The egalitarian principle being relied upon here is known as the "Pigou-Dalton transfer principle," which states that a transfer from someone who has more to someone who has less is an improvement, from the standpoint of equality.
5. William J. Baumol, *Superfairness* (Cambridge, MA: MIT Press, 1986), p. 19.
6. http://www.freepublictransit.org.
7. For the Economics 101 take, see N. Gregory Mankiw, *Principles of Economics* (Fort Worth, TX: Dryden, 1998), pp. 159–60.
8. This number is not entirely picked out of the blue. Charles L. Ballard, John B. Shoven, and John Walley, "The Total Welfare Cost of Distortions in the United States Tax System: A General Equilibrium Approach," *National Tax Journal* 38 (1985): 125–40, estimated the cost of the U.S. system between 13 and 22 cents per dollar. Canada would probably be at the lower end of that, given the presence of a VAT. Note that this is the *welfare* cost, not the "dollars and cents" cost, although I am finessing this distinction somewhat in the discussion. For a general discussion of how these estimates are done, and how changing a few assumptions can alter the outcome, see Joel Slemrod, "The Economics of Taxing the Rich," in Joel Slemrod, ed., *Does Atlas Shrug?* (New York: Russell Sage, 2000).
9. It is worth noting that the marginal cost of raising tax revenue no doubt increases (for example, the higher the tax rate, the greater the incentive to engage in tax evasion). Thus new public spending that requires new tax revenues must be subjected to a more sophisticated cost-benefit analysis.
10. John Maynard Keynes, *General Theory of Employment, Interest and Money* (London: Macmillan, 1949), p. 129.
11. For discussion, see Joseph Heath, "Reasonable Restrictions on Underwriting," in Patrick Flanagan, Patrick Primeaux, and William Ferguson, *Insurance Ethics for a More Ethical World* (Amsterdam: Elsevier, 2007).
12. See Herbert Emery, "Risky Business? Non-actuarial Pricing Practices and the Financial Viability of Fraternal Sickness Insurers," *Explorations in Economic History* 33 (1995): 195–226.

13. Joel Slemrod and Jon Bakija, *Taxing Ourselves* (Cambridge, MA: MIT Press, 1996), p. 138.
14. David M. Cutler and Richard Johnson, "The Birth and Growth of the Social Insurance State: Explaining Old Age and Medical Insurance Across Countries," *Public Choice* 120 (2004): 870–921.
15. OECD, *The Political Economy of Environmentally-Related Taxes* (OECD, 2006), p. 28.
16. John Stuart Mill, *Principles of Political Economy* (Amherst, NY: Prometheus, 2004), p. 869.
17. For a more up-to-date version, see Laurie Simon Bagwell and B. Douglas Bernheim, "Veblen Effects in a Theory of Conspicuous Consumption," *American Economic Review* 86 (1996): 349–73.
18. Robert H. Frank, *Luxury Fever* (New York: Free Press, 1999).
19. Roger D. Congleton, "Efficient Status Seeking: Externalities and the Evolution of Status Games," *Journal of Economic Behavior and Organization* 11 (1989): 175–90.

EPILOGUE

1. Peter Lindert, *Growing Public,* vol. 1 (Cambridge: Cambridge University Press, 2004).
2. Alec Nove, *The Economics of a Feasible Socialism,* 2nd ed. (London: HarperCollins, 1991), p. 96.
3. The paper that set off a lengthy debate on this subject was Benjamin Ward, "The Firm in Illyria: Market Syndicalism," *American Economic Review* 48 (1958): 566–89.
4. Beatrice Potter Webb, *The Cooperative Movement in Great Britain* (London: Swan Sonnenschein, 1907).
5. William Easterly, *The White Man's Burden* (New York: Penguin, 2006), pp. 3–4.

INDEX

ABOUT THE AUTHOR

Joseph Heath is an associate professor at the University of Toronto, where he teaches in the Department of Philosophy and the School of Public Policy and Governance. He is the author of four previous books, including the international bestseller *Nation of Rebels: Why Counterculture Became Consumer Culture* (with Andrew Potter). He lives in Toronto.